Pick Your Poison

How Our Mad Dash to Chemical Utopia Is Making Lab Rats of Us All

MONONA ROSSOL

WILEY

John Wiley & Sons, Inc.

Published by John Wiley & Sons, Inc., Hoboken, New Jersey
Published simultaneously in Canada

For general information about our other products and services, please contact our Customer Care Department within the United States at (800) 762–2974, outside the United States at (317) 572–3993 or fax (317) 572–4002.

Wiley also publishes its books in a variety of electronic formats. Some content that appears in print may not be available in electronic books. For more information about Wiley products, visit our web site at www.wiley.com.

ISBN (cloth) 978-0-470-55091-5; ISBN (ebk) 978-0-470-91875-3;
ISBN (ebk) 978-0-470-91876-0; ISBN (ebk) 978-0-470-91877-7

Printed in the United States of America

10 9 8 7 6 5 4 3 2 1

For my darling husband, Jack Fairlie.
Although I could easily lose sight of you in tall grass,
you are still the tallest man I've ever met.

CONTENTS

PREFACE

I'm a chemist, but I don't make my living mixing chemicals for a multinational company. Most of my colleagues in lab coats don't think much about the effects that their products will have on the rest of the world. Very few end up devoting their lives to education and prevention as I have, trying to get chemicals off the shelves and out of our homes, instead of onto and into them. How on earth did I end up on this side of the fence?

For one thing, I didn't start out in chemistry; I started out in vaudeville. Work began for me at age one when I was a prop in my father's magic act. I was a substitute for the traditional rabbit in an illusion specially conceived and created by my father. By age three, I was a professional entertainment worker and, like my father and mother, a member of the American Guild of Variety Artists. My sister, Ellie, a year and a half younger than I was, also worked professionally. Audiences couldn't tell Ellie and me apart unless we were standing together, so my father could create some rather baffling illusions using us as assistants. Soon we were also performing a rather cute acrobatic act together, and I was lip-syncing funny recordings and singing.

For those who don't know much about vaudeville, it was the primary form of entertainment until moving pictures progressively displaced it in the 1930s. Yet as vaudeville slowly died, the vaudevillians continued to live—and most continued to perform. They simply stopped playing the fancy Orpheum circuit theaters and began to work at state and county fairs, circuses and carnivals, Elks and Moose Club events, bar mitzvahs, and church picnics. We played those kinds of venues and shared the bill with the most spectacular acts you've never heard of—acts that had been on the road for forty or fifty years, ranging from single performer acts to entire vaudeville families of acrobats, comics, jugglers, high-wire walkers, sharpshooters, musicians and singers, and more.

If being onstage teaches you anything, it's self-discipline and the value of honing multiple talents. Instead of running away to join the circus, I ran away *from* the circus at seventeen to go to the University of Wisconsin. I worked my way through three degrees: a bachelor of science, a master of science degree, and a master of fine arts degree. This odd combination of degrees was not my idea. It reflected my attempts to find some avenue for a career when door after door slammed shut, only because I was a member of that half of the population that squats to pee.

First, I was a premed student. I had a backer who would have paid my way through medical school, so I filled out my med school application in 1956 with excitement. Before the applications were even acted on, there was a kind of orientation session. I remember that a woman administrator spoke, which made it worse. She said that the laws had changed and they were now forced to accept 10 percent women, and they didn't really want so many women in the school. Then she gleefully informed us that half of us would be flunked out after the first year anyway.

This was my first head-on encounter with discrimination. I had not seen this in show business. In entertainment, there will be equality as long as most men can't sing soprano or wear a brief costume effectively enough to misdirect attention away from a magician's gimmick. So I was unprepared for the med school speech. After working hard to make all A's in the required courses, I had expected to be welcomed. I stood up in the orientation, made a very expressive hand gesture, and left.

Finishing pre-med left me about a year away from graduating with a major in chemistry, math, physics, or zoology. I chose to major in chemistry and minor in math. My plan was to become a chemist, and I was already working in the chemistry department as student slave labor.

Just a few credits short of my degree, I ran out of money and went to work at Bjorksten Research Laboratories as a full-fledged research chemist. This firm was impressed with my work after a year and offered to pay for my education through graduate school. That offer evaporated, however, when the lab received a big government contract and found that it could not get security clearance for me. Apparently, being one of the few white members of the NAACP and participating in a few political events was enough to wreck your career in those days.

With another career down the pipe, I decided to switch majors completely. I had taken a large number of electives in art and found these courses very interesting. I finished my degree in chemistry and then applied for graduate school in studio art. My many art credits qualified me, but I was denied entry anyway. I was told that women couldn't be artists. Women had to enroll in art education to be art teachers instead.

My fury was barely controllable. I remember checking out a library copy of one of the primary textbooks for art education and reading it. With the tome under my arm, I walked into the dean of the art department's office, opened the book to page 1, and read the first convoluted, uninformative, verbose, useless sentence. I looked the dean in the face for a long, dramatic moment, then told him he had to be kidding. He enrolled me in studio art.

Now you at least know this about me: when I'm right, and someone else is wrong, I'm not afraid to let that person know about it.

When I graduated in 1964, I had a BS in chemistry with a minor in math, an MS in ceramics and sculpture, and an MFA in ceramics and glass with a minor in music. By this time I'd had three solo shows, I was an expert in glaze and glass chemistry because of my background, and I had won many awards for my ceramics and glass, including the Young Americans ceramics competition in 1962 and a purchase prize in the Twenty-Third Ceramics National competition in 1964. (A purchase prize means that when an artwork wins this award, it is purchased from the artist by some sort of organization, in this case a museum.) This prize piece is still in the permanent collection on exhibit at the Everson Museum of Art in Syracuse, New York. In addition, I had paid for my graduate education by working in minor faculty positions as a research project assistant in both the physical chemistry and the civil engineering departments. I had also been a graduate teaching assistant in the chemistry department, and I was one of only two graduate students chosen to teach undergraduate ceramics for two years in the art department. With this strong background in teaching, it seemed logical to me that I could teach glass and ceramics in a college somewhere. In order to obtain notices of college job openings, I went to the university placement bureau and filled out my application. The only thing I needed for the university to file the form and start to send me leads for jobs was the signature of Harvey Littleton, my major professor. Littleton refused to sign it, saying, "Women don't get those jobs."[1]

Instead, Littleton helped place all of the men in my class by introducing them to the right people, letting them know where there were job opportunities, and the like. All of them were teaching the year after graduation. And if you are in the art or crafts field, you probably recognize a few of my old classmates' names: Marvin Lipofsky, Clayton Bailey, and, a few years after me, Dale Chihuly. None of these and other male graduates had any significant competition from women for the first decade or so that they were establishing themselves. In fact, in the field of glassblowing, men still hold most of the cards.

If I wanted to continue working as an artist, I had to find the money to buy my own studio. Glassblowing, which I dearly loved, was simply too expensive to set up, and I had to give it up. I bought a small farmhouse near Madison, made pottery, and got a few local teaching jobs that paid very poorly. I barely survived.[2]

What does this have to do with product safety? Okay, I knew we'd have to get back to the real subject as soon as I finished settling some old scores. All of this background is important, though, because something special happened to me when I was working as a research chemist to put myself through art school.

One day as I traveled back and forth between the art and chemistry departments, I realized that the same chemicals were being used in both places—acids for etching, solvents for oil painting, minerals in ceramics, and the like. The chemistry department provided all students with safety training, eye wash stations, and special ventilation hoods. Yet there were essentially no safety precautions being taken in the art department for the same chemicals.

Worse, the art professors had a screwy notion in the 1960s: artists must not be neat or clean, and they should have intimate physical contact with their art materials. As a result, everyone was covered from head to foot with their paints, clays, and inks. Well, not everyone. I was minoring in music while in art school and had a heavy performance schedule as a singer. I showed up in class—even pottery and glassblowing—with my hair done and long fingernails and managed to leave looking pretty much as when I had arrived. I got a very large body of artwork done and received all A's, so don't tell me it can't be done.

My messy cohorts, however, covered in clay and paints, seemed to think that lead and cadmium compounds, which even then were known to be highly toxic, were somehow perfectly safe if they were in paints or ceramic glazes as pigments. It just didn't seem reasonable to me that changing your major from chemistry to art made you immune to toxic substances.

The fruits of this lack of safety awareness in the art department were also made manifest in many accidents and illnesses. Three of these are worth noting here.

1. The hot plate where we melted wax in the glaze room (which would have been done in a hood in the chemistry department) developed an ominous fog a few feet above the pot that suddenly exploded into a fireball. This is a well-known phenomenon to chemists—but not to the teachers and the students in the art department.
2. Some of us got acute lead poisoning when we were taught to make "dripped lead sculpture." We melted lead indoors without ventilation, cast it into bars, and used an acetylene torch to remelt and drip the lead into our molds. We thought we had some kind of flu that caused the vomiting and the diarrhea. No one in the art department, including me at that time, knew that an invisible fume of tiny lead oxide particles is emitted into the air whenever lead melts. And because the first effect of lead exposure is to lower the IQ, it may explain why I still remained in art school after this.
3. One of my classmates, Clayton Bailey, decided to build a salt kiln. This is a kiln into which salt is thrown when the kiln is at high temperatures. The salt dissociates into highly corrosive and reactive substances that attack clay, turning the ceramic surface into a glassy glaze. But Clayton decided it would be cool to build

the kiln indoors in the kiln room. The choking fumes emitted by this salt kiln resulted in the emergency evacuation of the entire art building.

These incidents made me aware that there was a need for someone in the arts who was knowledgeable about safety and perhaps had a little common sense.

Because we were required to present graduate seminar papers on art-related subjects, I gave mine on the safety aspects of ceramics. It was at these seminars that I first experienced the incredible hostility generated by some people at the mere suggestion that they might want to rethink their work habits. During the critique of my seminars, some of my classmates informed me that this subject had no place in the arts and knowledge about the toxicity of their materials would interfere with their creativity. I didn't think that death and disease would do much for their creativity either, so I persisted.

My interest in safety became known, and soon I was consulting on art safety, in addition to teaching at the Madison Art Center and the Madison Area Technical College. I certainly was no expert, but I had absolutely no competition because no one else seemed at all interested in the subject.

Then after I had worked several years at the Madison Area Technical College as one of only two ceramics teachers, the director decided to increase the department to three people and appoint a ceramic department head. I applied for the job. Instead, they hired a young man fresh out of school who had only a BS degree. They paid him twice what I was getting. I knew then that if I stayed in Madison, I'd probably kill someone.

I came to New York City in 1969, and from then on, I had no major discrimination problems. I must admit, however, that I fell back on my entertainment background, and my first paid jobs were singing and acting. In a kind of reverse logic in my life, whenever I was broke, I went back into show business.

In New York in the 1970s, the schools at which I taught were again calling on me to solve safety problems. But unlike the situation in Madison, I found that there were other people who were interested in art safety. Two of these people were Michael McCann, a Ph.D. biochemist, and Cate Jenkins, a Ph.D. chemist and National Science Foundation resident. In 1977, the three of us founded the Center for Occupational Hazards, later known as the Center for Safety in the Arts. Our aim was to provide the arts with health information and "industrial hygiene" services.

"Industrial hygiene": that job title sounds like we clean teeth in a factory. But it means that we analyze workplace hazards, assess the risks, and provide strategies for mitigating and limiting the risks, which includes providing special ventilation or protective equipment such as gloves, clothing, and respirators.

Applying industrial hygiene to the art and theater professions was a new idea in 1977. Although there are regulations and limits on your exposure to toxic chemicals if you work in a factory, a coal mine, or a laboratory, these regulations often are not applied to the arts. Yet the same toxic substances are used by artists, and their exposures to them are often more intimate and for longer periods of time than the traditional eight-hour workday.

There are also occupational regulations that protect workers from having accidents. For example, big healthy construction workers cannot go near a location where they could fall more than six feet unless they are wearing a harness tied to a five-thousand-pound anchorage or there is a rail built around the fall hazard. Yet performers are treated very differently. Performers, who may even be children or the elderly, are expected to work onstage one step from a ten-foot fall into the orchestra pit while powerful lights shine in their faces and toxic stage smoke is blown at them; then the stage suddenly goes black and they are directed to exit quickly in the dark. Something clearly is very wrong here.

Late in 1986, I left the center and started up another nonprofit called Arts, Crafts, and Theater Safety (ACTS) to do the same kind of work. Then in 1995, I took on a second job as safety officer for the United Scenic Artists, Local USA829 of the International Alliance of Theatrical Stage Employees (IATSE). As safety officer, I can recommend closing theaters or film locations for safety violations. Actually, I provided the expert advice that resulted in the union's stopping work on eight major film locations, which means that really important people hate me.

The research and the writing for my theater and art books required me to become intimately familiar with vast numbers of chemicals: pigments, dyes, solvents, wood, metal, minerals, plastics, acids, alkalis, pesticides (as preservatives, especially in art conservation), and much more. In a sense, there is no chemical, either natural or synthetic, that is not being used by some artist or in some theater scene or prop shop somewhere. I'm even an expert on the chemicals that are used in stage pyrotechnics, because my familiarity with them goes back to childhood and is enhanced by my knowledge as a chemist.

I vote on national standards (American Society for Testing and Materials) for product safety in the areas of art materials and consumer products. I even vote on two standards for the National Fire Protection Association on fire and pyrotechnic effects. I have qualified as an expert witness in many lawsuits that involve exposure to toxic chemicals that are used in the arts or in safety hazards associated with theater or art.

I have always considered the chemicals in the products that are needed to clean up that studio or shop or launder those costumes. And it was always evident to me that the same hazards, labeling, and regulatory issues should apply to these products. In fact, the hazards of these products are even more critical because of their widespread use and the fact that they are used in homes where mothers and infants may be exposed to them twenty-four hours a day.

I'm excited about explaining these issues to you in a way that will enable you to understand how to determine whose opinions you should trust and how to evaluate these products on your own.

CHAPTER 1

Your Body Is a
Chemistry Experiment

*Have We Given Ourselves Diabetes,
Autism, and Cancer?*

In 1895, the German physics professor Wilhelm Röntgen accidentally discovered that his cathode ray tube emitted previously unknown rays that could penetrate solid matter. He called them "X-rays" and electrified the world with an X-ray picture of his wife's hand. In 1901, Röntgen won the Nobel Prize in Physics for his invention, and the rush to make medical devices that used the new technology was in full swing.

The public did not dwell on the fact that a number of those early researchers died of cancer or X-ray burns. In 1918, for example, the *New York Times* reported that Dr. Eugene Wilson Caldwell, one of the inventors of the fluoroscope, died "as the result of burns he suffered many years ago while making experiments with the X-ray." Röntgen himself died of intestinal cancer in 1923.

Many uses and abuses of this technology occurred, under the direction of qualified medical doctors, as well as quack practitioners. One device that many older Americans have probably had experience with was invented and marketed by the Adrian Company of

Milwaukee, Wisconsin. Adrian's engineers had the bright idea of making a fluoroscope that would X-ray a child's feet to ensure that his or her new shoes fit. In the late 1940s and during the1950s, about ten thousand of these machines were in shoe stores throughout the United States. I remember many times watching my own bones through the fluoroscope's viewing port as I wiggled my toes in new shoes, while my sister and my mother looked through the other two ports.

Despite the fact that by 1940 it was well known that X-rays were not innocuous and the Adrian Company knew that these machines also leaked significant amounts of radiation into the surrounding area, Adrian still sold and maintained fluoroscopes for about thirty years. Early on, legislatures started to pass bans on the machines. By 1970, thirty-three states had banned these units, and restrictions on their use in other states were so tight that fluoroscopes were rarely used. In 1981, however, one was found still in regular use in a store in Madison, West Virginia. When the store manager was told that the machine was illegal in that state, the store donated it to the U.S. Food and Drug Administration (FDA) for its exhibits. (You can see a picture of a fluoroscope at www.museumofquackery.com/devices/shoexray.htm.)

All of the people who used fluoroscopes increased their exposure to radiation and upped their risk of developing cancer. How many people actually developed cancer as a result of watching their toes inside one of these machines? There is no way to know. This means that companies suffer little or no repercussions if they promote a product that causes cancer, because the disease doesn't develop until years after exposure to a toxic agent, making it difficult for consumers to determine the exact cause. Gruesome as it seems, it pays for manufacturers to make products that cause cancer.

The public's use of radium is an even better example of how companies can profit by harming both consumers and their own workers.

Marie and Pierre Curie discovered radium in 1898, and within a decade, others knew how to isolate the substance from various ores. Soon afterward, entrepreneurs, following the pattern of many a new discovery, incorporated radium into miracle patent potions to cure a variety of ills. When a discovery makes the news and the public has already heard about the new "miracle," this helps the quacks sell their products. It is unknown how many gullible people died from ingesting radium, but the risk was substantial and it certainly caused cancers.

In 1917, the U.S. Radium Corporation mixed radium with a little glue and water to make a paint that glowed in the dark. The company dubbed it "Undark" and decided to use it to make watch and instrument dials that were readable at night. U.S. Radium became a major supplier of radioluminescent watches to the military. Soon, ordinary citizens were clamoring for the glow-in-the-dark products.

At U.S. Radium, about a hundred workers, mainly women, were hired to paint the watch faces and the instrument dials. The workers were told that the paint was harmless. They used camel hair brushes to apply the paint to the dial numbers. The brushes would lose shape after a few strokes, so the supervisors encouraged their workers to point the brushes with their lips or tongues to keep them sharp. (My classmates and I were taught this same brush-pointing technique at the University of Wisconsin in 1958.)

By the mid-1920s, something was clearly wrong with the dial painters. The women were suffering from anemia, bone fractures, and necrosis of the jaw, a condition now known as "radium jaw." What followed was the same sickening scenario that repeatedly plays out in almost every worker's health dispute. Read the following chain of events and see whether a similar pattern might apply to other toxic products that were reported in the news during your lifetime:

1. Workers were told that the paint was nontoxic, although there was no factual basis for this declaration. The employers discounted evidence that cancers were claiming the lives of many radium scientists. The workers believed their superiors.
2. Health complaints were made in ever-increasing frequency. It became obvious that something was seriously wrong.
3. U.S. Radium and other watch-dial companies began a campaign of disinformation and bogus medical tests—some of which involved X-rays and may even have made the condition worse.
4. Doctors, dentists, and researchers complied with U.S. Radium's and other companies' requests and refused to release their data to the public.

5. Medical professionals also aided the companies by attributing worker deaths to other causes. Syphilis was often cited as the diagnosis, which had the added benefit to management of being a smear on the victims' reputations.
6. One worker, Grace Fryer, decided to sue U.S. Radium. It took Fryer two years to find a lawyer who was willing to take on U.S. Radium. Only four other workers joined her suit; they became known as the "Radium Girls."
7. In 1928, the case was settled in the middle of the trial before it went to the jury for deliberation. The settlement for each of the five "Radium Girls" was $10,000 (the equivalent of $124,000 in 2009 dollars), plus $600 a year while the victim lived and all medical expenses.

Remember the general outline of this scenario because you will see it over and over again: The company denies everything while the doctors and the researchers (and even the industrial hygienists) in the company's employ support the company's distorted version of the facts. Perhaps one worker in a hundred will finally pursue justice, one lawyer out of the hundreds of thousands in the United States will finally step up to the plate, and the case will be settled for chump change.

Killing workers through chemical exposure is even more profitable now that workers' compensation laws cover occupational illnesses, as well as the traumas they initially covered. Among the first states to pass workers' compensation laws in 1911 was New Jersey, where the Radium Girls worked.

At the time, workers' compensation covered only accidents. Occupational illnesses were not covered, which is the reason why the U.S. Radium workers could sue in 1917. Today, workers' compensation laws extend to occupational illnesses, and the five Radium Girls would not be able to sue. This means that workers must accept workers' compensation instead of suing. Now employers can do in or disable their workers, and the only consequence for the companies is that their insurance premiums rise a bit. Sometimes the spouses or the children of the dead or disabled workers can sue the company, but the sick or dying worker usually has to accept the pittance provided by workers' compensation. In New York City, where I live, full workers' compensation disability payments were $400 a week until 2007 and are not much more now. Try living on that anywhere, much less in New York City, where it won't even cover your rent.

In retrospect, our nation's experiences with radium and X-rays are shocking, but that's all in the past, right? Let's look at another more recent and less well known product that may relate directly to your life: phenolphthalein. Now, that's a big word to amaze your friends with, especially if you can pronounce it. It's easier than it looks— *fee-knoll-thay'-lynn*. If you've taken high school chemistry, you might remember this chemical. It is an indicator dye. It changes from colorless in acetic or neutral solutions to pink or fuchsia in basic solutions. The color changes are something like the ones that chemistry students see with traditional litmus paper, except that phenolphthalein changes color at a different endpoint.

Not long after phenolphthalein was invented by Adolf von Baeyer in 1871, some fool drank a little and found that it was a powerful laxative. Eureka! So, for more than a hundred years, phenolphthalein was used in many laxatives, ranging from early patent medicines like Citrolax to modern-day products such as Ex-Lax. Chances are really good that somewhere along the way you, too, have ingested phenolphthalein, with the results being as advertised.

Doesn't the FDA have rules about such compounds? Phenolphthalein couldn't be very harmful, because it's been used for years, right? And hasn't the FDA been testing the chemicals we ingest in food and medicines? After all, President Franklin D. Roosevelt signed the Federal Food, Drug, and Cosmetic Act way back in 1938.

It wasn't until the 1950s, however, that the FDA got serious about looking at the ingredients in food and over-the-counter products (OTCs) like laxatives. Thousands of chemicals were already being used at that time. The FDA really couldn't tell the entire manufacturing community to stop making all of these chemicals and wait until tests determined whether each one was safe, so it excluded from scrutiny any substance that was in common use before 1958. Phenolphthalein had been used since the late 1800s, and there were no reports of people dropping dead with the bottle still in hand. Therefore, it was excluded from testing. By 1985, when a more formal version of this policy was instituted, phenolphthalein was listed in Category I: Generally Recognized as Safe, or GRAS.

In other words, if enough people have ingested the stuff for a long enough time and there is no obvious body count, the stuff was considered GRAS. Hundreds of other chemicals were in the same category. The problem with this kind of human-use evidence is that cancer and other chronic effects don't develop for years or even decades after exposure. Then, when the cancers or chronic diseases do develop, it is almost impossible to associate a particular individual's disease with a specific exposure in the past.

To uncover the rest of the phenolphthalein story, we need to take a foray into my specialty, art materials, and talk about dyes. There are two chemical classes of dyes closely related to phenolphthalein. They are the triphenylmethanes and the anthraquinones. Some toxicologists or scientists should have noticed that although most of the dyes in these two closely related classes had never been tested for long-term hazards, the few that had been studied were shown to cause cancer in animals.

To figure out when toxicologists and regulators should have heard alarm bells about phenolphthalein, take a look at a triphenylmethane dye called "gentian violet" and some of the anthraquinone dyes.

Gentian violet is sold over the counter and recommended for painting babies' mouths when they get thrush, as well as for athlete's foot, jock itch, impetigo, ringworm, and a host of other fungal and bacterial infections. It is also commonly used to mark the location to pierce the skin of certain members of the younger generation, who, for reasons beyond my understanding, make holes in themselves. For this reason, getting some gentian violet under the skin when it is pierced is a real possibility.

In 1958, the first red flag went up when a German study showed that gentian violet caused tumors in animals and was a possible carcinogen.[1] No similar studies appear to have been done for the next twenty-seven years. Then in 1985 a study concluded that gentian violet "appears to be a carcinogen in mice at several different organ sites."[2]

Finally, a two-generation rat study was conducted and reported in 1989.[3] This study showed a significant incidence of adenocarcinoma (a cancer) of the thyroid gland for both male and female rats and a dose-related incidence of leukemia in the females.

In case you think that after this third study, some kind of warning label should have been required, you are right—but that's not how the world of toxicology works. Instead, the main cancer research agencies, such as the National Toxicology Program (NTP) and the International Agency for Research on Cancer (IARC), would have had to set up working groups and debate the evidence. This usually takes years.

Some countries and states move more quickly. For example, an Australian agency, the National Health and Medical Research Council (NHMRC), was looking at the same evidence, and by 1991 the council concluded that gentian violet (which the Australians call "crystal violet") is a carcinogen. By 1994, the NHMCR had canceled its registrations for over-the-counter use and veterinary-use medicine.

In the United States, however, the stuff is still readily available over the counter. A recent Google search showed that even common drug outlets such as Walgreens and Target have it. As is typical with old patent remedies, many natural and herbal outlets also continue to sell it.

One huckster markets it as a "natural antifungal traditional remedy," even though it is a synthesized chemical.

Anthraquinone dyes are also related to phenolphthalein. These anthraquinone dyes are common in our consumer products. Rit and other household dyes, art pigments such as alizarin crimson, and many natural herbs such as aloe and danthron contain anthraquinones. Only five of roughly three hundred anthraquinone dyes and compounds used commercially have been tested, and these five are now listed as known animal carcinogens and potential human carcinogens by various agencies, including the NTP. They are 2-aminoathraquinone; 1-amino-2-methylanthraquinone; 1,4,5,8-aminoanthraquinone (Disperse Blue 1); 1,8-dihydroxyanthraquinone (danthron); and 1-amino-2,4-dibromoanthraquinone.

The NTP scientist James E. Huff reportedly said that anthraquinones typically are mutagenic and carcinogenic in both genders of two rodent species. He predicted that the anthraquinones will also cause cancer in humans.[4]

As for cancer effects, 2-aminoathraquinone and 1-amino-2-methylanthraquinone were already on a National Cancer Institute list in 1978, and both were listed by the IARC as animal carcinogens by 1982. Did anyone consider taking the anthraquinones out of consumer products? Nope.

Then in 1990, 1,8-dihydroxyanthraquinone was listed as a carcinogen. This chemical is the main active component in the natural laxative danthron and several other natural laxatives. Did anyone consider warning people about the anthraquinone laxatives? Nope. Danthron continued to be listed by FDA as a Category 1, GRAS, natural laxative, and the public continued to ingest it.

Finally, the NTP studied phenolphthalein and some of the natural laxatives and released its findings in 1994. The FDA reviewed the available data, mulled over it for five years, and concluded in a final rule in the *Federal Register* in 1999 that

> Phenolphthalein caused chromosome aberrations, cell transformations, and mutagenicity in mammalian cells. Because benign and malignant tumor formation occurs at multiple tissue sites in multiple species of experimental animals, phenolphthalein is reasonably anticipated to have human carcinogenic potential.[5]

Even more important, the FDA concluded that "the exposures used to demonstrate . . . *in vivo* and *in vitro* genotoxic effects were in the range that could occur with human laxative use."[6] To state this again for emphasis, *the exposures used to test phenolphthalein both in live animals and in glass petri dishes were in the same range that people might be exposed to when taking laxatives.* The old argument that the animals were exposed to massive doses doesn't hold here.

In this same final ruling, the FDA declared that the OTC laxative ingredients phenolphthalein and danthron are not generally recognized as safe and effective (Category II) and had been misbranded. Effective January 29, 1999, no OTC drug products containing phenophthalein or danthron that were subject to this final rule could thereafter be introduced into interstate commerce.

When the rule was published, many laxative companies had to shift gears. If you were listening to the Ex-Lax television advertisements at that time, as I was, you would have heard that Ex-Lax was switching to natural senna because it was gentle. Ex-Lax uttered not one word about the cancer data on the chemical that the laxative company had been selling for decades. Nor was there any discussion of the FDA's report, which said that extracts taken directly from the dried leaves and pods of *senna*, the natural product they were substituting for phenolphthalein, contain many different compounds, some of which (the anthrones—also related to anthraquinone) are mutagenic on the Ames test (a bacteria test). Unless manufacturers show that commercially available senna preparations do not contain mutagenic or genotoxic components, the FDA said that it is unable to state that senna does not also pose a relative risk to humans.

To be fair, the laxative companies are probably refining their senna to eliminate these questionable compounds, but I think that you laxative users should seriously consider adding roughage to your diet instead! And speaking of laxative users, shouldn't someone be doing studies of the millions of people who have taken these compounds to see whether the increase in certain types of human cancers seen in the United States may be partly attributable to them? Instead, the NTP's *11th Report on Carcinogens* says,

> A few epidemiological studies have investigated the association between the use of phenolphthalein-containing laxatives and colon cancer or adenomatous colorectal polyps. No consistent association was found. Cancers at other sites have not been investigated in humans.

My translation of this statement is: A couple of fast and dirty epidemiological studies were conducted, in which scientists looked for the wrong cancers. They should have been looking for sarcomas, lymphoma, and pheochromocytoma, which are the anomalies caused by phenolphthalein in animals. As for danthron, no studies have been done of people who take it. If these studies were to be conducted, researchers should look for liver cancer, which is what danthron caused in animals.

At least thirty years before phenolphthalein and danthron were banned, good toxicologists should have known that these substances needed to be studied. And now toxicologists should be testing natural herbs, including aloe, many of which contain anthraquinones, anthrones, or phenylmethanes. Even more important, before the opportunity fades, they should be studying us—the lab rats—who have been ingesting these substances for more than a hundred years.

Our data should be mined thoroughly to salvage at least something from this needless human experiment.

Animal tests for cancer and organ damage are standard procedures, but many other, more complex physical manifestations of chemical exposure should also be researched. Recently, scientists investigated an organophosphate pesticide to look for such effects. The study's findings blew me away.

Most research on organophosphate pesticides focuses on the well-known cancer and neurological effects caused by these chemicals. But the scientists at Duke University took a new tack in a study called "Exposure of Neonatal Rats to Parathion Elicits Sex-Selective Reprogramming of Metabolism and Alters the Response to a High-Fat Diet in Adulthood."[7]

The seven-week experiment involved giving the insecticide parathion to laboratory rats during the first four days of their lives at doses of 0.1 or 0.2 milligram per kilogram of body weight per day. These doses fall just below and just above the threshold for detecting an inhibition of the enzyme cholinesterase in the blood. This enzyme helps the nervous system to function, and when it is inhibited, it creates the first typical signs of systemic toxicity in the animals. At the low doses given to the animals, they did not show overt symptoms, nor was their general health threatened.

After reaching adulthood, the rats were either given standard lab food or switched to a high-fat diet. Male rats on a normal diet that had been given the lower dose of parathion gained weight and showed signs of a prediabetic state, including elevated glucose levels and an impaired ability to break down fat. Male rats that were given the higher doses of parathion lost weight and exhibited additional metabolic defects, the study showed.

Female rats on the normal diet seemed more susceptible to metabolic problems and lost weight at both doses of parathion. On a high-fat diet, however, females that had been given a daily 0.1 milligram-per-kilogram-of-body-weight dose of pesticide increased their weight by nearly 30 percent by the end of the study, compared to a 10 percent gain for male rats.

The significance of this study is that researchers showed that exposure to organophosphate pesticides such as parathion early in life may play a role in the increasing incidence of obesity and diabetes that we already see in the general population. "Our results point to a lasting metabolic dysregulation as a consequence of neonatal parathion exposure," the researchers said. Their findings revealed that neonatal low-dose parathion exposure disrupts a body's ability to regulate glucose and fat "in a persistent and sex-selective manner."

If early exposure to low levels of parathion can potentially lead to the development of obesity and diabetes, it is likely that various other organophosphates or classes of pesticides and toxic substances may have very different effects on metabolism. There's no end to the speculation this engenders and to the unanswered questions we need to pursue!

Unfortunately, it is impossible to escape low-dose exposure to chemicals. Today, everyone on the planet has already been exposed to low doses of pesticides and other toxic chemicals from the womb to the tomb. No one anywhere on this earth is born without a bodily burden of DDT, polychorinated biphenyls (PCBs), dioxins, and more. The world's mothers provide the chemicals to their babies from their own bodies' fat and bones—chemicals that the mothers then mobilize to nourish their fetuses. Additional amounts may come from the food the women eat and the air they breathe during pregnancy.

Even babies born on South Sea islands or in the frozen wilds of Canada have toxic chemicals in their bodies. In fact, these populations usually have higher levels of toxins because the mothers eat fish and marine mammals that are now highly contaminated worldwide.

A classic example of a list of chemicals we may carry in our bodies is available on a Web site for a program called *Trade Secrets* that Bill Moyers did on PBS a couple of years ago (visit www.pbs.org/tradesecrets/problem/bodyburden.html for more information). In compiling his report, Moyers had his own blood tested for toxic substances. The analysis showed that his blood and urine contained eighty-four less-than-desirable chemicals: two organophosphate pesticide metabolites, two heavy metals (lead and methylmercury), thirteen dioxins and furans, thirty-one PCBs (polychlorinated biphenyls), three organochlorine pesticides and metabolites (including DDT), four phthalates (plasticizers), and twenty-nine semivolatile organic compounds (such as those used in paint thinners and hobby products).

In 2009, the Centers for Disease Control and Prevention (CDC) released its *Fourth National Report on Human Exposure to Environmental Chemicals*. In this report, the CDC monitored 212 chemicals known or suspected of being capable of causing long-term toxic effects such as cancer and birth defects. This massive study also found a majority of these chemicals in the blood, the serum, and the urine of twenty-five hundred human subjects, who ranged in age from one year to fifty-nine.

The data do not mean that these chemicals cause disease, only that many people are carrying low levels of these chemicals in their bodies. Although the amounts of these chemicals are small, so were the doses in the parathion animal experiment conducted at Duke University that caused such dramatic long-term effects. With 84 different chemicals being found in small amounts in Bill Moyers's blood and 212 chemicals in other people's blood, what is the combined effect of this chemical soup? No one knows. Yet perhaps we humans are showing the effects without really understanding the cause. The explosion of chronic diseases such as diabetes, asthma, and autism and the high rates of cancer just might be related. Consider that the American Cancer Society estimates that in the United States 40.84 percent of us will develop cancer in our lifetimes. That's roughly two people in every five.

Industry's argument that the increases in cancer and chronic disease are due to our living longer is bogus. Some of the fastest rising rates of cancer and chronic disease appear in children. Actually, people in the United States have shorter life expectancies than do citizens in approximately thirty other countries.

If the high rates of chronic illness and perhaps cancer are due to complex effects caused by exposure to low doses of chemicals early in life, as the Duke experiment suggests, how will we ever know? The majority of the hundred thousand chemicals we find in industrial and commercial products have never even had basic testing for chronic toxicity and carcinogenic effects. Industries don't want to spend the money for these basic tests and certainly will not embark on more complex tests such as the Duke pesticide study, especially when the results would only indict the industries themselves.

In addition, it would be almost impossible for epidemiological or human studies to prove that these low levels of chemicals are harmful. In order to prove harm, you would need to compare a chemically exposed population with a similar population that has not been exposed—and there is not a single group of people left on the planet that would qualify for the unexposed control group!

Only animals in laboratories can be raised in pollution-free environments, so the effects of chemical pollution will have to be determined from studies of animals. Yet now there is a movement to stop animal testing. You can expect industry to get behind this movement, under the guise of being the "good guys."

When I repeatedly suggest animal studies in this book, I don't do it lightly. I have been a vegetarian, abstaining from all meat and fish, since 1959, because I do not believe in killing anything we don't need to kill. When I was a child, one of my most beloved pets, Gwendolyn, was a white rat. Without animal tests, however, there can be no real progress in our understanding of toxic substances. If you need to know what a chemical will do in an intestine or a lung, you need to put it in one. Both the body and the chemicals are too complex in their interactions to yield good data any other way. Like it or not, we can't get all of the answers we need from a petri dish.

As for the validity of data obtained by testing a species other than our own, we are a lot more like rats than we want to believe.

The defensive attitudes displayed by manufacturers of chemicals and other products today are the same as in the past. Injured parties still must engage in protracted and unequal battles with corporations for their rights. A recent example was Erin Brockovich's battle with the chromium polluters. Her advocacy for the chromium workers looks a lot like the fight for justice waged by the Radium Girls. It's simply the same story with different details. Not one thing has changed.

Beware of pointing fingers at the lawyers or the courts. Basically, it is almost impossible for courts to hold industry liable for chronic diseases such as cancer, except in rare instances when the cancer can be traced to a specific exposure. The classic example is when an asbestos-exposed person develops mesothelioma, a rare cancer of the lining of the chest and the abdomen that is caused almost exclusively by asbestos. If, instead, a person develops lung cancer from exposure to asbestos, that case will be a lot harder to prove and may not be successful. If the asbestos caused the plaintiff to develop intestinal or other cancers, the case probably will never be proved and the plaintiff might as well go home to die.

If future studies reveal that significant numbers of people have probably died from exposure to gentian violet, anthraquinone dyes, or phenolphthalein laxatives, there is still no recourse. Defense lawyers can attribute the types of cancer that killed these victims to other causes. The animal tests showing that they are carcinogens are not evidence that will meet the standard of proof required in court.

One day, studies such as the pesticide test at Duke University may unravel the reason that we now are experiencing more diabetes, obesity, autism, and other chronic problems. Yet even then, this information will not threaten industry, because any person's individual case of diabetes, obesity, and autism cannot be traced to a single chemical exposure.

When epidemiologists study large numbers of people, even that evidence is usually not strong enough to meet the court's standard of proof. The exceptions to this rule are when epidemiologists can associate massive body counts with certain chemicals, such as the deaths that occur among smokers. Even then, by the time a smoker's court trial reaches a conclusion, the plaintiff is long dead, a fine is levied against the corporation, and the cigarette CEOs climb into their limos after the trial and go home to their opulent lifestyles.

All of this proves the main point of this chapter: big companies cannot be trusted to do a good job of product testing and of being the stewards of chemicals, because they have little to fear from the legal and regulatory systems.

CHAPTER 2

Dying for Your (Child's) Art

Why "Nontoxic" Doesn't Mean Not Toxic

A sbestos was a common ingredient in art materials in the 1960s and the 1970s. For example, one product was a powdered papier-mâché product for children marketed by Milton Bradley. It contained about 50 percent asbestos powder. Called FibroClay, the asbestos-containing product had a nontoxic approved product (AP) seal on it from the organization known today as the Arts and Creative Materials Institute (ACMI).[1]

Although the hazards of asbestos were known in the 1970s and the 1980s, the only required tests at the time by the Federal Hazardous Substances Act were the acute animal tests. Because asbestos didn't immediately poison the test animals, no law was broken by labeling this product "nontoxic."

The asbestos problem and other labeling issues were raised by a group of activists, including myself, when I worked with a nonprofit corporation later known as the Center for Safety in the Arts. The center presented the problem to the National Art Materials Trade Association (NAMTA) in 1979. NAMTA refused to work with us to amend the labeling laws to cover chronic or long-term hazards, however, so we took the issue to various states. We were joined by many groups, including the American Academy of Pediatrics, the American Association of School Administrators, the American Public Health Association, and Artists Equity—a huge coalition of trade associations, health professionals, and artists. Yet the U.S. Public Interest Research Group and its many state offices became the backbone of the lobbying efforts.

Seven state legislatures understood the insanity of labeling products "nontoxic" when they contain known carcinogens and passed laws that required the chronic hazard labeling of art materials. These states were California, Connecticut, Florida, Illinois, Oregon, Tennessee, and Virginia, and others considered similar legislation. Each state had slightly different requirements, which made it almost impossible for manufacturers to design a label that met all of the different rules. At this point, even NAMTA decided that it would be better to have a federal law to address this issue with a single set of regulations. Within a few years, a bill was drafted and introduced.

On October 19, 1988, Congress passed the Labeling of Hazardous Art Materials Act (LHAMA). Some of the provisions of LHAMA included requiring manufacturers to determine whether their products contained chronic hazards; requiring labeling on those products with chronic hazards, which included a statement that these products were inappropriate for children; prohibiting the purchase of such materials for use by children in grade six and below; and adopting the labeling procedures developed by the American Society of Testing and Materials for the labeling of chronic hazards in art materials, ASTM D 4236.

This sounds good so far, but there was a flaw in the ASTM D 4236 standard that none of us appreciated fully at the time. This standard requires a review of the list of ingredients by a toxicologist, who will then select the proper warning phrases and certify that this labeling will provide users with the information they need to use the product safely. If the toxicologist thinks there are no significant hazards, no warnings are required. His or her determination should be reached without any personal conflict of interest. But the flaw in this procedure is that the certifying toxicologist is paid for this work by the art material manufacturers—and handsomely.

The art material manufacturer is the toxicologist's client, either directly or through a certifying organization such as the ACMI. The more clients a toxicologist or a certifying agency has, the greater the revenues, so pleasing the client is an important objective. A serious conflict of interest is built into the regulation. (We saw the same sort of problem with Enron's accountants and the bond rating agencies during the banking crisis.)

Some certifying agencies such as the ACMI developed seals of approval that included the word "nontoxic." This word is not one of the label terms in ASTM D 4236, but it has been used so often by certifiers that schools to this day often require their art supplies to be labeled "nontoxic." In my opinion, very toxic art materials were and are still labeled "nontoxic" as a result of this conflict of interest.

Just what does the "nontoxic" label really mean? To understand, we first need to learn the vocabulary of toxicology and discover the many different ways a substance can be toxic.

Chemical toxicity is dependent on the dose, the amount of the chemical that enters the body. Each chemical produces harm at a different dose. Highly toxic chemicals cause serious damage with only tiny doses. Moderately and slightly toxic substances are toxic at relatively higher doses.

Even substances considered nontoxic can be harmful if the exposure is great enough. This is how people die even from drinking too much water. Overdosing on water can be called hydroneutremia, hypoxic encephalopathy, or water intoxication. It can happen when athletes replace water they lose from sweating without replacing electrolytes, when psychiatric patients abuse water, or when the drug Ecstasy impairs people's judgment about the amount of water they've had. Water can also be used to murder someone.

On March 26, 2003, eleven members of the Psi Epsilon Chi fraternity at the State University of New York College at Plattsburgh were collectively charged with 150 crimes, including criminally negligent homicide. A police investigation found that the members hazed a student, Walter Dean Jennings, by forcing him to drink gallons of water poured through a funnel.[2]

Compare the toxic dose of water that is needed to kill a person with the tiny doses of extraordinarily toxic substances that can kill. A fatal dose of ricin, a chemical extracted from castor bean plants, can fit on the head of a pin.

Chemical toxicity is also dependent on the length of time over which exposure occurs. The effects of short and long periods of exposure differ dramatically. Often the same chemical can produce what appear to be very different diseases, depending on the length of time over which the dose or doses were delivered. Most of these two types of diseases can be divided into acute or chronic illnesses.

Acute illnesses are caused by large doses of toxic substances delivered in a short period of time. The symptoms from short-term exposures usually occur during or right after the exposure and last only a brief time. Depending on the dose, the outcome can vary from complete recovery, to recovery with some level of disability, to—at worst—death.

Acute illnesses are the easiest to diagnose because their cause and effect are easily linked. For example, a glue sniffer who huffs solvents such as paint thinner or gasoline is immediately affected. Depending on the dose, symptoms begin with lightheadedness and a "high" feeling. If exposure continues, it may lead to more severe effects, such as headache, nausea, and loss of coordination. At even higher doses, unconsciousness and death could result.

Repeated low-dose exposures over many months or years can cause chronic effects. They are the most difficult to diagnose. Usually, the symptoms are hardly noticeable until severe permanent damage has occurred. Symptoms appear very slowly, may vary from person to person, and may mimic other illnesses.

If the same solvents that made the glue sniffer high are put in an industrial paint and if many workers use this paint for decades, significant numbers of these workers will develop chronic illnesses. The illnesses will not be the same for all workers. For instance, chronic exposure to solvents during a lifetime of painting may produce dermatitis in some individuals, chronic liver or kidney effects in others, and nervous system damage in still others.

The most common disease among industrial painters, however, is a type of brain and nervous system damage that causes coordination problems, short-term memory loss, and clinical depression. This is a combination of symptoms recognized by workers' compensation boards as a consequence of exposure to organic chemical solvents. Yet these are the same symptoms seen in alcoholics. When you dry out an alcoholic, you don't suddenly find him transformed into a happy camper. He usually has subtle coordination deficits, short-term memory loss, and clinical depression. He may go right from taking antiabuse drugs to antidepressants. It is now clear that all solvents, including grain alcohol in excess, can cause narcosis and will damage the brain and the nervous system permanently over time.

Other effects in varying degrees of severity can also occur. They fall in a range that is partway between acute and chronic, such as "subacute" effects produced over weeks or months at lower doses than those that cause acute effects. Such in-between effects are also difficult to diagnose.

Lead is a good example of a substance that produces these in-between effects. Acute lead poisoning will bring about severe diarrhea, vomiting, and central nervous system depression in extremely high doses, even killing you. Low-level chronic exposure causes IQ deficits that may not even be noticed by the victim. Yet the lead exposure levels in between acute and low-level chronic doses can produce a baffling array of symptoms, from alternating diarrhea and constipation to high blood pressure and kidney problems, nerve conductivity decreases, and a wide range of mental states, from irritability to outright craziness. Several cases of lead poisoning of which I am personally aware were first suspected by smart professionals in the mental health field. Blood tests later confirmed their suspicions that their patients' mental faculties were actually being affected by lead.

Every chemical is eliminated from the body at a different rate. Cumulative toxins, such as lead, are eliminated slowly. Repeated exposure will cause them to accumulate in the body. The rate at which each chemical is eliminated from the body is called its "toxic substance half-life." Alcohol, for example, has a very short half-life. If you don't test a suspected drunk driver's blood within hours, the amount of alcohol in the blood will drop greatly.

Other chemicals, such as lead, have a much longer half-life. Once the lead leaves your bloodstream and deposits in your bones, the lead has a twenty-five-year half-life in your body. This means that only half of the dose of lead you absorbed today from your food, air, and water will be excreted over the next twenty-five years. Lead is considered a cumulative toxic substance because the lead deposited in your body leaves so slowly that each successive dose adds to the amount that is retained.

Every single chemical has its own unique half-life in the body. There is a complete range of half-lives, from extremely short to almost a lifetime and everything in between.

Chemicals with short half-lives cannot be found on medical tests unless you are tested shortly after exposure. Yet although the toxic chemical is not accumulating, the damage it does to your body may be increasing. For example, a retired industrial painter will not have any solvents in his or her body, but the damage to the liver, the kidneys, and the central nervous system caused by the solvents may persist and be permanent. There is no way to physically prove that the damage was from the solvent exposure, however, other than through the work records of the individual.

The total body burden is the total amount of a chemical that is present in the body from all sources. For example, we all have body burdens of lead from air, water, and food contamination. If we also work with lead-containing materials on the job, this exposure can add to the body's burden. To determine the body burden of any single substance, we must know all of the exposures to that substance. Today, we are carrying body burdens of many chemicals and are often exposed to more than one chemical at a time. These chemicals may interact in the body in two primary ways: additively and synergistically.

Exposure to two chemicals is considered additive when one chemical contributes to or adds to the toxic effects of the other. This can occur when both chemicals affect the body in similar ways. Working with paint thinner and drinking alcohol is an example because both the paint thinner and the alcohol affect the body in similar ways. Synergistic effects occur when two chemicals produce an effect that is greater than the total effects of each alone. For example, many deaths were caused when people consumed what was considered a socially acceptable amount of alcoholic beverages and then took a prescribed dose of barbiturate sleeping pills. Now that the synergistic effect of these two substances is understood, there are warnings about drinking alcohol while taking medications such as barbiturates.

Many chemicals are similar. Old-timers like me remember a solvent called carbon tetrachloride. It was available in gallon cans in every hardware store and was used to remove and thin paint, to clean fabrics, to remove tar, and for a host of other tasks. Most fire extinguishers also contained this chemical. It is not available now because it was found to be synergistic with alcohol. People who drank a few beers while using carbon tetrachloride could end up dead. This is why it is one of the very few chemicals banned by the Federal Hazardous Substances Act for use in consumer products.

The problem is that synergistic chemicals are usually identified only after there is evidence in the form of human exposures. When there is a high-enough pile of dead people, experts can be motivated to study the effects of the two chemicals and their interactions in the body. Only a tiny fraction of the chemicals in commerce have been studied for long-term effects—even one at a time. Clearly, there is no plan to start studying all of these chemicals two at a time, to discover their synergistic effects. So, once again, we are the guinea pigs.

I am personally very concerned about the synergistic effects of chemicals that were inhaled by people, including myself, who lived in Lower Manhattan around September 11, 2001. We now know that the dust from the collapse of the World Trade Center contained hundreds of toxic chemicals from the fallen buildings. Five buildings, two of them skyscrapers, were essentially ground to a powder. The hundreds of chemicals came from all of the cement, asbestos insulation, fiberglass insulation, computers and their monitors, windows, fluorescent lights, plastics, plywood and paneling, and much more. Then the pile burned for more than two months. The fire was so hot deep underground that even metal beams melted.

Many of the first responders and the workers who labored there in the months after 9/11 are now sick, and some have died. Lawsuits and class-action settlements of various types make the news every few months. The synergistic effects of that soup of chemicals to which they were exposed are clearly part of the problem.

Unlike ordinary toxic substances, the effects of carcinogens are not strictly dependent on the dose. No level of exposure is considered safe. Yet, the lower the dose, the lower the risk of developing cancer.

For this reason, exposure to carcinogens should be avoided altogether or kept as low as possible.

No dose of a carcinogen is considered safe because, theoretically, it takes only a single molecule of a carcinogen in the right person, in the right place in a cell, to change the cell's genetic blueprint (DNA) and reprogram it as a cancer cell. Obviously, we can't be fanatical about single molecule exposures, but it does explain why, no matter how low the dose, if a large-enough population is exposed, someone will get cancer.

There are several mechanisms by which cancer is caused, other than by a toxin directly affecting a cell's DNA. For example, some substances irritate or damage organ tissues so they must repeatedly repair and regrow themselves. When cells in the body have to divide rapidly during regrowth, there is a greater risk that one of the cells will not divide properly and will create a cancer cell instead.

Occupational cancers typically occur five to forty years after someone has been exposed to a toxic substance. This period of time, during which there are no symptoms, is referred to as a latency period. Latency usually makes the diagnosis of occupational cancers very difficult. For example, the latency period for getting lung cancer after exposure to asbestos is ten to twenty years, while the latency period for developing mesothelioma from asbestos exposure is twenty to forty years.

Chemicals that affect fetal organ development—that is, chemicals that cause birth defects—are called teratogens. They are hazardous primarily during the first trimester. Two proven human teratogens include the drug thalidomide and grain alcohol. Chemicals that are known to cause birth defects in animals are considered "suspect teratogens." Among these are many solvents, lead, and other metals.

Often the teratogen is capable of causing damage only at a particular stage in the pregnancy. For example, thalidomide can cause limbs to fail to form only when the mother is exposed between the twentieth and the thirty-sixth day of pregnancy, while the fetus's arms and leg buds are forming and differentiating. Before or after these dates, thalidomide is harmless to the fetus.

The selectivity of teratogens will complicate any studies that attempt to determine reasons for the increase in autism, hyperactivity, and learning difficulties in children. The important factor is not only what the mother was exposed to; it is also likely to depend on exactly when she was exposed and what systems in the brain were being formed at that time. If these afflictions are due to the child being exposed after birth, it will have to be a significant exposure at exactly the time when certain brain development phases are occurring.

Toxic chemicals can affect the growth and the development of the fetus at any stage of development. Lead, for example, not only damages the fetus, it damages children and adults at any stage of life. Toxic effects to the fetus can result from very small exposures to the mother at any time during pregnancy.

Allergies are adverse reactions of the body's immune system. Common symptoms may include allergic dermatitis, hay fever symptoms, and asthma. Most allergies are triggered by plant and animal proteins that are found in natural substances, such as pollen, mold, pet dander, natural rubber, and wood dusts. A number of metals—for example, nickel and chromium—can cause allergies. And synthetic chemicals, such as dyes, and certain plastics, like epoxy resins, are good at causing allergies.

Once allergies have developed, they tend to last a lifetime, and symptoms may increase in severity with continued exposure to the trigger substance. A few people even become highly allergic—that is, develop life-threatening reactions to exceedingly small doses of something. Certain people become highly allergic to bee venom, but industrial chemicals have also produced similar allergic effects, including death.

It is also important to understand that an allergy cannot occur the first time that one is exposed to a substance. Allergies require time for the body's immune system to produce antibodies to a substance and then begin such a massive production of antibodies that this overreaction causes the typical allergy symptoms. In general, the more often one is exposed to a substance that can cause this immune reaction, the more probable it is that one will develop an allergy.

Chemicals inhaled into the lungs, however, are more likely to cause hypersensitivity reactions than allergic reactions. When irritating or damaging chemicals are repeatedly inhaled over time, the mucous membranes in the lungs may become damaged and inflamed.

Such damage results in increased sensitivity to airborne chemicals, in much the same way that a tight shoe causes the foot to be sensitive to chafing. This is called hypersensitivity, and it is not an allergy. It can be just as serious as an allergy, however.

Chemicals that can produce allergic or hypersensitivity reactions in significant numbers of people are called "sensitizers." The longer people work with sensitizers, the greater the probability that they will begin to react to them.

Now that we've seen how very complex toxicity is, we can look at how inadequate product label regulations are in providing warnings. The consumer label regulations are found in the United States Federal Hazardous Substances Act.[3] These rules primarily require toxic warnings on products that are capable of causing acute (sudden onset) hazards.

Hazardous products are identified in the regulations by tests that expose animals to a single dose or period of exposure by skin or eye contact, inhalation, and ingestion. These tests are called the lethal dose (LD) tests by ingestion, skin, or eye contact or the lethal concentration (LC) tests by inhalation. The LD50 test by ingestion, for example, would be the test at a single dose that kills 50 percent of the test animals within two weeks of administration. To be "nontoxic," the dose that kills 50 percent of the rats must be equal to or greater than 5 grams per kilogram of body weight. In other words, if 50 percent of the rats manage to survive for two weeks after receiving a large dose of 5 grams per kilogram of body weight, the toxicologist can call it "nontoxic."

Remember that this testing will only find the dose that kills half of the test group, not the dose that kills one animal. And it's only testing for acute reactions. For example, the powdered asbestos discussed at the beginning of this chapter was labeled "nontoxic," based on all of the LD50 and LC50 tests, because all of the animals would appear healthy after exposure. Cancer takes much longer to develop.

Many highly toxic substances have been and still are used in art materials. This will always be the case, because colors that will remain unfaded on paintings for hundreds of years require the use of substances such as lead, cadmium, chromium, cobalt, and a host of other toxic metals and some very complex organic chemical pigments. There is no way to make traditional art materials "green."

Yet if toxic substances must be used, the labels should provide the information and the warnings that consumers need to use them safely. When it comes to children's art materials, these toxic pigments should not be used at all. After all, how long does your child's grade school artwork have to remain unfaded on the refrigerator door?

After ASTM D 4236 was incorporated into the Federal Hazardous Substances Act, labeling toxic art materials "nontoxic" by toxicologists was accomplished in several ways. One was by devising tests to show that the amount of the chronically toxic substance was below a level of concern.

In one example, many zinc white paints were labeled "nontoxic." Yet, unknown to consumers, some of these white pigments also contained a small amount of lead. They carried no warnings because the certifying toxicologist decided that lead was not a hazard at these levels. When California passed a law called Proposition 65, setting levels at which consumers had to be warned of the presence of lead in products, the conflict became very clear. For a brief time, there were some zinc white paints labeled "nontoxic" under ASTM D 4236 that also carried a Proposition 65 warning about lead and birth defects and brain damage! Clearly, California's health department felt that products containing lead at these levels required a warning, while the toxicologists who certified art materials did not. Art material manufacturers quickly either chose a purer grade of zinc oxide pigment that wasn't contaminated with lead or dropped the word "nontoxic" from the label to eliminate this confusion.

Another method toxicologists employed to label a toxic art material "nontoxic" was to declare that the toxic ingredient in the art material is not soluble and so will not be released into the body if inhaled and ingested. The typical solubility tests involve placing some of the product in an acid solution, and if the toxic material does not leach out into the acid solution, it is assumed that it will not be released in the human gut or lung either.

The test sounds reasonable, but the body doesn't work like a beaker of acid. The failure of this solubility theory is best seen with ceramic art materials, such as ceramic glazes. The solubility tests, as applied to ceramic materials, have an interesting history that will point out once again how good intentions and deliberate ignorance end up killing people.

In the late 1800s in the British pottery industry, there were many deaths every year from lead poisoning. This occurred because powdered raw lead compounds, such as red lead (lead oxide) and white lead (lead carbonate), were used as glaze ingredients to make glazes melt at low temperatures. Pottery workers were exposed to the lead dust while they worked.

A process called "fritting" was developed, in hopes of making the industry safer. Lead frits are produced by melting raw lead compounds, silica, and other ingredients into a glass and reducing the glass to a powder. This glass powder is called a "frit." The frits made this way were not very soluble in acid, and well-meaning people thought that this also implied that the lead would be insoluble in the human gut or lung. And in fact, from the moment that lead frits were introduced into the British pottery industry, deaths from lead poisoning became rare. As a result, the British government has required industrial lead frits to pass solubility tests with hydrochloric acid from 1889 onward—and it still does today.

For almost a hundred years, acid solubility tests were uncritically accepted worldwide and with essentially no supporting experimental data. Most particularly, no one assessed the effectiveness of other measures that were introduced into British potteries at precisely the same time that frits were introduced. These measures included ventilation, wet cleaning, hand washing, protective clothing, and other hygiene practices. It is now clear that these changes in hygiene were the main reasons that lives were saved.

It wasn't until 1985 that the acid solubility theory was finally tested. The investigators first compared the solubility of two lead frits (lead disilicate and lead monosilicate) with raw red lead in acid. Then they exposed rabbits to these substances by ingestion and by inhalation and plotted their blood lead concentrations against time (six days for exposure by ingestion; more than twelve days for exposure by inhalation). The study concluded

[that] those compounds which exhibit a lower solubility in acidic media do not behave differently in *in vivo* [live animal] experiments from the other compounds and, in particular, from red lead. Moreover, the compounds which exhibit the lowest absorption levels via the . . . digestive system . . . do not show the lowest solubilities in acidic and biological media.

Consequently, the *in vitro* [in laboratory glassware] solubility of each compound does not predict the degree of absorption *in vivo* by experimental animals. . . . We therefore call for attention against the injustified [*sic*] feeling of safety that often accompanies the use of such compounds.[4]

I provided a copy of this study to the subcommittee that votes on the ASTM D 4236 standard and expected that it would cause the members to rethink their practice of labeling these lead frit glazes as safe, even for children. Yet no one accepted these data from animal studies. It took human poisonings to convince the subcommittee.

The Poison Control Centers in the United States have received hundreds of reports of people ingesting lead glazes over the years. There were 318 cases reported in 1991 alone.[5] A number of these incidents occurred because teachers and occupational therapists used lead glazes in activities in nursing homes and mental hospitals. The glazes were used in hospitals because medical personnel and therapists believed the claims of safety on their labels. In fact, these acid-insoluble lead frit glazes were often labeled both "nontoxic" and "lead-free"!

These ingestion incidents were not followed up by medical monitoring because the doctors and the poison control personnel did not believe that their patients could be lead poisoned by the glazes. Then in 1992, one nursing home patient swallowed some glaze that was labeled "lead-free." Unlike the other cases of ingestion, this patient's blood was tested, and it was proved that the lead was absorbed. Later in 1992, a patient died of lead poisoning from the glazes.[6]

So now it was clear: both soluble and insoluble lead glazes carry risks. The reason is simple: people are not composed of acid and water. People's bodies can employ acid, water, enzymes, heat, movement, cellular activity, and many other strong dissolving mechanisms. An acid test will not predict release in the human gut or lung.

The existence of both animal and human data made it easier for people poisoned by lead frit glazes to sue for damages. In 1997, there were two cases in which children were allegedly brain damaged by their parents' ceramic work.[7] In both cases, the plaintiffs obtained hefty settlements from ceramic glaze manufacturers. I was an expert witness for the plaintiffs in both of these cases. The witness for the defense of the ceramic glaze companies that were being sued was Dr. Woodhall Stopford, a toxicologist for the Arts and Creative Materials Institute, who approved of the labeling of the glazes and certified that they met the standards in ASTM D 4236.

In his deposition in one of the 1997 trials, Dr. Stopford referred to the 1992 nursing home incident in the following exchange:

> Dr. Stopford: And at that time one of the glazes that was being used was in the low soluble category and its ingestion was associated with an elevated blood lead level.
>
> Question: Say that to me again in layman's terms?
>
> Dr. Stopford: It appeared that the categorization between insoluble and soluble did not really have meaning from a toxicologic basis.
>
> Question: Did it have any meaning for the consumers?
>
> Dr. Stopford: Well, it's apparent that they would be at risk if they ingested either soluble or insoluble lead glazes.[8]

It should have been obvious to the ACMI, the glaze manufacturers, and the world that the lead frits were not reliable ways to prevent lead exposure. Before too long, the labeling of the glazes changed.

Yet neither the laws nor the lawsuits seemed to stem the tide of hobby, consumer, and hospital use. There were continued incidents and another death in 1997 in North Carolina.[9] Today, I still see lead glazes used in at least half of the schools and the universities I inspect. When I ask the teachers about lead frits, most of them quote all of the old textbooks on their shelves, which say that these fritted glazes are safe.

This story is meant to demonstrate that the art materials labeling law, however well intentioned, does not work. We use tests that don't reflect the way the body works. We rely on the opinion of a toxicologist paid by the manufacturer. Worse, most substances used in art materials, especially organic paint pigments and dyes, have never been tested for chronic hazards. Yet the toxicologist can label these unstudied chemicals "nontoxic." Many of these "nontoxic" pigments and dyes actually are members of classes of chemicals that the National Toxicology Program has suggested be listed as carcinogens, such as the anthraquinone dyes and pigments.

Plus, labeling a product "nontoxic" for only one kind of use ignores the hazards from materials that are used in ways other than how the label directs. Artists and teachers traditionally use materials "creatively": for example, melting crayons for candle making, for batik resist, or for other processes causes these "nontoxic" products to release highly toxic gases and fumes from the decomposition of the wax and from some of the pigments.

The only thing the art materials labeling law did effectively was to require labeling on products containing *known* chronic hazards in amounts that the interest-conflicted toxicologist considered signifi-cant. That was something at least.

This law applied only to art materials, however. All of your con-sumer products—wall paints, cleaning products, home-improvement products, and the like—were not covered. You could still legally label consumer products "nontoxic" when they contained asbestos and other chronically toxic ingredients.

Then on October 9, 1992, the Consumer Product Safety Commission (CPSC) finalized new art material rule actions, which included expanding the guidelines to cover *all* consumer products, not only art materials. Yet the rules the commission set up for art materials are very different from those for general consumer products. Nonart material manufacturers and repackagers are also supposed to label chronically toxic products, but they are not required to submit their formulas to a toxicologist, supply criteria for determining chronic toxicity to the CPSC, or prepare a list of their chronically toxic products.

The CPSC further says that all consumer products must now be appropriately labeled or the CPSC can bring enforcement actions against each misbranded product. Yet because manufacturers do not readily provide ingredient information, how can a misbranded nonart product be identified? Certainly not through the development of chronic diseases in users years later. Basically, no one is watching the store. Without an enforcement of strict standards, rather than guidelines, consumers should not rely on chronic hazard labeling of nonart consumer products.

To be fair, some manufacturers are ethical and try to do a good job of labeling, but there is a massive lack of data on the chronic toxicity of our chemicals. For this reason, even good manufacturers honestly may not know that the chemicals in their products are hazardous. Worse, they have every reason to want to believe people who say the substances are safe and that they are making good products. If ethical manufacturers place warnings on their product labels, they are likely to be competing with less ethical manufacturers who do not provide warnings and whose products consequently appear safer to the buyer.

This problem has been demonstrated by the ethical manufacturer Golden Artist's Colors, which makes acrylic artists' paints for adults. In April 2000, the company published in its newsletter, *Daily Hues*, a statement that said, "We have seen the leap made from the 'absence of known hazards' to the declaration that a product is 'non-toxic' under this Standard [ASTM D 4236]. We do not believe these phrases mean the same thing and our new labels reflect this."

Paints that Golden could have labeled "nontoxic" under the ACMI program carried the following statement instead:

Health and Safety. Based upon toxicological review, there are no acute or *known* chronic health hazards with anticipated use of this product (most chemicals are not fully tested for chronic toxicity). Always protect yourself against potentially unknown chronic hazards of this and other chemical products by keeping them out of your body. Do this by avoiding ingestion, excessive skin contact, and inhalation of spraying mists, sanding dusts, and concentrated vapors. Contact us for further information.[10]

Even a labeling curmudgeon like myself could not have said this better. It also shows that good and ethical companies are out there. Yet this company pays a price for honesty. It has to compete for the business of uneducated consumers with companies that label paints nontoxic when they contain these same untested pigments. Golden has since modified its warning statement to be a little less inclusive.

• • •

So maybe all of the products, even those containing asbestos, really didn't expose people to high-enough levels of the toxins and were actually safe? It would have been hard to refute this argument because we had to wait twenty years or more after exposure to assess the cancer data. Well, now more than twenty years have passed, and we are seeing the data, at least on asbestos. Artists and teachers are now dying of mesothelioma.

The CDC's National Institute for Occupational Safety and Health (NIOSH) analyzed annual multiple-cause-of-death records for 1999–2005, which are the most recent years for which complete data are available. For those years, a total of 18,068 deaths of people with malignant mesothelioma were reported, increasing from 2,482 deaths in 1999 to 2,704 in 2005. The annual death rate was stable at 14.1 deaths per million in 1999 to 14.0 per million in 2005.

The mesothelioma rate of fourteen deaths per million in the United States indicates that asbestos exposure in the past was significant. And for every mesothelioma death, there are estimated to be three or more lung cancer deaths and deaths from other cancers caused by asbestos, such as intestinal cancers.

Of particular interest in this report are the proportionate mortality ratios (PMRs) that are found for certain professions. PMRs are the fraction of all deaths from a given cause in the study populations (in this case, various professions), divided by the same fraction from a standard population. In other words, certain professions were found to have significantly higher rates of mesothelioma than that of the general population. Of the 163 occupations reported, 5 professions were found to have significant PMRs: plumbers, pipe and steamfitters, mechanical engineers, electricians, and *elementary school teachers*.

It is my opinion that this is not an anomaly. Because there is a twenty- to forty-year latency period between asbestos exposure and the onset of mesothelioma, the exposures that would have caused these cancers in 1999–2005 would have occurred mostly between 1965 and

1985. There were two well-documented sources of asbestos exposure during this period of time:

1. Asbestos insulation, vinyl floor tiles, and other building elements in the old elementary schools.
2. Art materials.

In the 1960s and the 1970s, asbestos was an accepted and common art material ingredient for elementary school classes. To illustrate how fully accepted it was, almost every elementary school in the state of New York had copies of the *Art for Elementary School* booklet published by the University of the State of New York's State Education Department in Albany. Printed in 1967, the booklet includes the following recipe for a modeling compound:

Asbestos

    3 cups ground asbestos or asbestos shorts (used for covering
        furnace pipes)
    1 teaspoon glue
    1 cup flour
    Water

Add enough water to make a dough of the right consistency for modeling. Ground asbestos is very inexpensive. When dry, it is light in weight, durable, a light gray color, and may be painted with powder paints.

The booklet also suggested that Zonalite and vermiculite be used for some projects. We now know that these products contained significant amounts of asbestos at that time. In fact, Libby, Montana, where W. R. Grace mined the vermiculite that went into Zonalite and similar products, is famous for the number of cases of mesothelioma in its workers and in the general population.[11] I could still find this booklet on school shelves until the mid-1980s. So it was used during the right time period for mesothelioma to occur in those teachers now. The teachers were at even greater risk than the students, because they were the ones who mixed these materials for their classes.

Another school art material that clearly demonstrates a human toll is talc, a mineral that we all know as talcum powder. The fine cosmetic talcs we use are usually safe, but the industrial talcs made from ores contaminated with large amounts of other minerals are not the same. One of these talcs, from upstate New York mines run by the R.T. Vanderbilt Company, also contains significant amounts of asbestos.

For generations, this talc has been an ingredient in art materials used at all levels of education, from elementary schools to universities. It was common in ceramic clays and glazes, water putties, modeling compounds, paints, and even children's crayons, to harden the wax. The white haze that develops on the surface of those old crayons is usually talc.

The Vanderbilts began to mine talc in upstate New York in 1948. Within twenty years, health professionals became concerned about the talc workers. The first formal study of Vanderbilt talc was published in 1967, and it concluded that asbestos-related diseases such as asbestosis and lung cancer were seen in the talc miners and millers.[12]

Two more studies came to similar conclusions in 1974.[13] A few more studies were conducted, and then, in 1980, a major report on the talc was published by NIOSH.[14] The lead researcher was John Dement, Ph.D.

The conclusions of the 1980 NIOSH study were made personal for me the year after that study appeared. I read a letter to the editor in a magazine called *Ceramic Scope* from a woman named Audrey Eichelmann, who was dying of mesothelioma. Eichelmann was a doctor's wife from Port Ewen, New York, who had never smoked and never worked outside the home. Her only known contact with asbestos was the talc-containing slip used in her doll-making hobby/business. I contacted her first by letter and later by telephone. She was fully aware that her exposure was from the talc, and I had hoped that she would speak out in order to help others. Yet I had to respect her wishes not to start a controversy. She died of mesothelioma on August 14, 1981, at age fifty-four.[15]

Then in 1988, the federal Labeling of Hazardous Art Materials Act passed. Surely now, the toxicologists would refuse to certify products containing this asbestos-contaminated substance. Instead, the Arts and Creative Materials Institute's toxicologist, Dr. Woodhall Stopford, continued to allow this substance in the art materials. He decided to believe R.T. Vanderbilt's argument that the fibers in the talc only *looked* like asbestos. Vanderbilt held that the structures that appeared to be fibers under the microscope were actually cleavage fragments and other needlelike particles created when the ore was milled. Dr. Stopford took the word of those researchers who supported Vanderbilt's assertions and ignored the other researchers, including Dr. John Dement, the lead researcher on the 1980 NIOSH study, who by this time was a faculty member at Duke University (the same school on whose faculty Dr. Stopford serves).

By this time, many toxicologists also understood that it was not relevant whether the mineral in the talc was asbestos. Research on other inert mineral fibers was demonstrating that any long, thin, inert fiber could cause asbestos diseases.

In 1990, NIOSH reviewed that 1980 data and reaffirmed its position that the talc did indeed contain asbestos. Still, Dr. Stopford continued to certify children's and adult art products that contained it.

Then on May 23, 2000, the *Seattle Post Intelligencer*'s crack investigative reporter Andrew Schneider reported that three major brands of crayons that he arranged to have tested were found to contain asbestos: Crayola, Prang, and Rose Art. The highest amount found was reportedly 2.86 percent in Crayola's Orchid color.[16] Even 1 percent asbestos in a product qualifies it as an asbestos material for adult asbestos workers.

The asbestos in the crayons was used to harden the wax, and it was traced to R.T. Vanderbilt's talc. The story reignited the debate about Vanderbilt talc contaminants and the ACMI labeling program. The ACMI had certified all three brands of crayons as "nontoxic." The statement written in 2000 by Deborah Fanning, the executive director of the ACMI, was still on its Web site as of May 2010. It says in part:

> Some ACMI members do use "talc" in crayon products and a principal talc supplier to crayon manufacturers is R.T. Vanderbilt Co. . . . Its talc mines and ores have been the subject of hundreds of tests and assays over the last twenty years. Its talc products have been found free of asbestos contamination. . . . In fact, Vanderbilt certifies to its customers that the talc is free of asbestos.
>
> Woodhall Stopford, M.D., with Duke University Medical Center and principal toxicologist of the ACMI Certification Program, stated that he has reviewed many of the analytical

test reports on Vanderbilt talc, which unanimously have found the talc to be asbestos free.[17]

Consumers should wonder about which "unanimous" studies he relied on for this opinion. By my count in the year 2000, there were four studies that supported Vanderbilt's position but eleven that came to the opposite conclusion. This includes the 1980 NIOSH report, whose lead researcher was Dr. John Dement.

By 2004, I had personally seen more than fourteen studies that concluded that the talc either contained asbestos or could cause the same diseases that asbestos can cause, namely, asbestosis, mesothelioma, and lung cancer. Still, the talc was in many ACMI-certified ceramic materials.

Yet 2004 was also the year that a fifty-three-year-old man named Peter Hirsch died of mesothelioma. Hirsch had operated a small pottery shop in New Jersey from 1975 to 1982. He used Vanderbilt talc in making his glazes.

Bonnie Parker, the widow of Peter Hirsch, filed a suit through Moshe Maimon of Levy, Phillips & Konigsberg, LLP, in New York City shortly after Peter was diagnosed. For the first time, a major asbestos litigation firm was going to take on the R.T. Vanderbilt Company, as well as Hammill and Gillespie, the dealer that sold Peter the talc. As is common in asbestos litigation, another firm, Georgia-Pacific, was also a defendant because Peter had used its asbestos-containing joint compound when he renovated his small shop.

I was one of the expert witnesses who testified in this ground-breaking lawsuit. Following a four-week trial in Middlesex County Superior Court and three days of deliberations, the jury ruled in the first-ever U.S. verdict that connected industrial talc with asbestos-related cancer. The estate of Peter Hirsch was awarded $3.35 million in compensatory damages on November 16, 2006, by a Superior Court jury in New Brunswick. The jury awarded $1.4 million for pain and suffering, $1.45 million for loss of earnings, and $500,000 for his widow's loss of companionship. On December 7, the punitive damage phase of the trial ended in a settlement of a confidential sum.

Almost more important than the jury awards were the revelations that came out during the trial. For example, at the start of the trial, attorneys for Vanderbilt admitted that there were eight confirmed cases of mesothelioma among its own workers. Yet a study of local death certificates by two of the other experts at the trial found five more cases of mesothelioma in workers. These deaths were entered into the record by stipulation, bringing the total to thirteen cases in a workforce of around a thousand people. Because only one death from mesothelioma in one million people is expected, this is clear evidence of asbestos exposure among the workers.

Another important revelation involved the four studies on which the defense relied to prove the talc was not hazardous. The researchers in two of those studies had disclosed that Vanderbilt financed their work. At trial, however, it was shown that all four of the studies favorable to Vanderbilt's position had been financed by Vanderbilt. Putting these four conflict-of-interest studies up against the roughly fourteen studies introduced by the plaintiff's attorneys probably made the decision for the jury much easier.

The next trial against Vanderbilt was even more successful. Johnny Franklin, the husband of Flora Franklin, sued R.T. Vanderbilt under product liability negligence. In 2005, Flora Franklin died from malignant mesothelioma at age sixty-eight, after suffering from this disease for a year and a half. She had worked as a tile sorter at Florida Tile in Lawrenceburg, Kentucky. Florida Tile used millions of pounds of R.T. Vanderbilt talc over the years, and the dust was everywhere in the plant, according to testimony from the plant manager and other workers. A Kentucky OSHA inspector also testified that when he measured the dust in the air, he identified tremolite asbestos in the talc.

This trial used all of the studies and the data assembled in the first trial. In addition, there was exquisite courtroom drama due to an extremely creative plaintiff's attorney, Joe Satterley. First, the owner of the talc mines and the scion of the Vanderbilt family, Hugh Vanderbilt Sr., sent his son, Paul, to oversee the defense team's jury selection process. In a surprise move, Satterley subpoenaed Paul while he was there. Paul Vanderbilt is the vice president, secretary, and director of environmental affairs for R.T. Vanderbilt. Yet at trial, he testified that he had no knowledge of the number of his workers who had developed asbestos-related diseases, nor did he seem to have an interest in environmental safety.

Joe Satterley's final question to Paul Vanderbilt elicited an incredible response:

Satterley. Final question: You'll agree that if it is determined that your product kills people, causes mesothelioma, the product should be banned from sale in the United States, correct?

Paul Vanderbilt. If it causes mesothelioma, yes.

Satterley. It should be banned, right?

Paul Vanderbilt. Yes.

Next, by using posters of enlarged photos taken by his experts that showed the fibers under a microscope, Satterley was able to demonstrate to the jury that the same kinds of fibers seen in R.T. Vanderbilt talc were also present in Mrs. Franklin's lungs.

Finally, stunning evidence was presented by one of Satterley's witnesses, Thomas Rogers, a seventy-two-year-old former employee of R.T. Vanderbilt with a tenth-grade education. He had worked twenty-seven years for Vanderbilt as a miner and a mechanic and in other capacities. Rogers was asked about an incident that happened sometime in the late 1970s or early 1980s after the John Dement NIOSH study found that the talc contained asbestos.

The jury heard testimony from Rogers that Hugh Vanderbilt Sr. stated that he would spend millions to fight the classification of the fibers in the talc as asbestos, and if that was not successful, he had a senator in his hip pocket. In Rogers's own words in deposition:

Well, they was having quite a spell on whether that [the talc] was going to be called asbestos or not and, of course, they had their own labs I guess and they was testing against NYAS [NIOSH] and he [Hugh Vanderbilt] said that in the end if all else failed he padded [patted] his back pocket he says, I got a Senator right here.

Rogers also said that the researchers from the labs that R.T. Vanderbilt used to defend its talc were supposed to come to the mines without notifying people in advance and take samples at any locations they thought appropriate. Instead, Rogers said that management told the workers from where to take the samples and to give these to the researchers. This is consistent with the phone conversation I had with John Dement in the early 1980s, in which he said he had noticed that asbestos occurs in pockets scattered throughout the ore. By carefully selecting samples, it would be possible to get ones that were asbestos-free.

The jury awarded $5,659,000 in total damages to Franklin. Those damages included in part $5,000,000 for pain and suffering, $20,000 for medical expenses incurred, plus punitive damages for clear and convincing evidence of fraudulent concealment and gross negligence in the amount of $450,000. The awards to the Franklin estate were reduced by 30 percent to reflect the jury's allocation of fault. Its members found R.T. Vanderbilt 70 percent at fault and a few other defendants (Ford Motor for brake linings, Georgia-Pacific for joint compound used in the house, and so on) were found jointly responsible for the other 30 percent. After apportioning fault, the court entered judgment against R.T. Vanderbilt totaling $4,090,000. The date of the verdict was September 10, 2007.

R.T. Vanderbilt moved for a new trial and a judgment notwithstanding the verdict. The trial court, after extensive arguments and a hearing on the matter, denied R.T. Vanderbilt's post-trial motions.

After the first trial, Vanderbilt's Web site said, "Contrary to some news reports, the jury did not find that Vanderbilt's talc contains asbestos." Actually, that is true. The jury was never asked to make a decision about this complex mineralogy. It was asked to determine whether the talc could cause mesothelioma, and the jury members responded with a resounding yes.

Dr. Stopford stopped certifying products that contain Vanderbilt talc but has maintained that this was due to public perception, not that he thinks the talc was hazardous.[18] And R.T. Vanderbilt closed its talc mines at the end of 2008.

But the problem is not over. I know of university art departments that have stockpiled the talc because they knew it was going off the market. The resulting mesothelioma cases will continue to be filed during the next forty to fifty years.

I have been retained in two more lawsuits. One plaintiff was a ceramics teacher of children with disabilities who died of mesothelioma at age fifty-seven. The case recently settled with a confidentiality agreement barring me from saying more. The other lawsuit involves a junior high school pottery teacher who is dying of mesothelioma. A trial date has not been set.

If you think you have escaped this hazard because you are not an artist, the Vanderbilt talc was in hundreds of other products as well. There are now mesothelioma lawsuits instituted by the families of users of a popular powdered water putty/plaster repair product that is mixed with water and used in home-repair projects.

Asbestos is an extreme example, which I used here to make a point, but many other "nontoxic" products could be full of toxic chemicals. I'm hoping this chapter leaves you with a general distrust of the nontoxic label, both in the past and currently. When you see "nontoxic" on a product, keep the following facts in mind:

- "Nontoxic" can still legally mean that there are no immediate, acute hazards as determined by the LD50 and LC50 tests.
- "Nontoxic" may mean there are little or no chronic data available on the substance. If the substance is not acutely toxic, and one can't prove it is toxic in the long term, many manufacturers feel that they have the right to call it nontoxic. Even if there are studies showing that the substance is toxic, manufacturers in the United States have traditionally waited for absolute, unequivocal proof, which in most cases is never available because we don't study our chemicals.
- An art material is "nontoxic" if a toxicologist paid by the manufacturer decides it is safe. The dramatic failure in this labeling procedure was illustrated with the lead ceramic glazes and asbestos-containing materials such as talc.
- Some art materials that have never been evaluated by a toxicologist may be labeled "nontoxic" illegally due to weak enforcement of the art materials labeling law. For example, in 1995, a cameraman and a reporter from Channel 9 in New York went with me to a major art materials outlet. That night on the evening news, we showed viewers about a dozen imported products that did not conform to the law, some labeled "nontoxic," which were being sold illegally. This is still true today, and a little research will lead you to many sources of noncompliant "nontoxic" products.

- Labeling of ordinary consumer products is pretty much up to the manufacturer and its paid advisers. Because there is no enforcement mechanism in the regulations for the chronic hazard labeling of ordinary consumer products, there is not much incentive to provide warnings.
- There is no regulatory requirement to warn consumers about damage to most of the body's organs, such as the lungs, the liver, and the kidneys. Only four types of chronic hazards are covered by the Federal Hazardous Substances Act regulations. These are cancer, and developmental, reproductive, and neurological damage.

Lawsuits are just about the only recourse for the public. Manufacturers often say that they fear lawsuits and that's why they do a good job of labeling. But in the case of chronic health effects that don't appear for ten to forty years, a company's CEO who makes that statement is not at risk from lawsuits. He will have his retirement income and his bonuses and be living in the Bahamas before the first case is filed.

CHAPTER 3

Calling a Product Green Doesn't Make It Stop Being Poison

The Chemical Substitution Game

I f you have ever owned or ridden in a new car, you already know what phthalates smell like. They are the primary substance in the typical "new car" smell. In addition, when a car is brand new, the seats are pliable and the dashboard has a nice finish. You may also have noticed that in cold weather, a greasy film condenses on the insides of the windows. That film usually consists of phthalates that have off-gassed from the plastics and condensed on the cold window's surface.

Old cars no longer smell of phthalates, and the seats are not as soft. The dashboard may even have cracks where the sun has beaten down especially hard. This means that almost all of the phthalates have migrated out of the plastic, leaving it brittle and slightly shrunken in size. Of course, you can fight back by buying an aerosol can of "new car" and spray the phthalates back on the dashboard's surface and into your lungs. I don't recommend this act of vanity.

The phthalates are not acutely hazardous, meaning that they have no immediately obvious effects, except in people who are exquisitely sensitive to them. Yet some phthalates are listed or suspected carcinogens, and many show that they can affect the reproductive development of both male and female children.

In 1988, California listed a cancer-causing phthalate on its Proposition 65 warning list. By 2007, the state had listed four more phthalates as developmental hazards. Still, our Consumer Product Safety Commission (CPSC) did nothing; it took an act of Congress to institute at least minimal consumer protections against these phthalates. Congress passed the Consumer Product Safety Improvement Act, which forced the CPSC to ban six of the most commonly used phthalates.[1] Effective as of February 10, 2009, the act made it unlawful for any person to manufacture for sale, distribute in commerce, or import any children's toys and/or child-care articles that contain these six phthalates at levels higher than 0.1 percent. (A "children's toy" means a product intended for a child twelve years of age or younger for use when playing, and a "child-care article" means a product that a child three and younger would use for sleeping, feeding, sucking, or teething.)

Plastic toy and child-care article manufacturers never missed a beat in their production schedules. They merely switched to unregulated substitute phthalates. The new phthalates will function almost the same as the old chemicals, and most new chemicals are rarely tested for long-term health hazards. The Environmental Protection Agency (EPA) may make the manufacturer protect its workers while the company is developing or manufacturing the untested chemical, but the chemical can be added to products without much fanfare, and you will probably not even notice the difference.

The EPA has Significant New Use Rules (SNURS) for brand-new untested chemicals. If significant amounts of a previously unknown chemical will be manufactured, the EPA looks for data on similar chemicals and makes a guess as to whether the new chemical will be hazardous to the workers producing it or to the environment. If the manufacturer's proposal includes precautions for workers to preclude their exposure and methods of control to avoid spills in the environment, the EPA may be satisfied and let the company begin production of the chemical. If the EPA guesses that the chemical still could cause environmental problems, it may require that the chemical be tested for its ability to harm fish or microorganisms or undergo some other test. The situation is a crapshoot, because the decisions are made on the basis of sketchy testing of similar chemicals, and there is no testing required for the consumer product in which this new and untested chemical will be used.

Think about that the next time you hear this claim: New and improved! New formula! It sounds great, but since the "new and improved" products usually function almost the same as the originals did, it's likely that one or more of the chemicals in the products have been exchanged for other chemicals that do the same job. This is called "chemical substitution."

Chemical substitution is possible because chemicals that are closely related by formula and structure also have similar physical properties. Therefore, chemical substitution is a way for manufacturers to alter their products to avoid regulation—often without making the products safer for us to use. For example, if a certain chemical is banned, manufacturers can look for another chemical that is almost identical to the banned chemical. Unfortunately, similar chemicals often have toxic properties that are similar as well. Frequently, the replacement chemicals are not as well studied and don't even have to be reported as toxic on labels or material safety data sheets (MSDS).

Some readers may be thinking with relief that a child born today will grow up in a safer world than we all have. After all, we know about asbestos and radium, and we've stopped putting mercury in thermometers and X-raying our feet at the shoe store. This chapter ought to put that idea to rest. We've become extremely adept at creating new chemicals, including some that look an awful lot like known hazardous ones, and this coming generation will be exposed to a mind-boggling number of chemicals. Someday people will be shocked that these chemicals were once commonly used.

Plus, we haven't actually banned asbestos.

Evidence that is strong enough for an outright ban on a substance usually requires a very large pile of dead bodies attributed to the use of the toxin. As we saw in the last chapter, thousands of documented deaths from lung cancer, mesothelioma, and asbestosis finally resulted in an EPA ban on use of asbestos in manufacturing. Then a coalition of manufacturers sued the EPA and overturned the ban. So bans are very hard to get, and even harder to keep in effect, if industry decides to oppose them.

The Bureau of Alcohol, Tobacco and Firearms (ATF) is supposed to have control over cigarettes. Yet decades of people dying and becoming disabled from smoking have not resulted in a ban on tobacco. There have been changes in the label warnings, however, and individual states and cities have banned smoking in certain locations, such as restaurants. As I write this chapter, it looks like control over tobacco will now leave the domain of the ATF and shift to the FDA, which may have better regulatory tools to control tobacco use.

The EPA, the ATF, OSHA (Occupational Safety and Health Administration), and the FDA cannot be directly involved in the banning of consumer products. Instead, regulation and bans on consumer products must emanate from the CPSC. This agency is responsible for enforcing and administering the Federal Hazardous Substances Act (*Code of Federal Regulations*, Title 16, Part 1500).

The Federal Hazardous Substances Act defines "consumer products" as products that can reasonably be expected to be purchased, stored, or used in or around a place where people live. The definition also covers products used or stored in a garage, a shed, a carport, or another building that is considered part of a normal household.

The CPSC has been routinely weak in its pursuit of consumer safety, due to an inadequate budget and uncomfortably close associations with the very manufacturers of the products it regulates. This agency is far more likely to work with manufacturers in voluntary programs than to assert its powers directly. Most of the major changes in the CPSC's regulations have been brought about by activist groups petitioning for action, by pressure from states that have passed laws stricter than those of the CPSC, or by actual acts of Congress mandating that the CPSC regulate or ban certain substances.

In the Bush administration, in particular, enforcement was lax. In 2008, Congress, frustrated with the do-nothing agency, passed the Consumer Product Safety Improvement Act. This act forced the CPSC to lower the levels of lead that it allows in children's products and essentially banned certain vinyl plastic additives (phthalates) in children's toys and child-care articles. The act also mandated an increase in the budget so that the CPSC would actually have the personnel to enforce the consumer regulations. The Bush-selected head of the CPSC, Mary Toro, declared that she didn't need or want the additional money. One of the last things President Bush did on his way out of the White House was to use his executive power to cancel that CPSC funding.

Consumers need to be fully aware that the CPSC has inadequate funding and a staff that is very reluctant to go head-to-head with U.S. manufacturers or importers on behalf of public safety. For one thing, if the manufacturers decide to defend themselves vigorously, the CPSC will be hard-pressed to find the money and the staff to fight back.

Let's look at the actual regulations enforced by the CPSC to see just how many chemicals and substances have been banned or restricted by the Federal Hazardous Substances Act. To compile this list, I went through several sections of the code and condensed and reorganized the following banned items:

1. Extremely flammable water repellents for use on masonry walls and floors inside homes and certain extremely flammable contact adhesives.
2. Carbon tetrachloride and mixtures containing this chemical.
3. Certain types of consumer-use fireworks that contain too much explosive material or do not meet certain performance requirements. Also included are reloadable tube aerial shell fireworks devices that use shells wider than 1.75 inches.
4. Liquid drain cleaners that contain 10 percent or more by weight of sodium or potassium hydroxide that are not packaged in child-resistant containers.
5. Products that contain soluble cyanide salts.
6. Asbestos in three limited forms: (a) general-use garments containing asbestos (e.g., asbestos gloves, aprons, etc.), (b) consumer patching compounds (e.g., spackle), and (c) artificial ashes and embers used in fake fireplaces that contain free-form asbestos that can be inhaled.
7. Aerosol spray can products that contain the carcinogen vinyl chloride, either as an ingredient or as the propellant gas.

8. Many types of toys that contain toxic substances or that present physical hazards (see the massive sections on toy regulations in 16 CFR 1500.85, 1303.1, and ASTM 963, whose tests for soluble antimony, arsenic, barium, cadmium, chromium, lead, mercury, and selenium are now mandatory).

9. Wall paints and other surface coatings that contain more than 0.06 percent lead and articles coated with lead paints, such as furniture, toys, and other articles intended for use by children, was the original ban, but the 2008 Consumer Product Safety Improvement Act required the CPSC to drop that limit to 0.01 percent.

10. As of February 10, 2009, the Consumer Product Safety Improvement Act made it unlawful to make, sell, or distribute children's toys and/or child-care products that contain any of six phthalate plasticizers in amounts equal to or greater than 0.1 percent by weight.

11. There are also Special Labeling Requirements and/or concentration restrictions on ethylene glycol, diethylene glycol, benzene, toluene, xylene, petroleum distillates, turpentine, methyl alcohol, and charcoal and for art materials that present a risk of chronic toxicity. This requirement for art materials is needed because children's and adults' art materials are exempt from all of the other bans.

So, there you have all of the laws that protect you from chemicals through the use of bans, limits, or special labeling. It's an odd and disorganized collection of products. The individual selections often reflect the efforts of citizen's groups that pressured for bans on certain substances. For example, highly flammable waterproofing products and contact adhesives are banned, but highly flammable solvents can be used in other products. Asbestos is banned for use in garments, spackle, and faux fireplace logs, but not in other consumer products, such as your brake linings. And the asbestos industry won the right in court to put asbestos in your vinyl floor tiles and other products.

For the odd handful of chemicals that the CPSC bans, such as vinyl chloride propellants, carbon tetrachloride, and cyanide salts, there are substitutes that can be used.

. . .

Suppose you were the manufacturer of a paint stripper that contained carbon tetrachloride when the CPSC was trying to ban this chemical in the late 1960s. First, you would form a coalition with other industries that use or manufacture carbon tetrachloride, and you would generate publicity about how great this chemical is and warn consumers that if the CPSC bans it, they will no longer be able to buy good paint strippers or else these products will be prohibitively expensive. That would buy you some time. In the case of carbon tetrachloride, however, it was hard to get the public on board. Carbon tetrachloride is not only toxic and carcinogenic, it has a unique way of interacting in the body with plain old grain alcohol. Some people who used this chemical while having a couple of beers were found dead. That's not good for your PR campaign.

So, it appeared as if the CPSC would get its ban in 1970. Okay, no problem. Carbon tetrachloride is a molecule composed of a single carbon atom with four chlorine atoms stuck on it. That's what the name "carbon tetrachloride" means: a carbon and four chlorides.

Yet everyone in the paint industry knows there is another substance, almost as cheap, that consists of a single carbon atom with two chlorine atoms on it, and it works about the same. It is called dichloromethane or methylene chloride. Now you can manufacture your paint thinner with this substitute solvent and advertise it proudly as "new and improved." You'll be able to do this for a couple of decades before it will be obvious that this chemical is also toxic and a carcinogen. Despite the knowledge about its toxicity, you can keep right on using dichloromethane because it is still not banned today.

For another example, suppose you were manufacturing a product that contained benzene, a common solvent used in paints, paint strippers, fabric cleaners, and many, many more products in the 1970s. When it was found to be a potent carcinogen and would require special warning labels that might put your customers on notice, you could find a substitute.

Benzene is simply a ring of six carbon atoms. Why not add another carbon atom with three hydrogen atoms in one spot on that ring? This chemical is now called toluene, and it works just about the same as benzene. Is toluene also a carcinogen? The EPA and other agencies say there are inadequate data available to make this determination. So we continue to encounter this chemical without knowing for certain what its long-term hazards really are.

Replacing benzene with toluene or carbon tetrachloride with dichloromethylene is called substituting in the same chemical class. Benzene and toluene both have benzene rings in them and are called "aromatic hydrocarbons," because all of the chemicals in this class have a typical solvent odor. Carbon tetrachloride and methylene chloride are both in a class called "chlorinated hydrocarbons," in which one or more chlorine atoms is placed on a hydrocarbon molecule.

To better understand class substitution, we need to delve into a bit of simple chemistry. For those of you who have never taken any chemistry classes, I guarantee that this is easy enough to follow. For others who know a little about chemistry, this will be a review. If there were any other way to explain this, believe me, I would do it, but the only way for you to make sound consumer decisions is to grasp a few of these basic principles. Otherwise, you are condemned to simply believe the manufacturers, the activists, or others who have axes to grind.

Without realizing it, you probably already know about classes of chemicals. For example, suppose you have an ink stain on your shirt that will not dissolve in soapy water, bleach, paint thinner, or nail polish remover (acetone). Then you try rubbing alcohol (isopropyl alcohol) from the medicine chest and find that it makes the stain disappear. In this case, it is likely that the stain can also be removed by grain alcohol and wood alcohol. This is because these alcohols are all in one class, called the "alcohols," and they dissolve similar materials.

What makes them "alcohols" is a hydroxyl group composed of oxygen and hydrogen atoms (-OH) stuck on one of the carbon atoms in the molecule. A carbon atom has four places on which you can stick another atom. Carbon is sort of like a tinker toy with four holes in which sticks can be placed. A single carbon atom with hydrogen on all four bonds is called methane. This molecule is the building block of all organic chemistry and the simplest organic chemical possible.

Methane is also the greenhouse gas chemical that is famously emitted in quantity by cows when they pass gas (and when we do the same).

If we replace one of the hydrogen atoms on methane with the -OH or hydroxyl group, we now have transformed methane to methyl alcohol. Also known as "wood alcohol," this is the stuff that burns in those little Sterno heating cans under the hot dishes on a buffet table.

If, instead, we start with two carbon atoms, each of which has given up one of its four hydrogen atoms in order to attach to each other, that molecule is called ethane. If we then replace one more hydrogen on one of those two molecules with an -OH, ethane is transformed into ethyl alcohol, better known as booze.

The same thing happens when we start with three carbon atoms stuck together in a row; this molecule is called "propane," the stuff in the tank that we fire up the barbeque with. If we replace one of those hydrogen atoms with an -OH, propane becomes propyl alcohol. And if we rearrange the three carbon atoms in propyl alcohol from a straight line to a "Y" or branched chain, we have "isopropyl alcohol" or rubbing alcohol. You get the idea.

All of these alcohols will have some similar properties, and they are similarly toxic.

As a group, the common alcohols will all bring about narcosis — and this narcosis is perceived as desirable, in the case of ethyl alcohol. At high doses, all of these alcohols will cause brain damage, unconsciousness, and even death. Chronic repeated exposure over the years to any of the alcohols can be expected to result in the same syndrome that is seen in alcoholics: liver damage and permanent nervous system damage, often manifesting in problems in coordination and mental deficits such as short-term memory loss and depression. These symptoms are well documented in alcoholics and industrial workers who have a history of solvent exposure. The difference in toxicity of the various alcohols is primarily in the amount of each alcohol it takes to cause these effects, plus certain side effects that are produced by particular alcohols.

For example, during the Great Depression in the 1930s, people who were desperate for a drink turned to wood alcohol, which was cheap and unregulated by the ATF. Yet wood alcohol (methanol) is much more toxic to people than grain alcohol (ethanol) is. In addition to the desired narcosis, methanol can do severe damage to the nervous system, which includes damaging the optic nerve to cause blindness.

It was also during the Depression that many people believed there were ways of making methanol safe. For example, some thought that filtering the methanol through a loaf of bread would change it into ethanol—a theory on a par with the ancient alchemists' recipes for converting lead into gold. Granted, the methanol would take on some of the grain flavor from the bread and would taste more like ethanol, but methanol itself remains stubbornly unchanged by this process.

There have even been people who from time to time have ingested other alcohols to become inebriated. The most famous is probably Kitty Dukakis, the wife of ex-presidential candidate and former governor of Massachusetts Michael S. Dukakis. Apparently to address a life long struggle with depression and alcoholism, Mrs. Dukakis tried drinking rubbing alcohol (isopropanol) in 1989 and ended up in the hospital. She completely recovered and wrote a book in 2006, *Shock: The Healing Power of Electroconvulsive Therapy*, which mentions this incident.

Obviously, grain alcohol is the safest of the alcohols. It is also used for cleaning and disinfecting surfaces, including your arm before you get an injection. Yet the Department of Alcohol, Tobacco and Firearms will not allow manufacturers to sell you pure ethanol because the hooch industry would be undercut. Why buy gin if you could add a little juniper flavor to pure ethanol and make your own 200 proof Beefeater?

For this reason, all ethyl alcohol must be sold "denatured," that is, sold with an additive mixed into it that will make it incredibly unpleasant or even poisonous to drink. There are about fifteen different legal denaturing ingredients, including jet fuel (which tastes terrible and is bad for you), methyl isobutyl ketone (it's toxic and it stinks), and methanol (this is poisonous). These are added in the range of a few percent, which is enough to ruin your day if you try to drink them. The denatured alcohol products, however, especially those with 4 percent methanol in them, are about the safest alcohols to use for cleaning and disinfecting surfaces or your skin prior to an injection. In fact, methanol-denatured ethanol is safer as a back rub than traditional isopropyl rubbing alcohol is.

The point of these stories is to firm up your understanding that all alcohols are in the same class and have similar chemical properties and toxicities. By looking at the data, you can pick out the alcohol that is safest to use. We can use these same principles to learn about other chemical classes, such as the glycol ethers.

Grain alcohol may remove certain stains, but it is not a good grease and soil cutter. If you want a really fast and efficient cleaning product, the commercial ones such as Formula 409, Simple Green, and Windex clean faster than any alcohol or soap and water could. This is because they contain small amounts, usually in the range of 2 to 6 percent, of one or more of the most powerful grease-cutting classes of chemicals known: the "glycol ethers."

Many people have heard of glycols, a class of chemicals that is used in antifreeze solutions in your car's radiator. Others may remember that ethers were used as anesthetics in the early 1900s. Yet the glycol ethers I will discuss are not at all like either glycols or ethers. Glycol ethers are in a class of their own.

Everyone has been exposed to the glycol ethers. You can't possibly have escaped. They are in paints, varnishes, stains, inks, brake fluids, perfumes, cosmetics, and, of course, a vast number of cleaning products. They mix with water, and many water-based cleaners and paints contain them.

Heavy overexposure to the glycol ethers can result in anemia, intoxication (as with alcohol), and irritation of the eyes and the nose. In laboratory animals, low-level exposure to some of the glycol ethers has been shown to cause birth defects and can damage a male's sperm and testicles. Some of the common glycol ethers haven't been studied for reproductive hazards or cancer. Yet there are enough data for the New Jersey Department of Health to state on its fact sheet that the most commonly used glycol ether (2-butoxyethanol) "may be a carcinogen in humans since it has been shown to cause liver cancer in animals."[2] With this opinion in mind, it is upsetting to consider that 2-butoxyethanol is also the active ingredient in one of the Gulf of Mexico oil spill dispersants and tons of it are being released into the sea.

You are exposed to the glycol ethers when you inhale them while using the cleaners that contain them. If the cleaner does not also have a lot of perfumes or odorants in it, you know you are exposed because you can smell the chemical. If there are strong perfumes, the odor of the glycol ethers can be covered up, so that the water-based cleaner appears to have no chemical solvents in it at all.

While you inhale them, you may also be exposed in another way. Most glycol ethers can silently penetrate your skin and enter your bloodstream without altering or damaging your skin, causing pain, or giving you any other warning.

If that were not enough, the glycol ethers will penetrate through natural rubber gloves and many types of plastic gloves without changing the gloves' appearance. So, while you are cleaning, you are being exposed both by inhaling the vapors as the cleaner evaporates and by exposure through your skin, even if you wear gloves. These are reasons why even the 2 to 6 percent of these chemicals commonly used in cleaning products can be significant.

The glycol ethers are all related to one another in a single chemical class. There are hundreds of them. We will look at only the first four members of the glycol ether class (see the table below).

The first two glycol ethers (2-methoxy- and 2-ethoxy-ethanol) are so very toxic that it is rare to see them in our products today. But if you were cleaning and doing household painting and repairs as I was from the 1970s to the early 1990s, these highly toxic glycol ethers

Common Glycol Ethers

Chemical Name	CAS Number*	Structure (by group)
2-methoxyethanol	109–86–4	Hydrogen—glycol ether—methyl
2-ethoxyethanol	110–80–5	Hydrogen—glycol ether—ethyl
2-propoxyethanol**	2807–30–9	Hydrogen—glycol ether—propyl
2-butoxyethanol**	111–76–2	Hydrogen—glycol ether—butyl

* Chemical Abstract Service numbers are assigned to chemicals for identification.
** These are the glycol ethers that are most likely to be in your products today.

were in most of the cleaning and paint products then. And if you were working as an artist or teaching art during this period of time, those glycol ethers were in your products in large amounts. Some of the new "safer" water-based paints and printmaking inks contained glycol ethers in amounts as high as 30 percent.

People who worked with cleaning products, paints, and inks in the 1970s through the early 1990s were often regularly exposed to these chemicals. It also occurs to me that at this time, we began to see a phenomenal rise in autism and learning difficulties in our off-spring. I know that every science writer seems to have a different theory about why these illnesses are on the rise, but I tend not to think the culprits are tiny amounts of pollutants in the environment or minuscule amounts of mercury in vaccinations—not when we've used billions of pounds of glycol ethers and many other types of toxic solvents, evaporating them into homes, where children and pregnant women often have twenty-four-hour exposure.

Today your products are more likely to use the glycol ethers that contain the propyl and butyl groups, which are presumably less toxic reproductive hazards but toxic nonetheless. You are especially likely to be exposed to 2-butoxyethanol. Many manufacturers use 2-butoxyethanol because in 2004, the Bush administration's EPA took this glycol ether off its list of Hazardous Air Pollutants (HAPs). Keep in mind that an HAP chemical is one that can participate in smog reactions or damage the stratospheric ozone layer. Yet the fact that butoxyethanol is not an air pollutant is unrelated to the toxic effects it may have on people who use it.

This means that if a manufacturer of a cleaning product wants to advertise his or her product as one that does not contain chemicals regulated by the EPA, this manufacturer is likely to use the butyl glycol ethers or the propyl glycol ethers, which never were on the list. And if the manufacturer's definition of "green" is the absence of air pollutants, he or she may even tout these products as "green."

I have included the Chemical Abstract Service (CAS) numbers in the table because they provide the best way for you to identify these chemicals in your products. You can't rely on the chemical name of the substance because there are many long and unpleasantly complicated synonyms for each of these chemicals. For example,

2-butoxyethanol can be called any of the following legitimate names on labels or material safety data sheets:

> 2-butoxyethanol; 2-butoxy-1-ethanol, 2-n-butoxy-1-ethanol; beta-butoxyethanol; ethylene glycol monobutyl ether; ethylene glycol n-butyl ether; ethylene glycol butyl ether; butyl cellosolve; n-butyl cellosolve; poly-solve EB; Dowanol EB; Ektasolve EB; butyl oxitol; EGME; and many more.

So you can't possibly know that this chemical is in your products if the manufacturer uses one of these synonyms.

CAS numbers, often found on the labels of products, have another important use. If your child accidentally drinks a product containing this chemical or any other, I hope for your sake that the CAS numbers of the various ingredients are on the label. This way, when you call Poison Control, you will not be trying to pronounce "methyl ethyl death"! Providing the Poison Control specialist with the CAS number or numbers of the chemicals in the product will enable him or her to immediately put the right chemical database up on the computer monitor.

I have also included these CAS numbers so that you can use them to avoid products containing these chemicals if you wish. I strongly suggest that you do. Investigate the cleaners that you consider using by researching online to find their material safety data sheets and look for these chemicals. Even in small percentages, they can be a significant hazard.

The problem, of course, is that I have greatly oversimplified the glycol ether situation in order to explain it. Actually, there are dozens of other, more complex glycol ethers and related chemicals, such as the glycol ether acetates, that could be in your products. There are almost no available toxicity data on many of these chemicals. Manufacturers can substitute these more complex glycol ethers, which have the same dizzying numbers of names and synonyms.

Now, more and more often, I see manufacturers withholding the identities of their glycol ether solvents. For example, I have six years' worth of material safety data sheets on All-Purpose Simple Green. Originally, it contained 6 percent 2-butoxyethanol, which was about twice as much as many other fast cleaners did at that time. This is probably why it worked so well. Then the material safety data sheets showed that the 2-butoxyethanol content had dropped to 3 percent. The latest MSDS indicates that there is only about 1 percent of this glycol ether in it. Yet because the product cleans just as well as the original formula did and the MSDS now states that there are other ingredients in the product that are not revealed, I have to suspect that some of these other glycol ethers are in the cleaner.

When a product cleans this fast, it ain't soap!

In fact, plain soap and water is a good substitute for the solvent-containing cleaners, if you are willing to use a little elbow grease and rinse the soap from the surface after cleaning. If you must use a fast cleaner that can be sprayed on and wiped off in one operation, however, then provide some ventilation, such as a window exhaust fan that draws air across your work area and blows it outdoors. Remember, don't use rubber or vinyl gloves, because these are quickly penetrated by the glycol ethers. Purchase some nitrile plastic gloves, and contact the manufacturer's technical service to find out how often you should change your gloves, because the glycol ethers will penetrate even these gloves in time.

A really cynical use of substitution by industry involved chemicals called PCBs, or polychlorinated biphenyls. These chemicals were based on a double benzene ring chemical called biphenyl that has ten different locations on which a chlorine atom could be placed. When more than two sites are occupied with chlorine atoms, it is common to refer to them as *poly*chlorinated biphenyls.

Because there are so many locations and combinations of locations at which chlorine can be located, these chemicals form a large class. They are extremely stable compounds with respect to heat, light, and chemical attack. They are perfect for high-temperature industrial applications, plasticizers, and fire retardants. Starting in the 1950s, these miracle chemicals were added to just about everything. One list compiled by the EPA states that PCBs were used in

> some wool felt insulating materials, plastics, paint formulations, small rubber parts, adhesive tape, insulating materials used in electrical cabling, fluorescent light ballast, potting materials, gaskets in heating, ventilation and air conditioning and other duct systems, caulking, coatings for ceiling tiles,

flooring and floor wax/sealants, roofing and siding materials, adhesives, waterproofing compounds, anti-fouling compounds, fire retardant coatings, coal-tar enamel coatings for steel water pipe and underground storage tanks . . . , and any number of other chemical uses such as additives and plasticizers.[3]

These miracle substances made all of the products last longer, look and function better, and resist fire. By the late 1960s, though, it was clear that they lasted just as long in the environment. PCBs are considered "probable human carcinogens" by the EPA. There is also evidence that they cause adverse effects on the immune, reproductive, nervous, and endocrine systems.

As a result, they were banned in 1977. One would think that was the end of this story—but it's not.

First, construction, demolition, and renovation workers today are still exposed to PCBs. The EPA requires testing of old paints, caulks, and similar materials only for lead, even though the EPA knows that these products are just as likely to contain PCBs. And although EPA regulations under the Toxic Substances Control Act (TSCA) stipulate procedures for handling and disposing of PCB-containing waste materials, the TSCA does not require that materials such as paints and caulking be tested for PCBs prior to a building's demolition.

Second, the story is not over because industry immediately replaced PCBs with substitutes. Manufacturers simply exchanged the chlorine atoms on the biphenyl molecule for bromine atoms. Bromine and chlorine are brother and sister elements in the chemical world. They have a great many characteristics in common.

So the polybrominated biphenyls were used in your paints, plastics, and other materials in commerce. Because there were little or no data on these brominated chemicals, industry had thirty years to use the various substitutes without legal or regulatory repercussions.

The cynical part of this story is that anyone with half a brain knew there was no reason to believe that the polybrominated biphenyls were any less toxic than their chlorine-containing siblings. Now, we are seeing them banned in the European Union along with the polybrominated diphenyl *ethers* (PBDEs) that look just like them except there is an oxygen atom in between the two phenyls.

. . .

Let's revisit phthalates, a chemical I opened this chapter with. One particular vinyl plastic product that is sometimes used by children provides the worst-case example of a potential for exposing consumers to phthalates. These are the brilliantly colored clays that can be hand formed into any shape and heated in a kitchen oven or a toaster oven to become hard, permanent objects. If you have school-age kids—anywhere from elementary to college age—they are likely to have worked with these clays as an art material sometime during their educational or recreational activities.

Exposure does not end with school for some people. Sculpting with this polymer clay is a hobby or a vocation that can be done easily, but not safely, at home. Every year when I judge artists' work for acceptance into the Washington Square Outdoor Art Exhibit, I am likely to see the work of one or two artists making jewelry or little figurines in polymer clays. Having read the biographies of applicants for the thirty-plus years I have been judging, I know that they often work in their homes while tending young children. The whole family will breathe the vapors of phthalates coming from the oven—often the same oven where both polymer clay objects and dinner were presumably heated.

If you've ever worked with these clays, you know that they have a greasy feel. If you put a lump of the clay on a piece of paper for a few minutes and remove it, an oily ring will be left on the paper. These are the plasticizers. Although regulators and activists are concerned about levels in the range of 0.1 percent in children's products, these polymer clays were documented in 1992 by the Vermont Public Interest Research Group (VPIRG) to contain 3 to 14 percent phthalates, depending on the color.[4] It may also be higher in certain products.[5]

VPIRG's study, called "Hidden Hazards: Health Impacts of Toxins in Polymer Clays," documented the results of laboratory analyses of ten samples from two brands of polymer clays, Sculpey and Fimo. In the following list, I have provided a summary of the phthalates that VPIRG found in these polymer clay samples, along with an assessment of their hazards and current regulations. Because VPIRG was vilified for doing this study, it is a pleasure to point out in print how right the group was in 1992.

- **DNOP** (di-n-octyl phthalate): VPIRG said that this phthalate is associated with birth deformities, reproductive disorders, and liver and thyroid effects, and when mixed with other phthalates, it is associated with gene mutation. Today it is restricted by law to less than 0.1 percent in children's toys or child-care articles that can be put in the mouth. It is also on California's Proposition 65 list as a developmental hazard.
- **DnHP** (di-n-hexyl phthalate): VPIRG said that this phthalate was associated with reproductive disorders and liver and thyroid effects. When mixed with other phthalates, it is associated with gene mutation. Today this phthalate requires a Proposition 65 warning of male and female developmental damage.
- **BBP** (benzyl butyl phthalate): VPIRG said that this phthalate was associated with reproductive disorders, birth deformities, nerve disorders, and miscarriages. It said that cancer studies are suggestive but inconclusive. Today this chemical is banned in children's toys and child-care articles in amounts above 0.1 percent, and its presence in a product requires a Proposition 65 warning about developmental damage.
- **DEHT** (di(2-ethylhexyl)terephthalate): The hazards of this phthalate were unknown in 1992 and are still largely unknown, and it is not regulated. DEHT was used to replace a closely related cancer-causing and banned chemical called DEHP (di(2-ethylhexyl) phthalate).
- **Unknown Phthalates**: Multiple unidentified phthalate compounds were also discovered. One of these phthalates, designated as "unknown #2," was found at a level of 46 milligrams per kilogram (46 ppm). Based on laboratory similarities, "unknown #2" closely resembled the cancer-causing DEHP. It seems clear to me that the process of substituting closely related unknown phthalates for those known to be hazardous had already begun.

One question VPIRG also addressed was how much exposure a person gets from manipulating these polymer clays by hand. The group arranged for a laboratory to assess human exposure. The researchers prepared and baked clay samples following the manufacturers' directions and measured releases of phthalates into the air and phthalate residues on users' hands.

First, the researchers worked 100-gram samples into the shapes of crude bowls, a typical project for children, with gloved hands for five minutes. Then the subjects washed, rubbed, and rinsed their gloved hands vigorously with distilled water for thirty seconds. Next, they rinsed their gloved hands again in a solvent (methanol). Testing of the solvent rinse revealed that large quantities of phthalate residues had remained on the gloved hands even after washing. To ensure that no phthalates came from the gloves themselves, the test was repeated without manipulating the clay. No traces of phthalates were found in the gloves.

The laboratory then calculated the amount of phthalates a typical child could ingest from his or her hands. Calculations were based on the U.S. Consumer Product Safety Commission's 50 percent hand-to-mouth transfer factor, which assumes that 50 percent of the material that is deposited on the hands will eventually be ingested by children. Researchers found that a child could ingest an average of 7,000 micrograms (7 milligrams) of phthalates when using 100 grams of polymer clay product for only five minutes.

To find out how much a person might absorb by breathing, the laboratory researchers baked the clay at 270 degrees F for twenty minutes, as the manufacturer directs consumers to do in their ovens. The researchers baked small samples of between 1 and 7 milligrams in vials to see how much phthalate vapor is released. They found that typical use of the product would release an average of 2 milligrams of mixed phthalates per cubic meter (mg/m^3) of air. One product, Fimo Lavender, was calculated to release the equivalent of an alarming 11.8 mg of phthalates per cubic meter of air during baking.

With these figures, the lab calculated that a person in an average-size kitchen, during and immediately after the baking process, would inhale an average of 0.5 mg/m^3 of air of the combined phthalates. During the baking of the worst emitter—Fimo Lavender—a person could inhale much more than 3 mg/m^3 of air of the three phthalates.

Using the calculation from both skin contact and inhalation during baking, VPIRG showed that exposures to phthalates approached and sometimes exceeded various workplace and environmental standards for related phthalates. The most dramatic finding was that for exposure to BBP from Sculpey by both ingestion and inhalation. VPIRG said,

The National Toxicology Program . . . Center for the Evaluation of Risks to Human Reproduction . . . panel . . . suggested that BBP was of only "minimal" concern for reproductive effects in humans because exposures in adults were assumed to be low—around 2 micrograms per kilogram of body weight. Yet VPIRG's research shows <u>a 20 kg (44 lb.) child using</u> <u>100 grams of polymer clay could be exposed to as much as</u> 130 *times* <u>the 2 micrograms per kilogram of body weight of</u> <u>BBP the panel identified as normal daily exposure</u> *after only* 5 *minutes of play.*

This and many other findings in the VPIRG report supported VPIRG's recommendation that "The Consumer Product Safety Commission should immediately recall polymer clay products containing phthalates. " At the very least, VPIRG called for label warnings "directing pregnant women and children not to use polymer clay products." And VPIRG said this in 2002!

Now, seven years later, most of the polymer clays contain substitute plasticizers that do not require warnings or labels. Their chemical compositions are considered trade secrets, and you will not even be able to find out their names. I leave it to you to decide whether you or your children should work with untested and unknown chemicals that are in the same class as those found at high levels in the VPIRG study.

Phthalates are also in your cosmetics and perfumes and in outgassing from your cars and other vinyl plastic materials, such as shower curtains. The combined exposure to all of these sources is not known, but phthalates are in everyone's bloodstream right now. Some experts think that phthalates are implicated in many types of developmental problems that are seen in children today.

The new administrator of the EPA, Lisa P. Jackson, thinks the phthalates are a problem, too. On September 29, 2009, Jackson outlined a set of agency principles for legislative reform. She added four classes of chemicals to the chemicals of concern list. Two of these are germane to this discussion: (1) phthalates and (2) a nasty group of chemicals called polybrominated diphenyl ethers, or PBDEs, that is related to the brominated biphenyls I discussed earlier. These brominated compounds are used as fire retardants in many plastic materials. Both the phthalate plasticizers and the PBDE fire retardants migrate out of our computers and into the dust in our homes. Inhaling and ingesting this dust may be one way these chemicals end up in all of us.

Identifying and quantifying the many plasticizers and fire retardant chemicals in household dust is becoming an important objective of various studies. For example, the Duke University chemist Heather Stapleton studied dust samples taken from homes in Boston.[6] She found many of these chemicals in her sample, but she also found one brominated chemical that she simply couldn't identify. She tried for months to pin down its structure.

Then, while attending a scientific conference, she happened to see the structure of a chemical flashed up on a PowerPoint screen during a presentation and recognized it instantly as her mystery compound. The substance is a chemical in "Firemaster 550," a product made by Chemtura Corporation for use in furniture and other products. This chemical was created as a substitute for an earlier flame retardant that the company had quit making in 2004 because of health concerns.

Now the story gets really interesting. Stapleton learned that the Firemaster 550 chemical is related to a known carcinogen and reproductive and developmental toxic substance recently banned by Congress from children's products: diethylhexyl phthalate, or DEHP. In fact, the structure of the Firemaster 550 chemical is identical to that of DEHP, with the exception of four bromine atoms stuck on the benzene ring structure in the center of the chemical. Even without any chemistry background, you could see that the business ends of this brominated chemical are the same as DEHP's.

So, here again we see the substitution principle: stick a few atoms on a bad actor and, whoopeie! We have a new chemical that is assumed to be safe! Chemtura officials said in a written statement that even though Firemaster 550 contains an ingredient that is structurally similar to DEHP, this does not mean it poses similar health risks. Well, then, we should ask why Chemtura didn't test the substance to determine whether the new chemical has similar risks. And why didn't Chemtura do these tests *before* it added the chemical to its products?

They deny this now! Yet the cat is out of the bag. Many of us are already carrying this chemical in our blood.

·   ·   ·

Before you think that all of the bad-acting chemicals are synthetic monsters created by big business, we need to look at one of many examples from Mother Nature's chemical factory. Diacetyl is a chemical that is found naturally in an ordinary pat of butter. It is primarily responsible for the buttery taste we all like. So smart chemists found ways to concentrate or synthesize it so that they could add the buttery flavor to foods without the fat and the calories.

This sounded just grand until the year 2000, when a rare lung disease called bronchiolitis obliterans was found in a group of workers at a microwave popcorn plant. This disease causes progressive shortness of breath, coughing, fatigue, and ultimately death, unless a lung transplant can be done.

Now it is becoming clear from experience with these and other workers that this natural substance can be deadly if it is inhaled. Yet as soon as the first lawsuits were filed in 2001 and articles about diacetyl made consumers wary, manufacturers began to develop substitutes for diacetyl. Today, consumers of microwave popcorn think that the problem is completely solved because diacetyl "substitutes" have replaced real diacetyl in their popcorn and other butter-flavored foods.

You can probably figure out where this story is going. The manufacturers will consider their substitute chemicals safe until proven otherwise, and we will see lung diseases occurring for decades until the regulations catch up with all of these chemicals. Ah, but this time, it is a little different, because David Michaels, the new assistant secretary of labor for Occupational Safety and Health, understands the problem. Speaking at the National Institute for Occupational Safety and Health's Going Green Workshop, in Washington, D.C., on December 16, 2009 (see www.osha.gov, click on "Newsroom," then "Speeches," and then search by date), Michaels said,

> Let me give one example that's causing our standards people fits: Diacetyl. We know that exposure to certain levels of this chemical—used in food flavorings like popcorn—destroy workers' lungs. Some companies have introduced "substitutes." You can't see it in my notes [here on the podium], but

I've put "substitutes" in quotes, because some of these "substitutes" are so chemically close to diacetyl that they really need to be classified as diacetyl. Other food flavoring additives may be further away chemically; they're not diacetyl, but they haven't been tested adequately to determine the health hazards they may present.

So, then, does it make sense to regulate diacetyl alone? Does it make sense to develop a standard or Permissible Exposure Limit, or just require engineering controls? Does it make sense to do all this work on diacetyl when we really need to be addressing a broader class of chemicals: "food flavoring additives"?

For the first time, there appears to be hope for ending the substitution game and finding a way to regulate the substitute look-alikes, as well as all of the untested chemicals in the flavoring additives area. Amazing! The head of a major government agency finally gets it.

Now you know that there are glycol ether solvents in your cleaning products and phthalate plasticizers in the plastic elements in your car, computer, and toys. Yet many more chemicals are out there.

You can use this knowledge to avoid entire classes of chemicals, such as the phthalates or the glycol ethers, until and unless individual members of these classes have been fully tested and shown to be safe for us to use.

CHAPTER 4

"All-Natural" Doesn't Mean Safe, Either

Mother Nature Is Out to Get You

The thick, white sap of *Hevea* trees is a natural rubber latex, a water borne suspension of a chemical (isoprene) that can be easily transformed into rubber resin. When humans found that this stuff could be used to make bouncy, stretchy items and glue (rubber cement), they established vast plantations of rubber trees. This seemed like a very benign endeavor, and only occasionally did medical literature mention that some people developed allergies to this tree sap or to the rubber products made from the sap.

When AIDS became an epidemic and the medical profession finally got serious about wearing rubber examining gloves, an epidemic of allergies followed. The increased frequency of exposure to rubber contributed to more people developing rubber allergies. It is estimated that around 15 percent of medical personnel are now sensitive to natural rubber.

Allergies to natural rubber can be serious. Symptoms include skin rash and inflammation, hives, respiratory irritation, asthma, and even systemic anaphylactic shock. Between 1988 and 1992, the FDA received reports of a thousand systemic shock reactions to latex. In June 1996, twenty-eight latex-related deaths were reported to the FDA.[1]

One death that was not reported to the FDA, because it did not occur in the United States, was covered in the *Express* in London in June 2000.

> A young fashion designer died after an allergic reaction to glue she was using to attach hair extensions.
>
> Nicola Faulkner, 28, who had been preparing for a dinner dance, collapsed in front of her boyfriend within minutes as her eye, lips and tongue started to swell and she fought for breath, an inquest heard yesterday.
>
> Her scalp started to itch intensely, and a skin rash spread over her body after her cousin attached the weave to the back of her head with American-made Super Hair bonding. Her lungs collapsed and pockets of air bubbled under the skin.
>
> Coroner Selena Lynch recorded a verdict of death by misadventure after hearing that Nicola had suffered an extreme reaction to the latex in the bonding and gone into anaphylactic shock. . . .
>
> Dr. Jane Norton, a pathologist from University Hospital, Lewisham, said the reaction to the latex had probably triggered a massive asthma attack. Nicola had used the glue once before without problems. "The first time the specified product is used there is no reaction," said Dr. Norton. "It is only the second time that you use the product that you react severely."[2]

I have provided this particular account because it mentions that Nicola Faulkner had used the same glue previously without incident. This is typical of allergic reactions. People usually get away with exposing themselves to allergy-causing substances for a while before the body suddenly and often without warning initiates a massive antibody reaction. For a small percentage of people, the reaction can be life-threatening.

How can latex be such a problem when it's all natural?

It's important to take care of our planet. Having a deep and abiding love of nature is a wonderful and uplifting emotion. Let me assure you, however, that Mother Nature doesn't love you back.

Don't take it personally. Nature's animals, plants, and insects have been busy carving out a living for themselves over these millions of years in a constant, intense, take-no-prisoners battle. They've developed their weapons: teeth and claws, stingers, choking vine tendrils, poison leaves, a host of chemicals used by insects and plants to repel or kill one another, and much more.

None of these battling species evolved because they knew that one day a grand animal called "human" would appear and find them useful. Instead, humans had to carve out their niche just as other species did, battling enemies from mammoths to microbes. And like all other species, it took us millennia to distinguish between foods and poisons. It's not easy to find safe food sources because the vast majority of the billions of plants on earth are inedible, cause severe allergies, or are outright toxic. A life-and-death, trial-and-error process was required to identify the very limited number of plants that we cultivate and eat.

It's a tricky selection process because sometimes the same plant can be both food and poison. Rhubarb stems, for example, can be made into a pie filling that has an almost religious significance to Midwesterners, but rhubarb stems grow under big edible-looking leaves that contain enough oxalic acid to kill someone.

When humans invade the world of plants and trees in order to build houses, make products from plants, or take food from them, we do so at our peril. Poisoning, cancer, and allergies await. In fact, if you have allergies, you are most likely reacting to natural things such as pet dander, dust mites, pollens, molds, poison ivy and poison sumac, or certain foods. Documented allergies to synthetic substances are not common. For example, I've never seen a study showing even one case of an allergy to petroleum distillate solvents. These solvents may cause irritation and a kind of aversion reaction or sensitivity to the odor, but this is not a classic immune system response allergy that can be proved with a blood test.

For outright toxicity, nature has a far more lethal arsenal than is found among synthetic chemicals. Aflatoxin, a substance generated by a mold that likes to grow on peanuts, is one of the most potent carcinogens known. Botulism toxin, which is released by bacteria that grow in our food, is another natural substance that can kill you when ingested in milligram amounts (note that the same toxin that can cause paralysis and death by ingestion can also be used by injection to immobilize facial muscles to reduce wrinkles).

In addition, two of the most toxic substances on earth are natural. Both are used in chemical warfare. One is called ricin, a chemical that is contained in castor beans. The other is anthrax, bacteria commonly found in soils worldwide. Pound for pound, ricin and anthrax are much more toxic than synthetic warfare gases such as phosgene.

We have no idea how many more highly toxic chemicals there are on earth because the Chemical Abstract Service registered the fifty millionth chemical on September 9, 2009, and is continuing to register them at a rate of a couple dozen a minute. The service isn't stopping to test these chemicals, so it's reasonable to assume that a fair number of them are highly toxic. Many of these registered chemicals are natural in origin. Some experts think that there are around 9 million natural chemicals, but that's a guess because we are still discovering new species of plants, insects, and sea life every day. Any one of these could produce unique substances or powerful poisons, such as those from a type of tropical rain forest frog, a tiny tidal pond octopus, or a certain stinging jellyfish.

We now know that certain chemicals we thought only humans could produce in their laboratories and factories are made by Mother Nature, too. One cancer-causing class of pollutants called "dioxins" is produced when plastics and other refuse are burned. Dioxin is one of the main reasons you aren't allowed to burn trash in your own backyard anymore. Yet in the 1990s, dioxins were found naturally occurring in deposits of clay, clay that had been undisturbed underground since the last ice age. Some bags of clay that are sold to potteries and art schools now carry dioxin warnings.

If you really want to get technical, petroleum products are natural because they are the product of plants or animals that were squashed and altered over millions of years by geological forces. So the next time you see the word "natural" on a product label, it should inspire instant skepticism. For starters, you know that the manufacturer is probably hoping that you are uninformed enough to think the product is nontoxic, based on its natural origins.

. . .

Of course, the all-natural products you prefer are hypoallergenic, so those are safe, right? Not exactly.

Regulations for the term "hypoallergenic" were first issued by the FDA in a proposed rule in the *Federal Register* in February 1974. The rule specifically applied to cosmetics. The FDA proposed to permit a cosmetic to be labeled "hypoallergenic" or make similar claims only if scientific studies on human subjects showed that it caused a significantly lower rate of adverse skin reactions than similar products did. The manufacturers of cosmetics claiming to be "hypoallergenic" were to be responsible for carrying out the required tests.

The proposed rule provoked numerous comments from consumers, consumer groups, and cosmetic manufacturers. Some people urged a ban on the use of the term "hypoallergenic" on grounds that most consumers don't have allergies. Others suggested that the term be banned because allergic individuals cannot use "hypoallergenic" products with any assurance of safety since an individual's allergic responses can be unique. A number of cosmetic manufacturers complained about the requirement for product comparison tests to validate claims of hypoallergenicity, especially because these tests would pose an undue economic burden on them.

In responding to the comments, the FDA pointed out that the proposed regulation was not intended to solve all problems concerning cosmetic safety. It was only intended to establish a definition for "hypoallergenicity" that could be used uniformly by manufacturers and understood by consumers.

The FDA issued its final regulation on "hypoallergenic" cosmetics on June 6, 1975. In this ruling, the FDA changed the comparative test procedures in ways that would reduce the costs to the manufacturers. Yet this was not enough for Almay and Clinique, makers of cosmetics that carried the hypoallergenic labels. They challenged the new regulation in the U.S. District Court for the District of Columbia. The two firms charged that the FDA had no authority to issue the regulation, but the court upheld the FDA regulations.

Almay and Clinique then appealed to the U.S. Court of Appeals for the District of Columbia, which ruled that the regulation was invalid. The appeals court held that the FDA's definition of the term "hypoallergenic" was unreasonable because the administration had not demonstrated that consumers perceive the term "hypoallergenic" in the way described in the regulation.

As a result of the decision, manufacturers may continue to label and advertise their cosmetics as "hypoallergenic" or make similar claims *without any supporting evidence*. Consumers have no assurance that such claims are valid. And ever since, the term "hypoallergenic" has been used by manufacturers to convince concerned customers that their products were unlikely to cause allergies, without having the proof to back up their claim.

Even today, the only applicable regulations for the term "hypoallergenic" apply to medical devices such as rubber gloves. The FDA regulations state, "Devices that contain natural rubber that contacts humans . . . shall not contain the term 'hypoallergenic' on their labeling."[3]

Yet there is no law barring manufacturers from using the hypoallergenic label on nonmedical devices that contain natural rubber, from shoes to undergarments or even cosmetics. And there is no law preventing manufacturers from using the hypoallergenic label on consumer products and cosmetics that contain other known allergens, such as terpenes (from pine oil) and various fragrances, nickel compounds, formaldehyde, and any of the known allergens. FDA guidelines only say that manufacturers *should* actually test cosmetics to determine whether they will cause allergies in significant numbers of people, but they are not required to do so.

It would be wise for consumers not to put much faith in the "hypoallergenic" label, along with similar labels like "safe for sensitive skin" or "allergy tested." If the manufacturers did test these products, just *who* did they test them on? It certainly wasn't you. You may react adversely to a substance that I could swim in without harm. Instead, get in the habit of reading ingredient lists and becoming familiar with substances that cause you to react.

You don't have to look into a jar of face cream to find evidence of Mother Nature's malice. It's right there on your breakfast table.

We drink a lot of orange juice, and that leaves a hell of a lot of orange peel waste. The stuff isn't good for animal feed because it contains a toxic substance. It isn't even easy to compost because worms avoid the toxin in the peels until after mold has turned it furry and green.[4]

Yet orange rinds have a use in commerce precisely because they contain a toxic substance. The orange trees evolved their fruit rinds to contain little pores full of a toxic oil to kill the insects that would try to spoil the fruit. You probably have seen this rind oil when, as a child, you bent the peel double to watch it squirt out. We used it in biology class to end our fruit flies breeding project. A little orange peel bent at the mouth of each vial of flies killed the little critters almost instantly.

This rind oil or citrus oil and its main ingredient, a chemical called d-limonene, have been EPA-registered pesticides for many years. The small amounts used in pesticides, however, do not make a dent in the vast mounds of orange peelings that we discard. Other uses had to be found.

These additional uses take advantage of citrus oil's other major property: it is a powerful organic chemical solvent. It is so powerful that it will take the paint right off your walls, all by itself. As a result, it is used in paint strippers.

If dissolving paint is easy, cutting grease is child's play for citrus oil and d-limonene. Citrus oil was therefore added to many industrial cleaners and thinners, such as those used in the printing and automotive industries.

Manufacturers looked for bigger markets and began to use the citrus oils as grease cutters in household cleaners, with the added advantage that the oils smell like oranges—an odor that consumers do not associate with toxic solvents. Because citrus oil smells good, let's put it in air fresheners and plug-in scent dispensers. And if it smells good and dissolves paint and grease, why not put it in hand cleaners, too?

As a result, the stuff seems to be everywhere. Ads promoting citrus products emphasize their natural origins and fail to mention that d-limonene and citrus oil are two of Mother Nature's own pesticides and are registered as fly killers by the EPA. Now if you are looking for a biodegradable pesticide, I highly recommend trying d-limonene before you choose other less environmentally friendly pesticides—but treat it with the same care that you would other pesticides. And treating it with care does not mean you should wash your hands in the stuff.

Instead of warnings on household products that contain d-limonene, the advertising usually points out that the FDA and the EPA allow small amounts of d-limonene and citrus oil in food as an additive. They do not tell you that in 1995, the EPA proposed banning the use of citrus oil to flavor food because it is usually contaminated with a cancer-causing pesticide called imazalil.[5] Imazalil and other pesticides, such as fenabutin oxide and the pyrethroid cyfluthrin, are commonly present in citrus oil.[6] These pesticides were used in the past and are still used today to protect orange groves from pests. (This is also a good reason to choose organically grown fruit when recipes call for grated citrus rind as a flavoring.)

The rule prohibiting citrus oil as a food flavoring was repealed after a previous court battle revoked the Delaney Clause, a rule that prohibited known carcinogens in our food at any level.[7] After the Delaney Clause was revoked, carcinogens were allowed in food if manufacturers could show that the risk to people eating a "normal" diet (whatever that is) is calculated to be very low, such as one person in a million.

Despite its pesticide status, d-limonene is sometimes labeled "nontoxic." This is not illegal, due to a quirk in our laws. D-limonene is acutely toxic to rats (4.4 g/kg) but just misses being acutely toxic to mice (5.6 g/kg).[8] This borderline status, especially when d-limonene is diluted with other ingredients, allows sellers to label their product "nontoxic."

The borderline acute toxicity of d-limonene has been known for more than twenty-five years. In 1982, a company was sued for failing to put an acute warning label on containers of d-limonene that it marketed as an artist's oil paint solvent. The product's fruity odor tempted a young boy to drink some. The boy was hospitalized. This company now includes an acute warning label.[9] All sellers should do likewise. And more than a decade ago, the Consumer Product Safety Commission proposed child proof packaging for d-limonene products.[10]

Yet these ingestion hazards are acute or short-term effects. What do we know about the long-term or chronic hazards of d-limonene?

One chronic (long-term) two-year study was reported by the National Toxicology Program in 1988.[11] This study concluded that d-limonene shows no evidence of causing cancer in female rats or in mice of both sexes, but clear evidence of carcinogenicity in male rats. These mixed results may be related to a mechanism that cannot be extrapolated to humans. So it is likely that d-limonene is not a carcinogen. Still, further tests should be done.

More important, the cancer study showed researchers other effects that were completely unexpected. The chronic liver effects in male mice and increased mortality in female rats caused by relatively low doses (0.5 and 0.6 g/kg) during the two-year study indicated to the NTP that d-limonene can be expected to be chronically toxic to humans at rather low doses.

Other studies indicated that d-limonene regresses induced mammary tumors in rats.[12] D-limonene was tested in England as an experimental treatment for human breast cancer.[13] It was not effective enough for further testing, but the studies show that d-limonene is a very pharmacologically active substance.

Because d-limonene is used on our skin, we should be aware that it is absorbed through the skin into the body. In addition, skin irritation and allergies have also been noted, especially in people who were previously sensitized to other "natural" solvents, such as turpentine and anise oil.[14] An animal study concluded that allergenic compounds form when d-limonene is exposed to air.[15] The German occupational standard for d-limonene also lists it as a skin sensitizer.

There is even a possibility that rags used to clean up d-limonene may spontaneously ignite and cause a fire. In 2003, the EPA proposed a rule that would lower the cost of disposing of solvent-contaminated industrial rags and reusable industrial wipes. As is required, a comment period followed, during which industry provided input. Regarding these comments, the EPA said,

> In the process of developing this proposed rulemaking, the Agency has learned that there are new, "exotic" solvents on the market, such as terpenes and citric acids [*sic* pine oil and citrus oil], that, while labeled as non-hazardous, could actually be flammable. . . . Stakeholders have told us that, under certain conditions that have yet to be determined, oxygen can mix

with the industrial wipes that contain these exotic solvents and spontaneously combust. According to some representatives of industrial laundries and fire marshals, resulting fires have caused major damage to facilities. Some stakeholders have suggested that EPA propose that generating facilities be allowed to . . . wet down the wipes with water prior to sending them off site. They explain that this is consistent with what laundries do now with their customers.[16]

It appears that the EPA was rather late to learn about the spontaneous combustion potential for citrus oil and d-limonene. Other prior references also said that citrus oil and d-limonene can spontaneously combust. For example, ten years before the EPA's comments were made on exotic solvents, a common reference for artists said that the oil could combust.

During use, the citrus solvents are also inhaled, so we should be aware of how toxic d-limonene is to the lungs.

The only current inhalation standard is that of Germany for workplace exposures.[17] These German standards are usually accepted by the European Union countries. They have set the eight-hour, time-weighted, average maximum contaminant limit for d-limonene at 20 parts per million. For comparison, this is the same level set by the American Conference of Governmental Industrial Hygienists for turpentine, 2-butoxyethanol (see chapter 3), toluene, and styrene—the toxic animal carcinogen from which Styrofoam is made.[18]

Yet by far the most amazing property of d-limonene is its behavior in the air in your home. This unusual behavior was first investigated by Charles J. Weschler, a chemist at Telcordia Technologies in Red Bank, New Jersey. He noticed that a white message board in his lab kept turning dingy. Weschler tested the surface and found that a thin coat of submicron particles of d-limonene, a chemical he was using in experiments, was building up on the board. This would be a surprise for any trained scientist who knows that most liquids evaporate into the air to create a vapor that will remain airborne and will dissipate on air currents. A vapor of an organic chemical like d-limonene is not supposed to re-form into liquid droplets and deposit on surfaces. Chemicals usually can only do this when they reach concentrations of around 100 percent as water recondenses from vapor when it rains. But d-limonene vapors were redepositing on surfaces from air containing vastly lower concentrations.

Weschler teamed up with chemists at Rutgers University in Piscataway, New Jersey, to determine how d-limonene does this. The New Jersey team sprayed a wooden coffee table for fifteen seconds with a lemon-scented wax and measured d-limonene's release of vapor into the air for the next three hours. Then they loaded a test chamber with concentrations of d-limonene vapor similar to those recorded during this process. Next, they added concentrations of ozone to the chamber, which are typical of indoor air on a smoggy summer day.

Within thirty minutes, particulates (tiny liquid mist droplets) began to form in the air. The particulates were less than 10 micrometers in diameter, which enables them to deposit deep in the lungs' air sacs (alveoli) if inhaled. The concentrations in the air of these particulates, in some cases, reached one-third of the EPA limit for particulates of this size.[19] In other words, the use of citrus oils can create a smog in your home that can approach levels considered to be toxic by the EPA! Scientists have long known that much of the haze shrouding eastern U.S. forests is from toxic particulates created in reactions of ozone with similar compounds (pinene and turpenes) emitted by evergreen trees. (Really? Evergreens help create smog? Of course. I've already told you that Mother Nature doesn't play nice.) Yet it was not known that this could happen indoors with d-limonene.

This finding interested other scientists. Researchers from the EPA conducted a study that was published in *Environmental Science and Technology* in 2004.[20] This study confirmed that a potentially harmful smog can form inside homes when air fresheners that contain either citrus or pine oil react with ozone air pollutant. The researchers noted that the smog particles exposed to ozone also contained formaldehyde, a probable carcinogen and a respiratory irritant and allergen. In other words, trying to improve the air with citrus or pine oil may actually increase formaldehyde levels in your home.

The researchers studied plug-in air fresheners as well. They found that the pinene (pine) and limonene (citrus) fragrances also react with ozone to release formaldehyde. The researchers concluded that opening a window on a high-ozone day could trigger these reactions.

The fact that pine and citrus oils react this way with ozone should give pause to misinformed people who use ozone generators or negative ion generators to "purify" the air in their homes. These devices add ozone to the air in your house, which may already contain more ozone from pollution sources than is good for you. The use of these ozone-generating devices can create indoor ozone levels much higher than those in the study.

The level of formaldehyde-related compounds created by the EPA research team from mixing ozone and air-freshening chemicals reached a concentration of about 50 micrograms in each cubic meter of air. This is near the EPA's Air Quality Limits for harmful particles.

Granted, this study was based on a room-size test chamber, rather than a house, but it seems clear that if you are concerned about indoor air quality, you should not introduce any extra chemical sources into your home, including volatile organic compounds such as d-limonene and ozone.

So, let's summarize. Citrus oil and its main ingredient, d-limonene, are pesticides, paint strippers, toxic solvents, and fragrances. Using them on your skin would be similar to cleaning your skin with turpentine, another very toxic natural solvent. Some of the solvent will be absorbed through the skin. The solvent can also be absorbed if you inhale its vapors. In addition, citrus oil and d-limonene can re-form into toxic mist particles in the air that will react with pollution levels of ozone to form particles that contain formaldehyde, a known carcinogen and allergen. You can actually increase toxic air pollution in your house with these air fresheners!

It might make sense to avoid products that contain these chemicals, but you may find it difficult. Simply reading the label ingredients may not be enough. For example, one manufacturer lists "terpenes and terpenoids" and "sweet orange-oil" on its label. It is only by reading the manufacturer's material safety data sheet (MSDS) that you can learn that "d-limonene is a major fraction of the sweet orange oil terpenes/terpenoids."

Some manufacturers will hide the citrus content of a product by using confusing synonyms for citrus oil on their labels. For example, four synonyms I've seen used for d-limonene are:

1-methyl-4(1-methylethyenyl) cyclohexene
4-isopropyl-1-methyl cyclohexene
p-mentha-1,8-diene
dipentene

These names or variations of them can be used on labels and MSDSs. D-limonene can also be called cinene or cajeputene, or it may be identified only by its class, which can be called terpenes, monoterpenes, bicyclic monoterpenes, or dipentenes. D-limonene can also be derived from other sources, such as oils of bergamot or caraway, and these oils may be listed on the label instead.

Ordinarily, I would tell readers to look for d-limonene's Chemical Abstract Service Registration Number (CAS RN), which is 5989-27-5. But there are many other sources of limonene that have different numbers.

The bottom line is that if a manufacturer is really determined, it can be almost impossible for ordinary consumers to determine whether d-limonene or citrus oil are ingredients in a product. Hell, it is sometimes difficult for me to tell, and I'm a chemist.

At least we have a few research studies on d-limonene. There are many other natural oils that may have similar effects about which we know very little. One very popular oil is tea tree oil, a product that is extracted from the leaves of the *Melaleuca alternifolia* tree. The first laboratory analysis I saw of this oil was on the Web site of a company selling the oil called Coldstream Plantation Pty Ltd in Australia in 1995. I was struck by the fact that it contained a total of forty-eight ingredients that were primarily terpenes and terpinols, including some limonene and pine oil. The main ingredient was terpinen-4-ol at 40.2 percent. Here's the breakdown:

Chemical	Percentage
Terpinen-4-ol	40.2
Gamma terpinene	20.5
Alpha-terpinene	10.2
1,8-cineole	3.6
Alpha-terpinolene	3.6

(continued)

Chemical	Percentage
Alpha-terpineol	3.1
Alpha-pinene	2.4
P-cymene	2.2
Limonene	1.1
Aromadendrene	1.1
Delta-cadinene	1.0
Sabinene	0.6
Globulol	0.3
Viridiflorol	0.3
Total	90.2

Plus smaller amounts of another thirty-four ingredients!

Aldrich Chemical Company is a supplier of terpinen-4-ol. Its MSDS dated from 1995 to 2004 clearly showed that the stuff is acutely toxic (as based on the LD50 tests). Yet the label on the tea tree products indicated that it is "nontoxic."

In addition, the Aldrich MSDS said there were no studies of human exposure or animal studies on the chemical's ability to cause cancer, birth defects, or other long-term hazards. All of the Aldrich MSDSs that were provided up to about 2004 said, "To the best of our knowledge, the chemical, physical, and toxicological properties have not been thoroughly investigated." Furthermore, the MSDS said, "For R&D [research and development] use only. Not for drug, household, or other uses." Yet tea tree oil was being sold in health food stores for all kinds of supplemental and medicinal uses during this time period and still is.

The 2009 Aldrich Chemical MSDS no longer includes the previous statement. Instead, the MSDS merely points out that there are "no data available" on acute toxicity, irritation and corrosion, or sensitization (allergy).[21]

The MSDS states that tea tree oil is not a human carcinogen listed by the IARC, but the IARC has never evaluated it, which translates to mean there are no cancer data available, either.

Tea tree oil and another common oil, lavender oil, are often used in cosmetics and personal-care products. In 2006, *Science News* reported an interesting story about such uses that indicate that further study of lavender and tea tree oils is in order.[22] The article noted that since the mid-1990s, the Denver-area pediatric endocrinologist Clifford Block has treated enlarged male breasts (gynecomastia) in a series of boys age ten or younger. Most had normal ratios of sex hormones in their blood, indicating that hormone production was not the problem. Block learned that at least five boys had been using toiletries containing lavender oil. One of the products also contained tea tree oil, and a couple of patients were putting pure lavender oil on their skin. The doctor advised the boys to stop using these products. Amazingly, the gynecomastia disappeared in a few months.

Block contacted Derek Henley and Kenneth Korach of the National Institute of Environmental Health Sciences in Research Triangle Park, North Carolina. In their lab, these two investigators exposed human breast cells to lavender oil and separately to tea tree oil. They found that both oils turned on estrogen-regulated genes and inhibited an androgen-regulated gene. Henley reported these unusual findings at the Endocrine Society meeting in Boston in July 2006.[23]

Although lavender oil may have created undesirable breast development in young boys, these same hormonal effects could be very useful to women under certain circumstances. Today, many postmenopausal women ingest plant-derived estrogen to replace hormones their bodies no longer make. Yet it wasn't long ago that most women were taking synthetic estrogen instead. In the 1990s, synthetic hormones designed to be almost identical to those produced by our own bodies were routinely prescribed to postmenopausal women. They restored a woman's menstrual cycle and kept the body functioning more as it did when they were younger. Women felt better, they looked better, and the drugs became very popular.

These hormone-replacement drugs were considered very safe. They had been studied and approved by the FDA using the proper double-blind protocol, meaning that half of the women took hormone-replacement drugs, the other half took pills that looked exactly like the hormones, and none of the women knew which pill they were getting.

Then, in July 2002, a study of hormone-replacement therapy was released that indicated that the drugs increased the risk of breast cancer, stroke, and heart problems. This study was different from the smaller studies that had been used for FDA approval. This double-blind study involved more than sixteen thousand women. Although the study was scheduled to go on for several more years, the danger became so clear that the study was discontinued, rather than put half of these women at increased risk of illnesses and perhaps death.

When this bad news went to the general press, I saw several national TV stations airing uncritical interviews with sellers of herbal supplements, urging women to use natural plant estrogens as substitutes for the synthetic ones. A lot of women switched to the plant-derived hormones, which are often called phytoestrogens. These plant drugs also caused the same basic effects on women's bodies that the synthetic ones had.

Yet a moment's reflection should make it clear that if the plant substances act the same way on the body that the synthetic hormones did, they probably have the same hazards. Even if the drugs could be synthesized to be exactly like our own hormones, as the manufacturers of the "bioidentical hormones" claim they can, these chemicals would still have the same drawbacks. Our own natural hormones probably can cause strokes and heart problems when used past menopause. And estrogen will stimulate growth of any estrogen-receptive cancers present in the body as well. It is not the substance itself or its origins that make it toxic; the effects that it produces in the body cause both the desired and the undesired side effects.

It is also worth considering that the plant hormones and the synthesized commercial hormones, which are somewhat different in structure from our own, may carry additional risks. We will never know, because there are no large double-blind studies of natural phytoestrogens or comparison studies between natural and synthetic hormones.

One argument that the phytoestrogen sellers use is that populations that eat a lot of soy products, which contain phytoestrogens, live longer than we do and are healthier than us. But then, people in thirty or more countries live longer and are healthier than we are. This effect probably has more to do with the amount we overeat, our defective medical-care system, and exposure to more chemical pollutants than to our lower consumption of soy.

This estrogen story also provides a good reason not to take any medication, natural or synthetic, based on the personal testimonies of users, including Oprah and Suzanne Somers. Women who take either synthetic or natural estrogen will tell you that they feel better and look better, their libidos have increased, and they have a sense of well-being. If feeling great were the only reason to take a medication, then we should all be on heroin.

I think it is abundantly clear that we simply don't know enough about all natural substances and should be more thoughtful about their uses.

Instead of a call to caution and more studies of natural products, I hear sellers of herbs and natural oils use pitches that are startlingly similar to those of the snake-oil salesmen who sold bottles of elixir off the tailgates of brightly painted trucks at the carnivals I traveled with sixty years ago. Those old spiels usually alluded to a brilliant doctor whose work was suppressed by the big drug companies, an Indian medicine man, or an ancient Chinese healer who discovered a miracle cure.

In fact, it was the wild claims of patent medicine sellers that prompted the formation and the passage of the Pure Food and Drug Act in 1906 that led to the founding of the U.S. Food and Drug Administration. Let me tell you from experience that this 1906 law was ignored by pitchmen in the 1940s, and pitchmen today are still convincing their gullible customers that requirements to test these products are merely a government plot to keep wonderful natural cures from the public and to force people to buy expensive tested drugs instead.

Deregulation also plays a part in the natural product game. In 1997, the Food and Drug Administration Modernization Act was passed. This act eliminated the need for premarket scrutiny, approval, or registration by the FDA of any substance that could be defined as a "dietary supplement." Now the wild and woolly herbal market was free to operate with relative abandon.

The mythical ancient Chinese healer of the 1940s carnival pitchmen reappeared in force, and the back of the carnival wagon was replaced by a bigger platform on television, on the radio, and in self-help books. Now eye of newt and oil of snake would be referred to by their obscure Mandarin names and labeled "dietary supplements" to avoid FDA jurisdiction. Yet herb sellers and the books they promote usually tout these herbal mixtures as medicines for specific diseases, to lose weight, or to increase body mass.

Today there is a sort of tacit agreement, even among many doctors, to ignore the law that requires these products not to make health claims. For example, many oncologists will encourage patients to combine chemotherapy with untested herbal remedies. The attitude seems to be, "What harm can this cause if the patient thinks these substances can help?" I submit that people don't really know whether they cause harm or not.

In particular, there is an almost religious fervor associated with Chinese herbal remedies. After all, how could you argue with a system of medicine that had been practiced for thousands of years? Well . . . maybe by noticing that its patients and practitioners are all just as dead as others who didn't follow this practice. Or perhaps by getting a good translation of the *Chinese Herbal Materia Medica* and reading it.

In 1998, the FDA translated one passage of this tome in the *Federal Register*, in a discussion about two natural minerals that have also been around for thousands of years, cinnabar and calomel:

> The Chinese *Herbal Materia Medica* reports that cinnabar (mercuric sulfide; cinnabaris, or zhu sha in Mandarin Chinese) and calomel (mercurous chloride; calomelas or qing fen in Mandarin Chinese) have been widely used as a sedative and detoxicant and to treat constipation and edema.[24]

In other words, the ancient Chinese docs prescribed mercury compounds for their patients! But surely the Chinese herbalists today would not prescribe mercury. The possibility that mercury was still present in these medicines prompted the California Department of Health Services to investigate Chinese traditional medicines in 1998. Regarding this California study, the FDA stated,

> 5 of 260 traditional Chinese medicines available in the retail marketplace, which they examined, listed cinnabar [mercuric sulfide] as an ingredient on the label. In this study, 35 of 251 products that were screened for mercury content were found to contain significant quantities of mercury. . . . Most of the

products that contained significant quantities of mercury did not list mercury sources on the label.[25]

Not only did a significant number of these medicines contain mercury, most of these mercury-containing products did not even list mercury sources on the label! Without labeling laws, consumers could not rely on reading labels to avoid mercury. And because the researchers tested the samples only for mercury, what else might lurk unlabeled in that stuff? Does anyone actually know what the active ingredients are in bat wings and bear gall bladders? Or their side effects?

A joke that has made the rounds of the Internet seems to best explain medicine men during the last two thousand years:

The natural minerals called calomel and cinnabar in the Chinese medicines sound so innocuous. These mercury compounds have also been used in makeup over the years.

In 1996, one of the better-documented incidents occurred that involved several Mexican-made, mercury-containing beauty creams. A *Physician's Bulletin* was released in May 1996 by the San Diego Department of Health Services. It warned doctors to be aware that a beauty cream manufactured by Manning Laboratories Vida Natural of Pampico, Tamaulitas, Mexico, contained calomel (mercurous chloride) at extremely high levels (19.5 percent by weight, three thousand times the amount allowed in U.S. cosmetics).

Although cases of poisoning from the cream were known in Mexico, the bulletin reported two cases in Texas and one in San Diego. It further warned that chronic exposure to mercury can result in damage to the kidneys and the central nervous system, resulting in personality changes, nervousness, tremors, weakness, insomnia, sensations of

A Brief History of Medicine

2000 BCE	Here, eat this root.
1000 CE	That root is heathen, say this prayer.
1850 CE	That prayer is superstition, drink the potion.
1940 CE	That potion is snake oil, swallow this pill.
1985 CE	That pill is ineffective, take this antibiotic.
2000 CE	That antibiotic is artificial. Here, eat this root.

numbness, memory loss, a metallic taste in the mouth, and other symptoms.[26]

In response to media announcements in Arizona, California, New Mexico, and Texas, 238 people contacted their health departments to report use of the cream. The Centers for Disease Control compiled the data.[27] Of the 119 people for whom urinalysis was completed, 104 (86 percent) had elevated mercury levels, defined as a level greater than 20 micrograms per liter in their blood. The levels found in the cream users ranged from 22.0 to 1170.3 micrograms per liter!

Because mercury can penetrate the skin so easily, elevated mercury levels were also detected in some people who never used the cream but were close household contacts of cream users. For example, both the mother and the son of a woman who used the cream for a year and a half had urinary mercury levels of 31.6 and 50 micrograms per liter, respectively.

Then yet another skin-care product, Nutrapiel Cremaning Plus, made in Tampico, Mexico, was found being used in New Mexico. It contained 9.7 percent mercury by weight.[28]

In the United States, the only use for mercury in cosmetics that is allowed by the FDA is in eye-area products in concentrations not exceeding 65 parts per million (0.0065 percent). These small amounts of mercury are allowed in eye-area cosmetics because they can prevent the serious eye infections associated with eye-makeup use. There currently is no more effective nonmercurial substitute.

When you call a mineral substance such as calomel by its chemical name of mercuric chloride, it helps us understand. Yet the whole idea of "natural minerals" is a dirty joke. The minerals that have formed naturally in the earth may contain highly toxic lead, mercury, chromium, uranium, and more. Asbestos and silica are also natural minerals. There is utterly no reason to consider any of these minerals safe because they occur naturally.

Currently, the sellers of certain cosmetics are touting "natural mineral" makeups. This term is meaningless, because natural minerals have been used in cosmetics since the dawn of time. The Egyptians in the Bronze Age used kohl eye liners whose main ingredient was a natural mineral called galena (lead sulfide). Minerals were still used in the court of Elizabeth I. People at that time used a white lead-containing natural mineral called cerusite, which caused skin damage and hair loss. One actress who was famous in the eighteenth century even died of lead poisoning from natural cerusite.

Even today, most makeups contain natural minerals. Included are the white replacements for lead, which are titanium dioxide, kaolin (a clay mineral), talc (talcum powder), and zinc oxide. (See chapter 6, where the hazards of titanium oxide are mentioned.) Many of the colorants used in eye makeup are metal-containing inorganic compounds that can be either synthetic or natural minerals, such as iron oxide (red), chrome oxide (green), and silicates that contain cobalt (blues).

Essentially, the salespeople who tout cosmetics made from "natural minerals" are only telling you that their makeup is made of the same stuff that makeup has *always* been made of. If the new makeup really does make you look noticeably better than other makeups do, this probably means that the minerals in this makeup are in nanoparticle size—particles so small that they will sink into your skin, look more natural, and cover better. These nanoparticle minerals have never been sufficiently tested for the sellers to be absolutely certain that there will not be ill effects years from now.

We've looked at the oils from tea tree leaves, from citrus fruit rinds, and from pine tree sap (pine oil). But what about wood from trees? Isn't that simply cellulose? Surely, that's not toxic.

Wood is nothing more than part of the stem of a very big plant. This stem transports all of the chemicals the tree makes to feed itself, the biocides and the pesticides it needs to resist insects and microbes, plant growth hormones, and herbicides to keep other trees from establishing themselves too close. Many woodworkers like to think that wood is almost pure cellulose, a very nontoxic and inert substance. Cellulose is white, however, and most woods have color that is imparted by the chemicals that are created or sucked up from the ground by the tree. In general, the darker the wood, the more of these substances that can be present. This, in part, is the reason that very dark woods such as walnut, rosewood, ebony, and teak are especially likely to provoke respiratory allergies and skin sensitization in many people.

There are workplace air quality standards for wood dust set by the American Conference of Governmental Industrial Hygienists (ACGIH). In its recommendations, the ACGIH notes that the "principal health effects reported from exposure to wood dust are dermatitis and increased risk of upper respiratory tract disease. Epidemiologic studies of furniture workers have indicated an excess of lung, tongue, pharynx, and nasal cancer. . . . Certain exotic woods . . . contain alkaloids that can cause headache, anorexia, nausea, bradycardia, and dyspnea on inhalation."[29]

The wood of the yew tree is so toxic that severe symptoms have been reported when the wood was used to make a food container or even a spoon to stir food. It is no accident that a highly toxic chemo-therapy drug can also be isolated from yew trees.

Some woods contain enough toxic substances to act as pesticides and fungicides. For example, Western red cedar can be used for roof-ing and shingles without staining or painting because it contains many chemicals that kill the molds and the dry rot mildews that will degrade other types of wood. Some forms of cedar that are used to make cedar chests contain sufficient quantities of these biocides to protect our clothes from moths for decades. As expected, the sawdust from these woods is especially known to cause toxic and allergic reac-tion in the woodworkers who are exposed to them.

Only a few woods have been studied sufficiently to declare them carcinogens, because it is rare to find a large number of workers who are exposed to only one type of wood dust. Yet enough data have accumulated for many agencies to classify them as carcinogens. The U.S. National Toxicology Program thinks that there are enough data to classify all wood dusts as carcinogens (see the table on the next page). I've used only a few examples of natural substances here, ones that I have followed over the years with a particular interest. I happened to pick on the Chinese practitioners because it is particu-larly easy to do. Yet folk medicines from almost every country, including our own, have similar hazards. The instincts of our ancient forebearers were not magically better than our own. There is no balm in Gilead.

Since the entire dietary supplement industry was deregulated, we shouldn't be surprised that there is mercury in herbal products or that there are no large double-blind studies of estrogenlike chemicals derived from plants. The basic principle here is that any industry (not only the banking industry) that relies on obtaining money from the sale of its products is eventually going to abuse its customers if no one is actively keeping it from doing so.

Cancer Ratings for Various Wood Dusts

Type of Dust	Agency*	Cancer Status
Beech and oak	ACGIH	A1: Confirmed human carcinogen
	German-MAK	1: Confirmed human carcinogen
	NIOSH	Ca: carcinogen
	NTP	K: Known human carcinogen
Birch, mahogany, teak, walnut	ACGIH	A2: Suspected human carcinogen
	German-MAK	3B: suspected carcinogen
	NIOSH	Ca: Carcinogen
	NTP	K: Known human carcinogen
All other wood dusts	ACGIH	A4: Not classifiable
	NTP	K: Known human carcinogen

* ACGIH = American Conference of Governmental Industrial Hygienists; German-MAK are Federal Republic of Germany standards that are usually accepted by the rest of the European Union countries; NIOSH = National Institute for Occupational Safety and Health; NTP = the National Toxicology Program

I hope these few examples of toxic plants, trees, herbs, essential oils, and minerals that I used will demonstrate that you should suspect "natural" substances of being able to cause all of the same toxic effects that synthetic chemicals do. The line between natural and synthetic is really phony when you realize that Mother Nature "manufactured" cancer-causing dioxin and put it in various clay deposits. Moreover, Mother Nature made all of the petroleum deposits in the world out of dead plants and animals.

Once we face the fact that there is no reason to consider natural substances to be any more or less toxic than synthetic ones, we are free to use our heads to sort out advertising claims more reasonably— and that includes personal testimonies from users.

If I go back to my carnival roots again, those old snake-oil pitchmen always had a stooge or two come out of the crowd to testify about the miraculous properties of the product. And if the snake oil had enough alcohol or cocaine in it, some of the townies who bought the stuff a day earlier might also testify because they really did feel a lot better!

Not only should we not trust the "feel good" testimony of users, we should also beware of testimony about "looking good." Women use both natural and synthetic hormone-replacement drugs to look better. Makeup that contains mineral nanoparticles makes you look better, yet there is no proof that it is safe.

Ideally, you should use the following criteria to select natural or herbal products:

1. Reject out of hand any manufacturer's claim that the product is safe based on its natural origins.
2. Reject products for which the manufacturer does not provide ingredient information on the label or in its material safety data sheets by common name, chemical names, or CAS numbers, so that you can look them up if you choose to.
3. Try to reject products that are known to contain nanoparticles, because there are currently little or no data on these tiny particles. Be aware that manufacturers may not reveal this information.
4. Reject products that require you to ingest them for any purpose, if no studies of the product have been done using significant numbers of animals and people.
5. Reject cosmetic products for which the manufacturer does not provide easy access to a material safety data sheet that lists all of the required information (see chapter 10 for reasons that MSDSs should be available on cosmetics).
6. Reject products if the manufacturer will not respond to your questions about toxicity with clear and informative answers.

The chances of finding products that meet all of these criteria today are slim to none. Yet the more of these criteria they meet, the greater your confidence can be. These are the criteria we should hold all manufacturers to in the future.

CHAPTER 5

Why Not Just Use Soap?

You versus the Environment

As the environment heats up, both literally and figuratively, people are seeing more and more manufacturers claiming that their products are green, biodegradable, environmentally friendly, eco-safe, and other similar terms. Does this mean we can simply look for a particular label and be assured that we are making the right purchase? And just how do manufacturers determine that their product deserves the label?

Determining whether a product is truly better for the environment is a complex process and must take account of the energy costs and the environmental damage at every phase of the product's existence, from cradle to grave. Factors that must be considered include the renewability of the resources that are used to make each ingredient in the product and the cost to the environment of any chemicals, such as pesticides or fertilizer, that help produce any of the raw materials, as well as the water to irrigate them. The energy cost must also include the energy that was needed to transport each ingredient to the manufacturing location and to make the product. Other factors are the toxic emissions created by the factory that makes or processes

all of the ingredients and the emissions from the engines of the transport vehicles or airplanes that deliver the product to market. Finally,
there is the cost to the environment of the discarded product or its
packaging when these are incinerated, dumped down drains, or
added to a landfill.

To really know whether a product is "green" requires data collection and calculations from economists, chemists, engineers, and
environmental scientists all working together. And they should be
specialists working for the public interest, not for the manufacturer of
the green product.

A lot of these people might also get it wrong. As an example,
consider the flurry of excitement that was generated by Willie
Nelson as he campaigned with activists who proposed making alcohol from corn. The plan was supposed to help small farmers and
reduce our reliance on petroleum. The enthusiasm for this idea
cooled when people considered the pesticides, the fertilizer, and the
water needed; the energy that would be used to cultivate and harvest
the corn, heat the stills, and transport the stuff; the problem of divert-
ing the corn from other industries and the world food market; and
other issues.

Corn ethanol is still around, but scientists are experimenting with
using grass and other sources, instead of corn, for the hooch stills.
The general lesson to be learned from this story is never to jump on
any environmental bandwagon, no matter how attractively painted
the wagon or charismatic its driver, until the vehicle has gone down
the road far enough to wear out its first set of tires. Keep a healthy
skepticism about ideas that sound too good to be true, especially ideas
presented with great fervor by people who mean well but have no
science background. Wait for more facts, facts that are presented by
people with qualifications and who are not paid by the companies
that will make money from the green product.

I'm only a chemist and an industrial hygienist. When I look in
the mirror, only one person looks back at me, so I will not be evaluating all of these complex economic and energy factors. I leave that to
the environmental specialists and the armies of activists in this field.
Besides, I want to concentrate on two considerations about these
"green" products that are often overlooked in all of the fervor to save
the earth. These issues are (1) the gaps in our knowledge about the

actual effects of "biodegradable" products on the environment, and (2) whether these green products are actually safer for you to use.

The best illustration of these issues can be found in the first class of products that was affected by environmental regulations: soaps and detergents.

Remember the old phosphate detergents and a whiz of a phosphate cleaning chemical called trisodium phosphate (TSP)? Nothing, and I mean nothing, will clean like TSP and the phosphate detergents. They were not very toxic, either. They were a little harsh if you got them directly on your skin or in your eyes, but there still don't appear to be any long-term hazards to people that are associated with TSP or the old phosphate detergents.

TSP and some of the phosphate detergents also broke down into the environment fairly readily. One of their degradation products was, of course, phosphorus, which is a major fertilizer ingredient. This phosphorus was eventually integrated into the environment by being incorporated into algae, plants, and trees, depending on where the phosphorus was released.

I remember an old woman in our neighborhood who had the best garden on the block. Her backyard did not have the best soil, and there was too much shade, but she threw her wash water onto the garden once a week, with all of the phosphates in it. Her plants grew like Audrey 2 in *Little Shop of Horrors*.

Way back then, however, all of people's wash water didn't go into gardens. People released large volumes of these cleaners into the drains in their homes. In cities, these waste lines terminate in waste-water treatment plants. No matter how effectively the waste-water treatment plant bacteria were at breaking down the detergents, the phosphorus itself was unchanged and was released into the environment. As a result, phosphorus got into our lakes and streams, causing the algae to bloom and microbes to flourish. The algae and the microbes used up oxygen in the water, and the fish died. In addition, a head of foam on streams was esthetically unacceptable.

So the detergents that contained phosphates were banned. They were replaced by the new biodegradable detergents and "phosphate-free" detergents. These don't release phosphate, that's true. But what do these cleaners break down to in the environment? Or better yet, what do consumers think they break down into?

To find out what people think, I went to Yahoo! Answers and asked what a biodegradable detergent was. The answer: "It means that over time the detergent will degrade into inert ingredients. A bio-degradable detergent is safer for the environment." This is probably what a lot of people think, because this was the "Best Answer—Chosen by Voters." But the definition of biodegradable is not a voting issue. This is a technical term that we need to understand, or we'll believe the same nonsense that the Yahoo! voters do.

First, let's begin with the knowledge that detergents are chemical molecules, often rather large molecules. The biodegradable ones are more easily attacked by the microorganisms in water and in sewage treatment plants, but the microorganisms only break the molecules down into smaller pieces. These little pieces are still pollution. They are not "inert," as defined on Yahoo! Answers.

Breaking something down into inert substances would not be a good idea, either. Inert means that the remaining bits do not change or alter with time or bacterial action. Truly inert substances remain forever in the environment, and that may not be desirable, depending on what the inert substance is.

In fact, whatever the bits and pieces that remain are, they can't be substances that can be used by microorganisms as food, or we would be right back where we were with phosphates. So, whatever is left of one of these big detergent molecules after it is broken down by water borne bacteria can't be incorporated or used as food by plants and other environmental elements—at least, not in the short run.

To get an idea of what these degraded bits and pieces might be, we need to first understand the structures of the main kinds of detergents and how they work.

Without getting too technical, I'll say that most soaps and detergents are substances that reduce the surface tension of water. This allows water to penetrate and wash away dirt. The types of dirt that are most difficult for water to penetrate are oils and grease because these substances are hydrophobic, that is, they actively repel water. So, most soaps and detergents are specifically designed to remove oils and grease. It's important to understand how they do this.

Contrary to advertising claims and common belief, soaps and detergents do not dissolve grease and oil. Only other oils or chemical solvents, such as dry-cleaning solvents, can dissolve or mix with grease and oil. In fact, that is why some liquid cleaning products actually do contain solvents.

Instead of dissolving oil, plain soaps and detergents emulsify oily materials. Most of them can do this because their molecules have two parts. One part either is itself an oil or functions like an oil. This part easily mixes with or attracts the oily dirt and is often called the "hydrophobic" or water-hating part of the molecule in much of the literature on detergents. Yet it is easier to think of this part of the molecule as oil-loving.[1]

The other part of the molecule is highly water soluble and is often called the "hydrophilic" or water-loving part of the molecule. This part allows the basically hydrophobic soap or detergent to be easily mixed with water.

In the cleaning process, the oil-loving parts of the molecules attach themselves to a bit of oily dirt. A group of them will surround the oil to form something called a "micelle." Together, they can float that bit of oily dirt away from the rest of the oil into the water, propelled by the water-loving parts of the molecules. In other words, they break up the oil into many tiny oil or oily dirt droplets that now float in the water surrounded by detergent molecules. And since "oil suspended in water" is a crude definition of an emulsion, the soap can be thought of as an emulsifier of oil.

Soap can be made from simple chemicals. Sometimes referred to as lye soap, simple soaps have been made and used for hundreds of years. The process begins with making lye, which consists of hydroxides of metals such as sodium and potassium. The first lye was historically made from fireplace ashes. During burning (which is oxidation), the heat converts the potassium and sodium compounds that the tree took from the soil as minerals essential for its growth into potassium and sodium oxides. Adding water to the ashes converts the oxides to potassium and sodium hydroxides or lye. When the ashes are filtered out of the water, a clear lye solution remains.

Next, a large kettle of almost any type of animal or vegetable fat is heated over a fire, and the lye is added. Within a very short time, the liquid fat appears to solidify or form a gel. This solid or semisolid material is soap.

Two ways we could describe this reaction are

1. Any oil or fat + lye = soap (the fat part attached to a sodium ion) + water

    or

2. Oil-loving substance + water-loving substance = oil/water-loving soap + water

Detergents are similar to soap, in that they have oil-loving and water-loving parts. The oil-loving parts of the detergent molecule are hydrocarbons that are very much like oils. Substances derived from either natural or petroleum oils can be used to make the oil-loving part of the detergent molecule.

These oil-loving portions of detergent molecules usually consist of from eight to thirty carbon atoms. Some have their carbon atoms lined up in a row; sometimes they are branched or in ring shapes. In general, those with their carbon atoms all in a straight line are more easily attacked by common water borne microorganisms and therefore more biodegradable. This is probably true because these straight chain or "linear" molecules are more like natural fats and oils. The less biodegradable detergents tend to be full of more complex structures, such as branched chains and six-carbon benzene rings.

A common straight-chain type consists of linear alkyl sulfonates, or LAS detergents. These have been specially tailored to be biodegradable. One of the most popular is called sodium lauryl sulfate, which is made from palm oil. The detergent is touted as natural, but the manufacturing process can produce impurities such as dioxins, and the product may also be damaging to our skin. Many health activists recommend against this type of detergent. So, despite being better for the environment, it may not be better for the user.

On the other end of the biodegradable spectrum are the alkyl benzene sulfonates, or ABS detergents, which are not linear but often have branched chains and ring configurations. Today, these are frequently replaced by the LAS detergents because the ABS detergents break down to release benzene and other substances that are undesirable in water.

Yet benzene is a ring-shaped structure, and because LAS detergents are actually linear alkyl (benzene) sulfonates and the ABS detergents are alkyl benzene sulfonates, both contain at least one alkyl benzene group. So neither is completely benign in the environment. The LAS detergents are simply less polluting than the ABS ones.

Even more important, the ability to degrade in the environment is not related to toxicity to the user. This is a separate issue that must be determined product by product, by analysis and testing.

On almost every chemical cleaning product label, you will see the word "surfactant." This simply means something that will cut grease and clean your clothes, dishes, or whatever. Coupled with that word, however, you will see the product described as "anionic," "cationic," or "non-ionic." These are classes of detergents, and the class depends in part on how the fat-loving part of the molecule and the water-loving part of the molecule are bonded. To understand, we need to know that a part of a molecule that carries a charge is called an ion. A positively charged ion is a cation. A negatively charged ion is an anion. If nothing else, these definitions should help you with crossword puzzles, because the terms are frequently the answers to questions.

One type of phosphate-free non-ionic detergent consists of nonylphenol (NP) and nonylphenol ethoxylate (NPE) detergents. When phosphates were banned, these detergents became rather popular. I won't go into the chemistry of these detergents, but there were good reasons why they became popular. Some proponents still support the use of these detergents for the following reasons:

1. They are very powerful cleaners.
2. They are so good that very few additives to strengthen or whiten are needed, which results in fewer chemicals in the waste stream.
3. They are one of the most studied surfactants available. There are far more data available on these than on the other families of detergents.

4. The detergent industry argues that they actually are biodegradable, because a number of studies in the United States have shown that sewage-treatment plants remove, on average, 95 percent of nonylphenol and its ethoxylates from wastewater.
5. The industry reports that studies have also shown that nonylphenol and nonylphenol ethoxylates do not tend to bioaccumulate in the bodies of fish and other animals. This would mean that they do not become a part of the food chain.
6. Concentrations of NP/NPEs in the environment measured by some studies are typically below 1 part per billion.

This sounds good, but unfortunately for the detergent industry, it appears that although 95 percent of the NP and NPE detergents biodegrade, the remaining low levels of nonylphenol, as low as a few parts per billion, can have endocrine-disrupting effects on aquatic organisms, fish, reptiles, and amphibians. The feminization of animals by nonylphenol leads to a condition that can be oversimplified as the "teeny weeny peenie" syndrome.

We actually had good reason to suspect that nonylphenol had endocrine effects decades earlier, when it was first used in medicine as a spermicidal lubricant.

It is also possible that people are exposed to these emasculating substances simply by breathing the air in certain locations in the country. A 1999 study of urban and coastal areas near the lower Hudson River estuary showed that small amounts of estrogenlike nonylphenols were present in the air, presumably from the rapid evaporation and spray from waves of water that contained these detergent residues.[2]

I have a theory that can't be proved, but it seems to explain what happened next to the nonylphenol detergents. This theory predicts that chemicals that are found to be *male* reproductive hazards will be regulated worldwide more quickly and with less confirming data than chemicals known to cause cancer, birth defects, or damage to the female reproductive system. In any case, as my screwy theory predicts, a European Union Directive banning most uses for the NP and NPE detergents was issued in June 2003, and by January 17, 2005, all member states had implemented it.

Our country has been slower to act. On June 6, 2007, the Sierra Club, the Environmental Law and Policy Center, the Pacific Coast

Federation of Fishermen's Associations, the Washington Toxics Coalition, Physicians for Social Responsibility, and UNITE HERE petitioned the EPA.[3] They were concerned not only about nonylphenol in our water but also about the secondary degradation of nonylphenol into yet other chemicals that have not been tested. Their petition can be summarized as requesting the EPA to:

1. Require manufacturers and importers to conduct chronic aquatic safety studies on nonylphenol and several of the secondary degradation products of these detergents that may be even more endocrine disrupting;
2. Require labeling on all products containing nonylphenol (NP) and nonylphenol ethoxylates (NPEs); and
3. Limit the use of NP and NPEs where the use of these substances presents an unreasonable risk to public health and the environment.

The EPA agreed only to initiate chronic aquatic toxicity testing, but it denied the request for testing some of the secondary degradation products of the detergents or labeling and limiting the use of the detergents. The Sierra Club and the other signers of the petition have also pressured some of our legislators to introduce bills that would ban the nonylphenol detergents. As a result, some of the "green" companies no longer sell them. Yet so far, nonylphenol detergents are still around.

The lessons we can all take from the history of nonylphenol detergents are

1. Phosphate-free does not equal biodegradable.
2. Sometimes very small amounts of chemicals in water can have rather dramatic effects on the reproductive systems of aquatic organisms.
3. Biodegradable substances break down into more than one set of chemicals, which are usually called primary and secondary degradation products. Any of these may be toxic.

The demand for fast and efficient detergents has also caused the detergent industry to create more detergents. In order to make them do an even more impressive job of getting your dingy socks white, the industry produces a flock of additives to make them work better. I've listed the main types of additives in appendix A.

Two of these additives, dyes and enzymes, deserve special consideration.

Blue and white fluorescent dyes have been added to our detergents to fool our eyes into thinking our clothes are cleaner than they actually are. Theatrical costumers have long known that if garments are washed in detergents, they will glow in the dark. This becomes a problem when a scene ends with a dramatic blackout that turns unexpectedly comical when disembodied white shirts and socks are seen moving silently off stage.

The dyes are used in such high concentrations in some products that many theatrical scenic artists have found that they can substitute concentrated detergents for expensive black light paints. When painted on scenery, the detergent cannot be seen in regular light but will glow eerily under special theatrical black lights. That glow is emanating from a group of dyes whose hazards are essentially unstudied.

The enzyme additives also deserve special consideration. They appear to be biodegradable and are often added to detergents to attack certain kinds of stains and soil and also to help break down the detergent itself to make it more biodegradable. Yet the safety of these enzymes has come into question over and over again. Recently, detergent enzymes were cited as a reason for a local Canadian recall of these products.

On February 26, 2010, the Canadian Broadcasting Corporation reported that two of the largest school boards in Montreal banned green cleaning products that contained enzymes. Dr. Louis Jacques, who works for Montreal's public health department, was reported as saying that he has studied research on such products and is worried that the enzymes that make the detergents green could cause allergic reactions in children. He wants further study and perhaps regulation of those enzymes.

Dr. Jacques explained that "Based on the studies that have been done among workers, we know that these products can cause asthma, rhinitis, conjunctivitis, and dermatitis. But the most frequent health problem that was caused or aggravated by these products is asthma."

I agree with Dr. Jacques and have also seen the studies of the workers who manufacture and package enzyme detergent products. Considering that asthma is one of the most prevalent respiratory problems in schools, keeping these enzyme products out of schools until more is known about them is common sense.

This incident points up once again that we don't know all of the health effects of the many ingredients in biodegradable detergents, and we certainly haven't got a clue about the environmental fate of all of these additives.

So, why not just go back to soap? Soap has served us well for many years. Soaps are cheap, and they are manufactured from a renewable source, whereas many of the synthetic detergents are made from petrochemicals. Soaps are also biodegradable, and we know a little more about their degradation products because soap is made from common fats and oils.

Soaps have been replaced by detergents, however, partly due to their tendency to clog sewage systems. Fifty years ago, when soaps were the main cleaning agent, the grease traps of most homes had to be pumped periodically because they were clogged with soap. Now that most homes are connected to sewers instead of traps, this soapy buildup could be expected to deposit in sewer lines and water treatment plants.

When soap is used with hard water, that is, water that contains a lot of minerals, precipitation occurs. The calcium and magnesium ions, which give hardness to the water, form insoluble salts with the fatty acid in soap, and a curdlike precipitate is created that settles on whatever is being washed. By using a large excess of soap, it is possible to redisperse the precipitate, but it is extremely sticky and difficult to remove. And this goo can lead to deterioration of the fabric and odor when bacteria begin to degrade it.

If you live in an area where the water is extremely soft, you might be able to return to using soap for almost all cleaning tasks. Yet the dreaded soap precipitate will still form if the dirt you are washing out of your clothes contains metal compounds such as calcium and magnesium, which are found in soil or fertilizers. Then, once again, the precipitate deposits will build up in the fabric.

Many environmental activists swear that they can make a perfectly good laundry product out of soap, however. The most common recipe floating about is to grate enough ordinary bar soap to make a cup of flakes, add one-half cup of borax and one-half cup of washing soda (sodium carbonate), and mix these ingredients with water. The formula often varies the amount of washing soda, from less than one-half cup in soft water to more in hard water. It's worth doing.

The principal lesson that detergents teach is that biodegradation cannot make nothing out of something. If we start with a big complex detergent molecule, there are going to be a lot of bits and pieces left for us to deal with. At this stage of research, we aren't even sure what all of the substances from the various detergents are or what they do in the environment. And then there are the residues of the additives. It is likely that we will get some rude surprises from them as well.

In addition, biodegradability is utterly unrelated to the product's toxicity to the user. Even highly biodegradable sodium laurel sulfate detergent, made from natural palm oil, may have significant amounts of toxic contaminants due to by-products of the manufacturing process. Enzymes may cause allergic reactions, and many of the other additives' side effects are not known.

Another common product that has lessons for us in biodegradability is water-based paints.

One reason I have trouble convincing people that there can be significant amounts of volatile toxic solvents in water-based paints is that they assume the EPA regulations prohibit this. They have seen paint cans that list the required data on volatile organic chemicals, or VOCs. People seem to think that if they use paints labeled as containing "low VOCs" or "no VOCs," it means there are no significant amounts of volatile solvents in the paint.

Actually, this term refers only to chemical solvents that are regulated by the EPA because they participate in atmospheric photochemical reactions; that is, they create smog. Many solvents may be toxic but might not cause smog in the atmosphere. For example, a bottle of nail polish remover containing almost 100 percent of either acetone or methyl acetate could legally be labeled "no VOCs." This is because these solvents react negligibly in the atmosphere. Even highly toxic perchloroethylene or perc, used in dry cleaning, is not a VOC. These chemicals are called "exempt compounds" and do not come under the VOC rules. The VOC regulations, like the biodegradable rules, are related to environmental safety and not to the safety of the users.

Even more disturbing is that some of the complex and untested glycol ether solvents that are considered VOCs by the EPA are exempt from the VOC regulations when they are used in consumer products. So, your "no VOC" household product could actually be full of toxic solvents that are not disclosed by the regulations either because they don't cause smog or because the EPA has decided that the solvents occur in lesser amounts than are contained in industrial-use products.

Paints teach us once again that there is often is no direct relationship between the safety of the environment and the safety of the user. Simply meeting the environmental VOC regulations, making products water based, showing that they are biodegradable, or declaring them "green" because they are safer alternatives to existing products are requirements that have nothing to do with whether the product is safer for you to use. Most of these products, such as paints and detergents, are filled with additives about which we know even less and that may also be hazardous to the user.

We have looked only at soaps, detergents, and household paints as examples in this chapter. Yet we could learn the same lessons from other types of household cleaners, cosmetics, toiletries, textiles, plastics, building and construction materials, arts and crafts products, and much more. Research is needed to develop data on the actual environmental fate of all of these products, and comprehensive toxicity testing will be needed to make any real sense of this.

Taking all of these factors into consideration, my advice is to consider your health first and the environment second. I know there are fine scientists working to create more environmentally friendly products, but they are so far from their targets and there is so much they don't know that I suspect many of the "green" products sold today will be found not to be better for the environment in the long run. Concentrate instead on using simple products such as soap, using less of all products, and putting less into the drains and into the trash.

The greenest product is the one that was never made or used.

When you must paint your house or use a complex cleaner, investigate these products. Don't merely accept the limited information on the product's label. One of the best ways to do this is to ask manufacturers to provide you with more data in the form of a material safety data sheet.

CHAPTER 6

Of Wall Paint and Face Paint

How Labels Can Mislead You

We've had a very long look at nontoxic and hypoallergenic labels, but other labels are equally misleading. It is partly our fault. We like to put the best interpretation on the manufacturer's claims for our own comfort. We'd like to feel confident that the manufacturers wouldn't sell us something if it weren't thoroughly studied and found safe.

Instead, we should think like lawyers whenever we read a label: What kind of trade secrets did they add to make it new and improved? What criteria are met for the product to be labeled Generally Recognized as Safe? And are water-based products safer than the old oil-based ones?

Smelly, toxic petroleum solvents were the solvent of choice in both consumer and industrial products in the past. Essentially all older paints, varnishes, and other household and industrial surface coatings contained these petroleum solvents, or the products had to be thinned and cleaned up with petroleum solvents. The solvents were also used to clean grease and oil from industrial equipment and machinery parts. And petroleum chemicals modified with the addition of chlorine, called "chlorinated solvents," were used to dry clean clothes.

In a sense, we can think of the period up to 1980 as the "petroleum product age," because gasoline powered our cars and petroleum-based chemicals figured so strongly in all of our lives. The reason the solvents were used so extensively is that they were really good at what they did. They quickly "cut" grease, dissolving it so that it could be wiped or rinsed away from machinery or clothes. The petroleum solvents could also dissolve both natural resins, such as linseed oil from old oil-based paints, and new synthetic plastic resins, such as acrylic, to make the base for all types of paints. Some of the old oil paints and varnishes released so much solvent vapor that a day's painting could leave you high from solvent inhalation. In the past, work for some house painters amounted to paid time for glue sniffing!

Although these solvents were good for commerce, they were bad for the environment. When they evaporate from all of these products and disperse into the air, they react with sunlight, smoke from the burning of coal, oil burners, car exhaust, and other pollutants to create a toxic, smoky fog or smog. The smog was a hazard that everyone could understand because people suffered from eye irritation and breathing problems when this visible, odorous cloud appeared in cities and industrial areas. Once scientists determined that the chemical reactions that cause smog depended on volatile petroleum solvents plus combustion by-products from petroleum and coal, it was clear that the use of volatile petroleum solvents must be reduced.

Chemicals that create smog from air pollutants and sunlight are called "photo reactive." Environmental regulations began to restrict the use of photo-reactive solvents in surface coatings, household cleaning, dry cleaning, automotive parts cleaning, and many other products. One of the replacements was the new water-based products. Industry touted the greater safety of these products for both the environment and its customers, but were they really safer?

The petroleum-solvent cleaners for both household and industrial use had to be replaced with water-based ones. Water doesn't dissolve oil, though, so other chemical solvents had to be found that would mix with water and still dissolve grease. The first generation of these water-based solvents did this well: they were the extraordinarily toxic

primary glycol ethers that are known to cause male and female reproductive damage. The original primary glycol ethers were so toxic that
they were eventually replaced by more complex glycol ethers, which
seem to be less toxic. Yet many of the more complex ones have not
been evaluated for toxicity, and the entire glycol ether class appears
to cause reproductive effects and other organ damage in animals.
Some may even be carcinogens. Later, many of the glycol ether solvents would also be regulated as causing environmental damage.
Today, a couple dozen of these glycol ethers and their acetates are
commonly used in our products. All are technically listed under the
VOC regulations, but many of the more complex glycol ethers, most
of which are untested for long-term hazards, are exempt from the
VOC regulations when used in *consumer* products! So it is possible to
have a "no VOC" product that is full of these chemicals without the
labeling indicating this. Sometimes these glycol ethers are not listed
on the material safety data sheets, either.

The best example of the problems with the new water-based technology is seen in paints. The paint industry was faced with a challenge. The most common natural paint resin, linseed oil, would not
dissolve in water at all. And the new plastic resins, such as acrylate
and vinyl resins, were hydrophobic, meaning that they "hate" water
and refuse to dissolve or mix with it.

A whole new method of producing paints had to be used. The
model was similar to another certain natural water-based oil mixture:
cow's milk. Milk is primarily water, but butterfat, which is also hydrophobic, is a major constituent. If cow's milk is left to stand,
the cream, which is high in butterfat, rises to the top. Yet if it is
homogenized—that is, shaken or stirred until the butterfat globules
become extraordinarily small—the fat will no longer separate from
the milk mixture.

When oils such as butterfat are suspended successfully in water,
this is called an emulsion. A similar emulsion is seen in nature as the
white sap of rubber trees, only this emulsion is commonly called
latex. The whitish sap of this tree consists of water with microscopic
globules of natural rubber in it. You see the same kind of white latex
if you cut a stem or a leaf of the milkweed plant.

Industry's goal was to make plastic resins form an emulsion or a
latex with water. Soon, this was accomplished.

Of course, the new water-based paints were immediately touted as safer for users, as well as for the environment. This was not actually the case, however. It took some very unusual chemicals to keep this latex from separating out like butterfat. In addition, small amounts of special solvents were needed in the plastic to keep it liquid and soft so that it would fuse and form a layer when the water dried. These chemicals were (and often still are) some of the glycol ethers discussed earlier.

The early water-based acrylic paints had an additional problem born of the fact that the acrylic plastic on which they were based really was almost nontoxic! This presented the manufacturers with a huge problem. Putting a nontoxic acrylic water-based emulsion in a can was an invitation for bacteria and fungi to take up residence there. To give the new acrylic paints a proper shelf life, industry needed a really powerful preservative.

Mercury compounds make good preservatives. They had been banned in the old oil-based paints since 1976 as being too toxic, but mercury was used in the early acrylic water-based paints.[1]

Then, after a 1989 incident in which a four-year-old boy in Michigan developed mercury poisoning from the volatilizing of mercury preservatives from the walls of his parents' freshly painted home, pressure was exerted to get mercury out of latex paints as well.[2]

Effective September 30, 1991, the sale of paints containing the most popular phenylmercuric acetate preservative ceased.[3] It is still not clear whether there could be other mercury compounds in the water-based paints, but you can be sure there is some kind of biocide in them that is strong enough to keep microbes and fungi from lunching on the paint while it's in the can or when it is on your walls.

In plain words, these early mercury-laced, acrylic, water-based paints were more toxic than the solvent-based paints they replaced!

The labels on most household paints today will usually list four or five ingredients:

1. Water
2. One type of plastic emulsion in the paint, such as acrylic latex or vinyl latex
3. A filler or an extender, such as silica (fine sand) or one of the silicate minerals

4. Titanium dioxide or some other white pigment
5. Some form of antifreeze, such as ethylene glycol or propylene glycol, to keep the emulsion stable in cold weather (note: these are glycols, not glycol ethers)

Although some of the antifreeze chemicals can be toxic, the amounts are usually not high enough and evaporate too slowly to be a hazard during brush painting. The silica can cause respiratory problems and even silicosis, but only if it is inhaled, for example, during spraying or sanding.

Titanium dioxide is also a hazard by inhalation. It was the white pigment of choice after lead white pigments were banned from household paints in 1978. Titanium dioxide certainly is less toxic than lead, but it is now listed as a possible carcinogen by the International Agency for Research in Cancer. Plus, the titanium dioxide in paints is likely to be in nanoparticle size, making it more toxic than ever by inhalation.

Aside from the hazards of these five ingredients, unfortunately, there are probably thirty to forty other chemicals in small amounts that are not listed on the paint label. A good number of these are known to be hazardous, and many more have never been tested for long-term hazards.

Probably the most toxic of the unlisted chemicals are the biocides, better known as pesticides and fungicides. There are two types in almost all paints:

1. Biocides to protect wet paint in the can, which usually evaporate into the air as the paint dries [4]
2. Biocides that remain in the paint to protect the dry film. [5]

In addition, latex paints may include any of the substances in the following list:

Adhesion Promoters

Antioxidants

Antisag and settling agents

Antiskinning agents

Flow Modifiers

Freeze-thaw stabilizers

Light stabilizers

Mar and slip aids

(continued)

Adhesion Promoters	**Flow Modifiers**
Antistatic agents	Moisture scavengers
Coalescing agents (e.g., Texanol)	pH (acidity) control agents
Defoamers	Plasticizers
Dispersants	Rheology modifiers
Driers (to speed drying time)	Rust inhibitors
Emulsifiers	Surfactants (detergents)
Flame retardants	UV (sunlight) absorbers
Flatting agents	Wetting agents

Most of these additives are complex chemicals with names as long as your arm. The majority have never been tested for their effects on people. Some are expected to be toxic, based on their chemical class.

Remember, chemicals like these for which there are no toxicological data can legally be labeled "nontoxic" by manufacturers.

One example of these additives is a solvent called Texanol. The length of its actual name (2,2,4-trimethyl-1,3-pentanediol monoisobutyrate) is a good reason to simply call it Texanol. It is one of the most common coalescing agents in water-based paints and one of the very-high-production-volume chemicals for which there are essentially no published chronic data, including for carcinogenic or reproductive effects. Texanol is also one of those chemicals I mentioned that is considered a volatile organic chemical but has been exempted from the VOC regulations when used in a *consumer* product. Texanol and the dozens of other unidentified chemicals in your household paints are sometimes the reason these "nontoxic" paints cause symptoms in sensitive people. It is wise never to consider an ingredient label on a consumer product to be inclusive of all of the substances in the product.

Clearly, if a label proclaims that the product is protected against insects, rodents, and mold, it is probably full of pesticides, rodenticides, and fungicides.

My first run-in with these labels came when I was inspecting a grade school that had a limited art budget. To save a few dollars, the teacher was using a wheat paste, thinking that wheat would be safe for children. Yet this wheat product was packaged as a wallpaper paste. As such, it had to last for many decades without being attacked by insects, mold, or rodents. The teacher saw the pest-proof/rodent-proof claim on the label but never thought about how this was accomplished. Of course, it was laced with pesticides and rodenticides.

This incident also points out two other labeling lessons:

1. **Never use adult products with children.** Products clearly meant for adult use on the job or for professional maintenance or repair can be labeled without warnings because the manufacturer assumes they will not be misused or eaten. Only if the product is meant for householders to use in the home are there likely to be appropriate warnings about exposure to children.
2. **Do not use a product for a purpose other than how the label directs, unless you are prepared to accept full liability for that use.** The manufacturer has no responsibility for your unorthodox use of the product. And beware of household hint columns and craft magazines that suggest these off-label uses for products.

You should also watch out for labels that go to great lengths to tell you all of the ingredients the product doesn't contain, while neglecting to tell you what the product actually does contain.

If you see "contains no phosphates" on a detergent, this only tells you that one of dozens of various types of detergents has been excluded, not which detergent is actually in the container. This label is still required by New York law (see chapter 11), but it is not informative because the phosphate detergents have been banned since the 1970s in the United States. This label does not inform you of anything other than that the manufacturer is complying with the law.

You're also not getting anything special when you see "contains no CFCs, which deplete the ozone layer." These are the chlorinated and fluorinated carbon compounds that have been banned for years. The manufacturer is telling you nothing other than that it is abiding by the law, as every other manufacturer is also doing.

It's hard to imagine what "chemical free" could possibly mean. I've seen this term used even on pesticide product labels. Clearly, the world, including your body and everything in your house, is made up of chemicals. This also applies to the stuff in that "chemical-free" product. There simply couldn't be a more ridiculous label than this one.

When you see "no synthetic chemicals," you can believe it, but it doesn't mean anything useful. As far as your health is concerned, you shouldn't really care. Toxic stuff can be made by both God and Goodyear. Chemicals can be just as toxic when they have been extracted from a plant or a tree as when they are synthesized in a laboratory. The origin of the chemical is irrelevant to toxicity. It may mean that the method of manufacture is better for the environment, but this is not really clear unless you know all of the costs of extracting it from nature, the transportation costs, and other factors.

Unfortunately, "no animal-tested ingredients" or "cruelty-free" could be put on a large number of ordinary consumer products because there have been no tests on the majority of chemicals we use. These labels are particularly misleading on a cosmetic product because only certain FDA-approved ingredients can be used for such products. These FDA-approved chemicals usually have already had significant animal testing before they are approved for limited uses in certain types of cosmetics, and they are often "batch approved," meaning that the primary manufacturer from whom the cosmetic company buys its ingredients has analyzed each batch and certified that it is of the purity the FDA requires. Perhaps the manufacturer has not retested its specific mixture of FDA-approved ingredients, but such testing is not even required.

At last, we come to a phrase you may soon learn to dread: "generally recognized as safe (GRAS)." This term is specifically used by the U.S. Food and Drug Administration primarily for food ingredients and food-related uses. Sometimes this term is misused in product literature or material safety data sheets to imply that the product is safe enough to eat.

Some GRAS substances are not intended to be eaten at all. These are chemicals restricted to use in food packaging or as disinfectants and soaps to sanitize food-processing utensils and similar purposes in which they would not be ingested. For example, highly toxic substances can be GRAS for use in food packaging if manufacturers can prove that the toxic GRAS chemicals do not migrate from the packaging into food.

Those GRAS substances intended for actual use in foods are approved by the FDA only at specific levels or in accordance with "good manufacturing practices." For example, acetic acid is GRAS because a good manufacturing process would limit it to the roughly 5 percent in vinegar. Concentrated acetic acid, often referred to as "glacial acetic acid," is not GRAS. It is so corrosive, flammable, and reactive with other chemicals that it can cause explosions when mixed with them.

Many GRAS common substances used as flavorings are acutely toxic as determined by their oral lethal dose tests (LD50s) for rats. For example, vanillin, sage oil, and clove oil are acutely toxic.

Even some carcinogens are GRAS. One of these is titanium dioxide, which has been considered a carcinogen by the National Institute for Occupational Safety and Health for more than twenty years and is now also listed as "possibly carcinogenic to humans" by titanium dioxide the International Agency for Research on Cancer. Yet is considered GRAS by the FDA when the amount used is 0.5 percent or less in your candy, ham, cake icing, and many other foods.

Titanium dioxide is a good example to illustrate the most important assumption of the GRAS definition, namely, that the food-use substances are approved by the FDA for ingestion. Titanium dioxide is a lung carcinogen when inhaled but is apparently not a hazard when ingested.

Mom was right: don't inhale your food.

Another large group of GRAS substances, like so many other chemicals we use, have never been tested for their toxic effects. In the 1950s, when the FDA began to look at food additives, there were already thousands of chemicals in use in the food supply. So the FDA simply excluded from scrutiny any substance in common use before 1958. In chapter 1, we discussed how a common over-the-counter GRAS laxative ingredient was finally studied in 1985 and banned from use because it was found to be a powerful animal carcinogen. How many other hazardous chemicals are among the untested chemicals is unknown.

In summary, GRAS means that either the ingredient has been used for years without testing or the FDA has tested and approved it for some very limited use related to food, food packaging, and so on. If it is approved for food, it still may be acutely toxic in large amounts and even a carcinogen under certain circumstances. And GRAS status certainly is not an indication that the chemical is safe if inhaled.

Even the phrase "FDA-approved" can be misleading. It's used to describe ingredients in products that require FDA-approved ingredients by law. For example, it would be an unfair trade practice for a manufacturer to advertise that the ingredients in its cosmetic products are FDA-approved, which would imply that the ingredients in other cosmetics may not be approved by the FDA.

The term is also used improperly if it refers to an ingredient that is not used in the manner for which the FDA approved its use. For example, ingredients approved for use on the cheeks may not be approved for use around the eyes or on the lips and the mucous membranes. Different requirements apply to chemicals that are intended for use on each of these three body parts. Most important, cosmetic ingredients and additives are not approved for inhalation.

The most well known abuse of the FDA-approved label is when it is applied to spray tanning products. The FDA's Office of Cosmetics and Colors referred to the restrictive nature of the approvals for cosmetic ingredients in 2003 when the new DHA-spray sunless tanning booths became popular. In these booths, consumers receive an airbrush mist or spray application of dihydroxyacetone (DHA), a cosmetic chemical that gives the skin the appearance of a tan.

DHA is regulated by the FDA as a color additive. On its Web site, the FDA explains the color additive rules:

> The Food, Drug, and Cosmetic Act (FD&C Act), Section 721 authorizes the regulation of color additives, including their uses and restrictions. These regulations are found in Title 21, Code of Federal Regulations (21 CFR), beginning at Part 70. If a color additive is not permitted by regulation or is used in a way that does not comply with the specific regulation(s) authorizing its use, it is considered unsafe under the law. Such misuse of color additives causes a cosmetic to be adulterated.
>
> DHA is listed in the regulations as a color additive for use in imparting color to the human body. However, its use in

cosmetics—including sunless "tanning" products—is restricted to external application (21 CFR 73.2150). According to the CFR, "externally applied" cosmetics are those "applied only to external parts of the body and not to the lips or any body surface covered by mucous membrane" (21 CFR 70.3v).

In addition, no color additive may be used in cosmetics intended for use in the area of the eye unless the color additive is permitted specifically for such use (21 CFR 70.5a).[6]

When someone is exposed to an airbrush mist in the tanning booth, it is difficult to avoid exposure to DHA in a manner for which it is not approved, such as in the area of the eyes, the lips, the mucous membranes, or even internally by inhalation. Consequently, the FDA advises you to ask the following questions when considering commercial facilities where DHA is applied by spraying or misting:

- Are consumers protected from exposure in the entire area of the eyes, in addition to the eyes themselves?
- Are consumers protected from exposure on the lips and all parts of the body covered by mucous membranes?
- Are consumers protected from internal exposure caused by inhaling or ingesting the product?[7]

If the answer to any of these questions is no, the consumer is not protected from the unsafe (and thus illegal) use of this color additive. Clearly, this applies to all of the new and very popular consumer and theatrical airbrush makeup ingredients as well!

Currently, I am not aware of any airbrush makeup for which all of the ingredients are FDA-approved for use on the skin (for example, the cheek), as well as around the eyes and on the lips. And I know of no FDA-approved cosmetic ingredients that are approved for inhalation. In my opinion, all of these popular new airbrush makeup products are misbranded and technically illegal.

This is even more distressing when you consider that some makeup ingredients, such as silica and titanium dioxide, are lung carcinogens. They are perfectly safe when applied to the skin but not when inhaled.

And now many cosmetic ingredients are in nanoparticle size, meaning that they are so tiny, they can get deep into the lungs and perhaps go through the lung into the bloodstream or through nasal tissue into the brain. These issues have not been well studied and certainly should be before products like this are made available to the public.

I wish I could tell you that you could simply look at the ingredients list to figure out what's safe, but you might also see this on the label: "trade secret or proprietary." These are words to run from. Now the manufacturer has put you on notice that you will not be able to find out what you have been exposed to.

Of the 84,000 chemicals regulated under the 1976 Toxic Substances Control Acts, the EPA estimates that nearly 20 percent— that is, 17,000 chemicals—have trade secret protection. Of the trade secret chemicals, 151 are made in quantities of more than 1 million tons a year and 10 are used specifically in children's products, according to the EPA.

This means that the names of these chemicals and their physical properties are guarded from consumers and virtually all public officials. Their identity is also kept from medical professionals, state regulators, and even emergency responders who would have to clean up a spill of the chemicals or respond to a fire involving them.

One story to illustrate how hazardous this can be was reported by Susan Green, a columnist for the *Denver Post*, on July 24, 2008. A man appeared at a Durango, Colorado, hospital who was complaining of dizziness and nausea. Reportedly, his work boots were damp, and he reeked of chemicals. He said that he had been involved in a chemical spill at a gas-drilling site. The man recovered, but two days after he was admitted, the fifty-seven-year-old nurse who treated him was fighting for her life.

Nurse Cathy Behr told a Denver reporter that her liver was failing and her lungs were filling with fluid. Behr said that her doctors diagnosed chemical poisoning and called the manufacturer, Weatherford International, to find out what she had been exposed to.

Weatherford provided safety information, including hazards, for the chemical, known as ZetaFlow. But because ZetaFlow has confidential (trade secret) status, the information did not include all of its ingredients. Mark Stanley, the group vice president for Weatherford's pumping and chemical services, said in a statement that the company made public all of the information that was legally required.

Behr said that the full ingredient list should have been released. "I'd really like to know what went wrong," said Behr. She recovered but still has respiratory problems. "As citizens in a democracy, we ought to know what's happening around us."[8] I agree with Nurse Behr.

Thirty-three years ago, the Toxic Substances Control Act was designed to protect trade secrets in a highly competitive chemical industry. If a company's competitors were to find out the identity of a new chemical, they could use it in their products without spending the money to develop the chemical. But critics—including the Barack Obama administration—say the secrecy has grown out of control, making it impossible for regulators to control potential dangers or for consumers to know which toxic substances they might be exposed to.

Obama's EPA head, Lisa Jackson, has said that the 1976 law is both outdated and in need of reform. It remains to be seen whether reform will actually occur. Until then, I suggest avoiding products that contain trade secret chemicals.

CHAPTER 7

You Have the Right to Know

How the MSDS Can Help You Protect Yourself (When No One Else Will)

We now know that label terms often don't mean what we think they mean, and some will outright lie. So, what's a consumer to do?

The next step you can take is to obtain additional technical information in the form of a document called a material safety data sheet, or MSDS. It is usually intended to inform workplace users, rather than consumers, but good companies will make MSDSs readily available to all customers.

The first such documents were created in the 1940s when the Manufacturing Chemists' Association, now known as the Chemical Manufacturers Association (CMA), began to produce *Chemical Safety Data Sheets*. These sheets contained information on the "Properties and Essential Information for Safe Handling and Use." Ultimately, about a hundred of these *Chemical Safety Data Sheets* were produced. They were very detailed in their coverage of each chemical, to the point of being almost a stand-alone book on the product. The longest was forty-six pages.

The CMA no longer produces these *Chemical Safety Data Sheets*, but soon various chemical companies began to compile similar data sheets for the customers of some of their high-volume chemicals. By the early 1980s, these sheets were produced by most major manufacturers.

In 1983, the Occupational Safety and Health Administration (OSHA) published the Hazard Communication Standard, better known as the Right to Know law. This law gave about twenty million chemical manufacturing workers the right to obtain detailed information about the chemicals they were exposed to on the job. Under this new law, manufacturing employers were expected to provide proper chemical labeling, to produce and supply access to safety information in the form of MSDSs on all potentially hazardous chemicals, and to offer workers formal documented training by a qualified person on the hazards of their jobs.

The fact that the law covered only workers engaged in chemical manufacturing was not acceptable to workers in other jobs. Many unions petitioned to get their workers included under the hazard communication regulations without success. Unable to get federal action, these unions and organizations lobbied for, and got passage of, Right to Know laws in many states.

For example, New York State had an effective Right to Know law by 1985. It covered almost all types of private sector workers. The law was enforced by the state's attorney general's office. This particular Right to Know law affected me directly when, in 1986, the attorney general issued the first-ever citations to a theater production company. They were issued to *La Cage aux Folles*, which was operating from the Palace Theater on Broadway in New York City.

Think again if you believe that singers, dancers, stagehands, costume dressers, rigging and lighting technicians, and other theatrical workers couldn't possibly have significant exposure to chemicals. At the Palace, there was a 55-gallon drum of potentially carcinogenic perchloroethylene (perc) dry cleaning solvent right offstage in the wings so that makeup and other soil from costumes could be removed instantly. Because the show involves a lot of dancers and actors in drag, some of the costumes were padded in the bust area. These costumes could soak up the cleaning solvent, which would then be next to the actors' skin or evaporate from the fake cleavage just under their chins, a location from which inhalation of the vapors was essentially guaranteed.

The theatrical workers were also using a fog machine to create an atmospheric effect in certain scenes. People who were inhaling the chemical mist emitted by this machine at *La Cage* now had a legal right in New York State to know what they were snorting every night.

The chemicals that were used to create the fog at *La Cage* in the 1986 production were trade secrets, identified only as "glycols." Some fogs used at that time were actually ethylene glycol, the typical anti-freeze chemical. Certain fog products also contained (and some still do today) diethylene glycol, a chemical that has killed children when it was substituted for glycerine in cough medicines by unscrupulous manufacturers. Other glycols common in theatrical fog include tri-ethylene glycol, propylene glycol, and butylene glycol.

Exactly which of these glycols were being inhaled by the *La Cage* cast is not known. Yet I bothered to list all of them (see the following table) because many of you go to the theater and have seen this stuff. The fog doesn't know it is supposed to stay onstage, so you've proba-bly inhaled some of these glycols as well.

Glycols Used in Theatrical Fog

Ethylene glycol (used primarily in the past)
Diethylene glycol
Butylene glycols (1,2-, 1,3-, and 1,4-butanediols)
Triethylene glycols
Polyethylene glycol (E 200, made by Dow Chemical, used in
    the past)
Polypropylene glycols (not commonly used)
Monopropylene glycol (propylene glycol; 1,2-propandiol)
Dipropylene glycols
Glycerin (glycerol; 1,2,3-propandiol)

The reason the identity of the glycol fog chemicals was of particu-lar concern at *La Cage* was that the fog machine did not produce very uniform mist particles, and a portion of the droplets of fog chem-icals would settle on nearby surfaces. One fog machine was located in the wings, right above a prop table where filled champagne glasses were waiting to be taken onstage. As a result, some actors in *La Cage* were also exposed by ingestion.

In addition, the cast used makeup and hairsprays that were potentially toxic. The sprays are especially hazardous when a lot of people are using them in a crowded dressing room. When makeup and hairsprays are used by consumers, these cosmetic products are not covered by the Right to Know laws. But as soon as they are used under workplace conditions, they come under the law.

In any case, MSDSs on the fog, the cleaning fluid, hairsprays, and other potentially toxic products had to be collected and made available to the cast and the crew. I was brought in to do the official documented training that is also required by the law. The training session was held in the Palace Theater house on a Wednesday between the matinee and evening shows on February 19, 1986.

States such as New York had their own Right to Know laws at this time. It made life difficult for trainers like me, because we had to comply with a different set of regulations in each state. The situation was partly resolved after 1987. That year, after many legal maneuvers by unions and workers' groups, and after OSHA was faced with a possible contempt citation from a federal court to show why all workers should not be included under this law, OSHA expanded coverage to another fifty-nine million workers.

The law now covered most jobs in which chemical products were used, including two groups of workers that had been excluded from a number of OSHA regulations in the past: people working in the construction industries and in the service and health-care industries.

Today, some twenty years after the federal hazard communication law was passed, most private sector workers come under either the federal law or a state law that is identical or very similar to it.

Public sector workers have not fared as well as those in the private sector. There is still a patchwork of coverage for public sector workers, such as teachers in public schools and universities, workers in state libraries, art conservators in museums, and the like. Some public sector workers—for example, those in New York and New Jersey—come under an OSHA-approved state plan. Certain states allow the federal OSHA jurisdiction over their public sector workers. Yet in twenty-five states, public workers are not covered and their public institutions are exempt from federal safety inspections.

I have worked in all but three states in this country and have seen how the lack of these laws affects schools. If any relative of mine wanted to send his or her child to a public college in one of these uncovered states, I would advise my relative to reconsider or do some heavy research on accidents and lawsuits filed against the school. Even when these states have set up an independent state agency to deal with workplace safety and have rules that look good on paper, it is my experience that they don't work. I think that one state agency is loath to try to exert pressure on another state agency.

The other reason I would be leery of public schools in states where public employees are not covered is directly applicable to this chapter. These schools usually do not have a program that provides MSDSs or training about them to teachers and students. It is not only safety, but education about safety, that is deficient in these schools.

Everyone who uses potentially toxic products should be familiar with MSDSs. The federal law requiring access to MSDSs is not restricted to construction workers, painters, plumbers, carpenters, pesticide applicators, and other workers who obviously use chemicals. The law also applies to health-care workers, people in any industry who use cleaning and maintenance products, auto-body shop workers, cosmeticians and beauty operators, gardeners and lawn-care workers who use fertilizers and herbicides, swimming pool maintenance workers, teachers of art and science classes, and many more. Even workers in the restaurant trade, including fast-food chains such as McDonald's, are owed hazard communication training that covers products such as those used to clean and sterilize.

Sometimes office workers also require hazard communication training and protections. For example, workers need training if old-fashioned liquid or powdered copy-machine toners have to be poured into the machines, rather than provided in a closed cartridge, or if adhesives and spray products are used. Certainly, the service people who come in to repair or maintain office business machines and use solvent sprays and wipes and the workers who clean the offices after hours require training under this law. When these workers come to an office with their chemical products, they should also be able to provide the regular occupants of the office with MSDSs on their cleaners if any office workers have concerns or a reaction to these products.

Even if you don't work with chemicals yourself, but others around you do, you may come under the law. OSHA provided an example to explain this difference. It said that a bookkeeper employed by a chemical manufacturer will not need training if her office has a separate entrance and she does not come in contact with the chemicals or the vapors from them. If the bookkeeper has to walk through the plant to get to her office, however, she needs the same training that the workers do.

With all of these categories of jobs and potential exposures in mind, I'd like readers to think about the jobs they have held during the last twenty years. Did any of those jobs involve being around or using chemical products of some kind? And if they did, were you made aware of this OSHA law and did you receive the required training or access to MSDSs?

I'm willing to bet the proceeds from this book that less than half of my readers who were entitled to training actually received it. My guesstimate is based on the fact that the workers and the teachers I train often tell me that this is the first such training they have had, despite the fact that their employers have been required by law for decades to provide it.

So I will assume that only a portion of you will know that if chemical products are used in your workplace, OSHA or some state agency probably requires your employer to provide you with the following:

- **A written plan to address job hazards that must be made available to you on request.** As part of that plan, the employer must provide an up-to-date inventory that lists all potentially hazardous chemicals located on your worksite.
- **Proper labeling of all chemical products.** This includes the name of the substance, the name and the address of the manufacturers, and any hazard warnings that are required by law. In particular, it means that the common practice of pouring chemicals, such as paint or cleaning materials, into an unlabeled container and scribbling a word or two on the container with a marker is

prohibited. (Actually, the practice is not prohibited if you use up the product in the container during your shift, but containers of chemicals that are improperly labeled cannot be left in the workplace unattended.) All products in a workplace must be labeled so that anyone coming into the workplace for the first time, including firefighters and emergency medical responders, will be able to find proper labels on all products.

- **A file of MSDSs on all potentially toxic materials.** This file must be made available for reference at all times to workers.
- **Training by a qualified trainer.** Training must be provided for all potentially exposed workers, whether they are using the chemicals or are exposed in proximity to them. Training must cover the workers' rights under this law, the hazards of the chemicals the workers use, label terminology, MSDSs, and safe handling procedures.

If this training were done the way the law requires, this chapter would be old news for anyone who has ever held a job that involved chemical products. In fact, I believe that if the training required by OSHA were done properly, most people in the United States would also be informed consumers who insist, as I do, on labeling reforms and testing.

MSDSs are useful whether or not you work with chemicals on the job. They can be used to evaluate your household and hobby products. They should be easy to get, even though the federal OSHA regulations do not require companies to make MSDSs available to consumers. A few states, such as Connecticut, have a consumer Right to Know law that entitles you to MSDSs, but good companies provide them to anyone.

In fact, failure to find MSDSs easily on a manufacturer's Web site should be your first clue that the manufacturer may have something to hide. After all, what reason could a manufacturer have for not providing the additional safety and ingredient information on the MSDS?

Manufacturers who try to hide behind the exemption to provide MSDSs for consumer products should be aware that this exemption applies only if they *never* sell their products to people who intend to use them on the job. If cleaning products, cosmetics, art materials, and other consumer products are sold to people who use them to clean, apply cosmetics or hair products, or teach arts or crafts with these products *on the job*, then the employers of these people must have MSDSs for them.

Certain basic information is supposed to be present on all MSDSs, as dictated by the OSHA regulations. Do all MSDSs actually contain the required information? No. Will you see all of this information on the MSDS you get from the Web site of your products' manufacturers? Not likely.

This is a story you have heard over and over in this book: no one is watching the store. Absolutely no person or government agency is overseeing the accuracy or completeness of MSDSs. OSHA requires manufacturers to write them for the protection of workers during the manufacture of the chemicals and requires employers to have a file of them in the workplace for the edification of the workers. Yet OSHA checks to see if this file exists only if it is inspecting the workplace, which is a rare occurrence in U.S. workplaces. On these occasions, it would be even rarer for OSHA to check the accuracy and the completeness of the information on the MSDSs in that file.

Instead, the issue of accuracy or completeness of the information on an MSDS is likely to be raised only after an accident, an injury, or a lawsuit, when the quality of this information bears directly on a proximate cause of the accident and establishing liability. So the majority of MSDSs are abysmally insufficient. Nonetheless, MSDSs are usually more informative than labels are.

The order in which the required information is presented also varies greatly from one MSDS to the next. Manufacturers objected to being forced to present their data in the format that OSHA developed, so OSHA gave them the right to organize the required information in any order they chose. The result has been chaos.

You may have to hunt for specific information through a document that can range in length from one page to ten or more and that can be divided into sections, usually, but not always, numbering from twelve to sixteen.

Technical sanity is once again arriving from the world community. Spearheaded by the European Union, the United Nations adopted the Globally Harmonized System of Classification and Labeling of Chemicals in 2003. The GHS classification system promotes common, harmonized criteria for the classification of chemicals and a template for a worldwide compatible MSDS. In the process, the UN dropped the "MSDS" name and simply called the new documents Safety Data Sheets.

We'd better get used to taking our orders from the United Nations and the European Union if we want to sell products to the rest of the world. Considering our safety record, it is a good idea that others are taking the lead. Many countries have adopted these standards and already demand the Safety Data Sheets.

OSHA saw this coming. On September 30, 2009, OSHA published a proposed rule to update the Hazard Communication Standard by adopting the global UN classifications of chemicals and the new Safety Data Sheets.[1] OSHA said that these new international standards would enhance environmental protection and public health and reduce trade barriers by using universal hazard statements, pictograms, and signal words to communicate hazard information on product labels and safety data sheets. The new sheets will also be more usable for workers, consumers, and nontechnical people.

The comment period on the OSHA rule closed at the end of December 2009, and now the comments are being reviewed. Of course, most of the comments were from companies that were not likely to want these changes. I've already read the long litany of objections filed by Proctor & Gamble. On the other side is the American Industrial Hygiene Association, which likes every single proposal. Guess which organization has more clout? So we will have to see what happens.

The new Globally Harmonized Safety Data Sheets will provide great advantages over our old MSDSs. We can see examples of these advantages by comparing the current OSHA regulations with the new Globally Harmonized ones for two groups of chemicals: carcinogens and chemicals that pose a hazard to health.

The current OSHA regulations require the listing on the MSDS of any substance considered a carcinogen by the International Agency for Research on Cancer (IARC), the National Toxicology Program (NTP), or OSHA that is present in the product at 0.1 percent or greater. Yet we already know that only around 900 chemicals have been evaluated for their cancer potential out of the 140,000 registered for use in commerce in the European Union or the 50 million chemicals registered by the Chemical Abstract Service.

As a result, many of our MSDSs state something like this: "Not listed as a carcinogen by IARC, NTP, or OSHA." An untrained worker might assume this means that the chemical is not a carcinogen. Instead, this merely indicates that the chemical has not been evaluated by these agencies because there are not enough data.

The new Globally Harmonized Safety Data Sheets will tell the user whether the substance has been studied for cancer effects. In this case, telling users what is not known is as important as telling them what *is* known. This will also begin the process of alerting workers to the fact that most chemicals have never been tested for cancer effects.

Our current regulations define a health hazard as "a chemical for which there is statistically significant evidence based on at least one study conducted in accordance with established scientific principles that acute or chronic health effects may occur in exposure employees." This sounds good until you realize that many chemicals have never had that first study that is required to show it is a hazard. Many chemicals exist for which there are no acute data and even more that have had no chronic testing.

The Globally Harmonized Safety Data Sheets will be very different. Although the GHS system can't change the fact that most chemicals have not been tested, the new GHS Safety Data Sheets will provide blanks for the various toxicity tests. If the test has not been done, the statement "No data available" is required to clearly tell product users that this test was never conducted.

You can find these rules and all of the others for the new GHS Safety Data Sheets in a large publication with a purple cover that is available online from the United Nations. It is designed to help manufacturers write Globally Harmonized Safety Data Sheets and is often called the GHS Purple Book. You can try finding it on the UN's Web site, but doing a simple Internet search for "GHS Purple Book" should bring you to a Web site that will allow you to download a free copy in English and other major languages. In the Purple Book's annex (appendix) 4, the following advice sums up the misleading statements about untested chemicals we currently see here in the United States and how these statements are no longer acceptable:

A4.3.11.4 General statements such as "Toxic" with no supporting data or "Safe if properly used" are not acceptable as they may be misleading and do not provide a description of health effects. Phrases such as "not applicable", "not relevant", or leaving blank spaces in the health effects section can lead to confusion and misunderstanding and should not be used. **For health effects where information is not available, this should be clearly stated.**[2]

Although we can hear the cavalry blowing the call to "charge" in the distance, U.S. consumers will still have to contend with the crap that constitutes most U.S. MSDSs today. Still, I advise consumers to get them on any product they consider purchasing.

To begin evaluating any product, you need to determine whether the item is defined in the law as a chemical product or an article. Items such as furniture, computers and machines, kitchen utensils, and the like may emit chemicals, but they are considered articles. They do not have MSDSs. For example, there is no MSDS for your car. Yet there are MSDSs for the gasoline and the oil you put in the car.

MSDSs are limited to goods that are chemical products, such as cleaners, cosmetics, spray products, paints, or any other items composed of chemicals to which you could be exposed.

Once you know that a product should have an MSDS, the following steps can be taken.

1. Find out who the manufacturer is. The company running the Web site on which you see the product offered for sale may not be the actual manufacturer. Web sites, hardware stores, department stores, and similar distribution outlets do not have to supply MSDSs for the hundreds of products they sell. Each product's manufacturer should be listed on the label of that product, however.
2. Go to the manufacturer's Web site. If there are no MSDSs available on the site, that's a bad sign. Often, I quit considering the product for purchase at this point. Or you can go to step 3.

3. Contact the manufacturer by e-mail or phone and ask for an MSDS.
   (a) If the manufacturer says its product doesn't require one because it is a consumer product, that's a deal breaker. It does require one.
   (b) If the manufacturer tells you it provides MSDSs only to employers or large commercial buyers, that's also a deal breaker. Unless you live in a state that has a consumer Right to Know law, the manufacturer has the right to refuse to give you an MSDS. But I don't recommend dealing with companies that will not provide MSDSs to consumers.
   (c) If the manufacturer has other reasons for not providing MSDSs, you can listen to these reasons, but I can't think of anything the manufacturer could say that would justify not having MSDSs.
4. Don't purchase the product until you have the MSDS. If it can't be downloaded from the manufacturer's site or can't be sent to you immediately as an attachment or a fax, this is a very bad sign.
5. When you get the MSDS, determine whether the product is a single-component substance or a mixture.
   (a) **MSDSs for single-component substances.** MSDSs for single-component products are like to be fairly correct and complete, especially if they are from a chemical catalog supplier or a large primary manufacturer. For example, science teachers who order chemicals for student experiments have access to large chemical catalog suppliers, such as Sigma-Aldrich, Sargeant, and Fisher.

   If you intend to buy a quart container of a single-component product, such as a solvent, and the MSDS tells you to wear a self-contained breathing apparatus and a Tyvek moon suit, you will know that the small secondary supplier of your quart container has not taken the time to rewrite the proper precautions for your use of the product. The information is probably the same as it would be if you were ordering a tanker full.
   (b) **MSDSs for products that are mixtures.** The majority of the products you use are not single chemicals but are mixtures

of chemicals. In 1987, when OSHA issued the Hazard Communication Standard in the *Federal Register*, it estimated that there were at least 575,000 hazardous products used in the workplace. The estimates have risen.

An example of a mixture is a kitchen counter cleaner that may contain water, a solvent or two, a disinfectant chemical, and one or two detergents. The company that formulates and sells this cleaner would first order the individual ingredients from larger manufacturers and mix them. Now the formulator is faced with the problem of looking at the MSDSs for each of the several ingredients and figuring out how to cobble all of these data together into a single MSDS.

A critical look at the MSDS should tell you whether the manufacturer has done a good job. If there is a lot of missing data or confusing advice, it is likely that the company doesn't have the technical staff to provide a good MSDS.

6. Evaluate the information. Once you have the MSDS and know whether the product in question is a single component or a mixture, you are ready to go through the MSDS critically. I've included an explanation of how to read one in appendix B, and I highly recommend that you look at it. It's not as complicated as it sounds.

I don't expect that you will have complete mastery over MSDS terminology simply by reading appendix B, but I assure you that it gets easier if you keep reading the MSDSs. In a few years, when the Globally Harmonized Data Sheets become standard, it will be even easier.

In the meantime, I'll be happy if you simply bug a lot of manufacturers of consumer products into sending you MSDSs. If consumers don't ask, manufacturers won't provide them.

If you are a member of the International Alliance of Theatrical Stage Employes, you have the right to ask me to evaluate an MSDS or two for you. I work for Local USA829, but we have extended this service to all IATSE members. If you are an artist inquiring about an art material, you can contact me through Arts, Crafts and Theater Safety (via e-mail to ACTSNYC@cs.com).

You may also have access to advice about MSDSs from professional safety people if your employer or school has a department dedicated to safety or environmental compliance. As a rule, people do not go into the safety field to become rich and famous. Most of us love what we do and will use any excuse to help or enlighten people. Talk to us.

CHAPTER 8

Your Air Filter May Be Polluting Your Air

Understanding Chemical Exposure

Again and again, I've been called by individuals and citizen's groups about widely varied problems, including emissions from a nearby cement factory and neighbors complaining about activities in adjacent apartments that range from people setting off a pesticide bomb for bedbugs to others secretly welding metal sculptures. I've also investigated homes and businesses inundated with World Trade Center dusts and odors.

My first job is to explain to people that they can't make any intelligent judgments about these issues until they have a basic knowledge of air pollutants. Without this basis, they can be taken advantage of by fast-talking product manufacturers, landlords, or officials.

They need to be able to use the terminology properly, so that they can ask the right questions, questions that have to be taken seriously by experts and officials. They also need this information if they intend to discuss environmental issues intelligently, rather than allow the dialogue to become emotional rhetoric. I have often watched citizens who were clearly justified in their concerns over a particular air pollution issue destroy their own credibility by using emotionally charged, exaggerated, and incorrect terminology.

I would like to see every high school teach the basics about air pollution, but we'd have to start by teaching the teachers, who usually don't know about it, either! It's not difficult, because there are only six classes of air pollutants that can be in the air you breathe. Each of the six affects you differently. These six are gases, vapors, mists, fumes, dusts, and nanoparticles.

Gases

Scientists define gas as a formless fluid that can expand to fill the space that contains it. Now, this definition is likely to leave most people confused. Yet it's simpler than that.

Instead, think of the whole world as being made up of molecules, tiny molecules too small to be seen except under an electron microscope. Then look around and realize that whether things appear to be solids, liquids, or gases is determined by how close these molecules are to one another. If they snuggle up tightly with strong bonds or attractive forces between them, you have a solid, such as in your door, your spoon, or a chunk of coal.

When the molecules are farther apart, they are liquids. There are still bonds between the molecules, but they are weaker and they allow the liquid to flow and take the shape of the container into which the liquid is poured, such as a bottle, a swimming pool, or the basin of a lake.

If the space between the molecules is vastly greater, however, then they fly freely around and only occasionally bump into one another by accident. This configuration of molecules makes up a gas. Because molecules are too small to be seen, gases are invisible. And since the molecules are flying around and bumping into one another, this causes gases to fill any space you release them into.

This means that if there is a leak in your gas stove or heater, it won't be long before everyone in the house will smell the gas as it expands into every corner. (As you may know, natural gas has no odor. A very stinky gas is added to natural gas so that we will know when we have a leak.) The farther the gas is from the stove, the weaker the odor, because the concentration of cooking gas molecules gets lower and lower as the gas molecules fly farther apart.

Ordinary air is a mixture of gases, such as nitrogen, oxygen, or carbon dioxide. Gases released in small amounts, such as from a leak in your gas stove, mix and disperse evenly in all directions. Once the gas escapes into the air in a room in your house, it's easy to get rid of it by simply opening the windows. A breeze will accelerate the mixing. The open window allows the cooking gas molecules to try to expand into all outdoors, becoming less and less concentrated indoors.

The fact that gases will simply keep floating on air currents, mixing and expanding indefinitely, is also the reason that chlorine- and fluorine-containing hydrocarbons used in aerosol spray can propellants and air-conditioning gases have traveled all the way up to the top of our planet's atmosphere and have damaged the stratospheric ozone layer.

Gases vary greatly in toxicity. They can be irritating, acidic, corrosive, poisonous, and so on. Some gases, such as those in ordinary air, are not toxic, but they can be dangerous if they are in quantities unlike those found in air. For example, oxygen should be in the range of 21 to 20 percent in the air. If other gases are introduced into the air in amounts that reduce the oxygen significantly, say to 16 percent, we will die from lack of oxygen.

For another example, we all exhale carbon dioxide gas. It is not very toxic in the quantities we expel, which are only a fraction of a percent. Yet 7 percent in the air would be fatal. One potential source of such high concentrations can occur on theatrical stages when dry ice is used to create fog. Dry ice is very cold and will create a water-mist fog when the change in temperature condenses water vapor in the air. In the midst of that fog, however, are very high concentrations of the carbon dioxide gas that was released from the dry ice. And because the fog is cold, it sinks to the floor.

A graphic demonstration of this problem was seen at a well-known opera company that was performing *Electra*. Clytemnestra, one of the characters in the opera, "dies" in the last act and lies on the floor for about ten minutes. To make the scene more interesting, the designers had the singer fall near a pool of water from which emanated low-lying dry ice fog. After only a few minutes, she lost consciousness and began to have seizures. Fortunately, alert cast members and a stage manager got her off the stage and into an ambulance in time to prevent any long-term damage.

This loss of consciousness happened so quickly precisely because gases are molecules. When they are inhaled, they are small enough to go right through the membranes of the tiny air sacs in your lungs and directly into the little capillaries adjacent to the air sacs. In other words, gases can get into your bloodstream rapidly when you inhale them. This is a good thing when you are inhaling oxygen, which is needed by your body. It is not good if the gas is toxic because that gas, too, is almost immediately taken into your bloodstream. Inhaling a gas is one of the fastest ways to absorb a chemical into your body.

Vapors

Vapors are the gaseous form of liquids. For example, water vapor is created when water evaporates—that is, when some of the molecules of water jump out of the surface of the liquid and begin to fly around like the gas molecules. Once released into the air, vapors behave like gases and expand into space. At high concentrations, however, they will recondense into liquids. This is what happens when it rains.

Gases and vapors may seem to be the same, but they are not. Gases are always gases at room temperature and ordinary barometric pressures. But vapors are made from substances that can also exist in another form, such as a liquid at room temperature. In addition, there are a few solids, such as mothballs, that give off vapors without going through a liquid phase. Solids that do this are said to "sublime," rather than evaporate like a liquid.

Vapors, like gases, may vary greatly in toxicity, flammability, and reactivity. Examples of common toxic vapors are those from solvents such as gasoline, paint thinners, and cleaning fluids.

Because vapors are also molecules in the air, they, like gases, immediately go through the air sacs in your lungs and are as rapidly absorbed as gases. This is why an addict who sniffs glue can get enough solvent into his or her bloodstream in seven seconds to be intoxicated. Drinking the same solvent would take much longer to get this effect.

Mists

Mists are tiny liquid droplets in the air. Any liquid, water, oil, or solvent can be misted or aerosolized. The steam above the tea kettle and the spray from an aerosol paint can are examples. Some mists, such as the paint spray, also contain solid material. (Note: When steam from the kettle seems to disappear, it has been converted by evaporation from a mist composed of visible water droplets to a vapor, which is composed of individual water molecules floating separately and invisibly in the air.)

A mist of a substance can be more toxic than a vapor of the same substance at the same concentration. When the droplets are inhaled, they deliver the mist in little concentrated spots to the respiratory system's tissues. Vapors, on the other hand, are more evenly distributed in the respiratory tract when you breathe them in.

The location in the lungs in which the mist droplets land will depend on their size. Large spray mists will land in your sinuses and upper respiratory tract. Very tiny droplets can get all the way down into those little air sacs, where they are likely to do more damage.

Fumes

This term is regularly misused to mean any kind of emission. For example, it is common to refer to "gasoline fumes," when the technically correct term is "gasoline vapors."

Fumes are actually very tiny particles that are usually created in high-heat operations, such as welding, soldering, or foundry work (for chemists, we will not cover certain chemical reactions that also create fumes without heat). Fumes are formed when hot vapors cool rapidly and condense into fine particles. For example, lead fumes are created during soldering. When solder melts, some lead vaporizes. The vapor immediately reacts with oxygen in the air to form a metal oxide molecule that has a slight electrical charge. Other molecules of metal oxide being created near it are attracted, and the molecules condense (clump together) into tiny, invisible lead oxide fume particles.

In addition to many metals, some organic chemicals and plastics will create fumes if heated to the right temperatures.

Fume particles are so small (0.01 to 0.5 microns in diameter) that they tend to remain airborne for long periods of time. Eventually, however, they will settle to contaminate dust in the workplace, in the ventilation ducts, in your hair or clothing, or wherever air currents carry them. Although individual fume particles are too small to be seen by the naked eye, in large numbers they sometimes can be perceived as a bluish haze rising like cigarette smoke from soldering or welding operations.

Fuming tends to increase the toxicity of a substance because the small particle size enables it to be inhaled deeply into the lungs and because the fume particles dissolve much faster in lung fluid than do larger particles. Once the fumed substance has dissolved, it, too, can enter the bloodstream.

Dusts

Dusts are usually formed when solid materials are broken down into small particles by natural or mechanical forces. Natural wind and weathering produces dusts from rocks. Sawing and sanding are examples of mechanical forces that produce dusts. Yet it is important to know how small the dust particles are, because this influences their toxicity.

The finer the dust, the deeper it can be inhaled into the lungs and the more toxic it usually is. "Respirable" dusts—those that can be inhaled deeply into the lungs—are about 0.1 to 10 microns in diameter. The respirable dust particle sizes are in the same size range as fume particles. This means that both respirable dusts and fumes can get all the way down into your lungs' air sacs (alveoli), the most delicate structures in the lung. Once there, they will either dissolve and go through the air sacs' walls into your bloodstream, or, if they are inert and do not dissolve, they will remain in the air sacs for the duration of your life.

Lead fumes and dusts are examples of substances that will dissolve and enter your bloodstream. Asbestos and silica are examples of inert substances that will remain in your lungs essentially for life.

The EPA divides respirable dusts even further into particulate matter that is between 10 and 2.5 microns in diameter referred to as PM_{10}, and particulate matter that is 2.5 microns in diameter and smaller, referred to as $PM_{2.5}$. There are significant data to support the assumption that the $PM_{2.5}$ air pollution particles are more toxic.

Heavier dusts, ranging in size roughly from 10 to 100 microns, will deposit farther up in your respiratory system, in your sinuses, throat, bronchial tubes, or some of the bronchi (smaller tubes). These dusts may be called "inhalable," or "total," dust, meaning that the amount of dust includes both small and large particles.

The surfaces of the sinuses, the throat, and other bronchial structures are lined with cells that secrete mucus. The heavier dust particles bump into one of these locations and stick.

If all of the dusts we have inhaled stayed in the sinuses and the bronchial tubes, we would soon be filled with dust and unable to breathe. Fortunately, these surfaces in the lungs' tubes also have cells with little hairlike structures called cilia that repeatedly and steadily raise the mucus up and up, all the way to the back of your throat—at which point, you are faced with a decision.

Usually, you decide to swallow without being aware of it. So the large dust particles you inhale end up in your stomach and digestive tract, where you can also extract toxic substances from the dust and allow them to enter your bloodstream.

Clearing of the lungs by cilia is not possible for smokers. The first puff of cigarette smoke in the morning paralyzes the cilia for the day. This means that everything a smoker inhales stays longer in his or her lungs and can do more harm. If you want to know what the results of this problem sound like, listen to a smoker get up in the morning! The smoker has to hack up a night's worth of phlegm, the amount that normal people raise up without a fuss on a continuous basis during the night. This revolting hacking sound alone should be enough to inspire one to quit smoking.

Nanoparticles

The new kids on the block are the very fine dusts called nanoparticles. They are less than 0.1 micron in size and are so small, they begin to behave like gases. Some can go right through the sinuses and into the brain, through the skin, or through the air sacs and into the bloodstream. We are only now learning about the hazards of these tiny particles, which are currently found in the air and in some of our consumer products, such as makeup.

Some fume particles are also in the nanoparticle size range. It has now been demonstrated that welders working with mild steel that contains manganese have higher rates of a neurological disease that is essentially the same as Parkinson's disease. Manganese has long been known to cause this disease, and it is suspected that the manganese fume particles from welding are going through the sinuses and directly into the brain. An experiment with rats showed that manganese nanoparticles can do this.

Smoke

Smoke is formed from burning organic matter. Burning wood, leaves, paper, coal, oil, or any organic hydrocarbon will produce thousands of chemicals, many of them the same types of chemicals. The smoke will also include most and sometimes all of the air pollutant classes I described earlier. For example, cigarette smoke probably contains more than four thousand chemicals, including carbon monoxide gas, benzene vapor, a mist of thick liquid tar, and soot particles in fume and nanoparticle size.

See the following figure, which shows the different types of particles in their typical range of sizes in micron units. The bottom section of the chart shows the range of particle sizes in microns that common mechanical filters can capture.

For example, the sizes of viruses and nanoparticles are clearly outside of the capture range of the best high-efficiency particulate air filters (HEPA filters). Experts think that a high percentage of certain types of nanoparticles, fumes, and viruses are captured by electrostatic forces on these filter fibers, but there are little or no data on the smaller nanoparticles in the range of 5 to 50 nanometers in diameter.

Because it is likely that 100 percent protection against these small particles is impossible to achieve with any known filter technology, workers exposed to nanoparticles may need to use respirators that supply air from a compressor or from compressed air tanks, rather like firefighters.

The chart also makes clear the idiocy of the old-fashioned cloth masks worn by physicians for so many years. A cloth mask might prevent the doctor from sneezing on you, but his viruses will go through the cloth and the mask won't protect him from any airborne viruses or bacteria from you or others. Hospitals have been slow to upgrade their respiratory-protection and infection-control procedures. Only now are they beginning to comply with the respiratory-protection requirements that have been accepted in other industries for decades.

PARTICLE DIAMETERS IN MICRONS (μm)

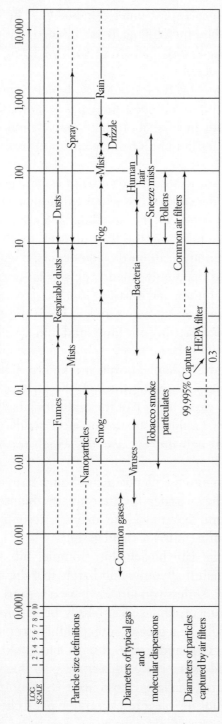

The top of the figure shows the range of sizes of various particles, and the sections at the bottom show the common mechanical filters that are available to capture these pollutants. A more complete chart can be found in the American Society of Heating, Refrigerating and Air-Conditioning Engineers' standard called "Ventilation for Acceptable Indoor Air Quality," ASHRAE 62–2001, figure 2. The figure here has been simplified to support the points made in this chapter.

To cause harm, chemicals must enter our bodies. The three main ways they do this is when the chemicals are inhaled, are ingested, or contact the skin. Toxicologists call these ways of being exposed to chemicals the "routes of entry."

Preventing exposure by these routes will make you safe from chemicals. In order to develop good strategies to prevent chemicals from entering your body by inhalation, skin contact, and ingestion, it requires a deeper understanding of chemicals and how you absorb them.

The lungs are meant to absorb oxygen and expel carbon dioxide. They are a complex network of bronchial tubes that range in size from large bronchial tubes to the small-diameter bronchioles. At the ends of all of these tubes are the little air sacs, or alveoli, where the exchange of oxygen and carbon dioxide occurs. The air sacs are also the entry point for many unwanted toxic substances in the form of gases, vapors, mists, fumes, and dusts.

To review: gases and vapors, being molecules in the air, can pass right through the tiny air sacs in your lungs and into the bloodstream. *When you inhale either a gas or a vapor, you are immediately exposed.* It is the fastest method of chemical exposure known. This is a good thing in the case of oxygen passing through the air sacs to immediately provide this vital gas to the rest of the body. It's a bad thing if the gas is toxic and enters the bloodstream to cause bodily damage. An example of such a gas is hydrogen cyanide, which was used in gas chambers.

Yet not all gases go into the bloodstream. Some gases are so corrosive or reactive that they damage the lung tissues themselves, rather than go through them. Examples are ozone, ammonia, chlorine bleach, and hydrochloric (muriatic) acid gases.

If you are cleaning with bleach, for example, the amount you inhale could be so small that you would barely feel the insignificant damage that is caused. Unless you already have a serious lung condition, this small amount of damage can easily be repaired, and the only consequence might be a greater susceptibility to colds and lung infections because bacteria and viruses can get a foothold more easily in damaged or irritated tissues.

At higher exposures, such as those seen in people who have incorrectly mixed chlorine bleach swimming pool chemicals, the damage could be serious enough to severely impair their lungs. In the worst case, the tissues are so severely affected that fluid leaks from the injured tissues to cause chemical pneumonia that can kill the person.

The small particles in dust and fumes can be inhaled deep into the lungs. Once the particles are there, they can either dissolve and go through the air sacs to cause bodily damage or remain in the air sacs for a person's lifetime. An example of a substance that will pass through the air sacs is lead, which could be in the form of dust from sanding lead paint or lead fumes from soldering.

Dusts and fumes that are inert, meaning they don't dissolve or change, will remain in the air sacs until the person dies. Some dusts and fumes produce lung damage by creating scar tissue or causing cancer. The most well known of these is asbestos, which can scar the lungs to produce a disease called asbestosis. Asbestos can also damage cells in a way that causes lung cancer or mesothelioma (a cancer of the lining of the lung).

Other inert dusts that cause lung damage include silica (from sand and rocks), kaolin (a clay), and talc (talcum powder). If your mom was a little too enthusiastic while powdering your tush when you were a baby, you may still be carrying evidence of this event in your lungs. Although the amount of scarring from these brief exposures to talcum powder is negligible and using a baby powder made of cornstarch is a better choice, the best practice would be to prevent inhalation of dust by not using powder at all on a baby.

A few types of dust and fumes stay in the lungs but don't seem to cause any harm at all. One of these is barium sulfate, the same stuff you swallow with great reluctance to undergo medical X-rays of your intestinal tract. This insoluble form of barium is also harmless if inhaled as a powder in the lungs, except for the fact that it is opaque to radiation and can fog your X-rays, which interferes with the diagnosis of other lung abnormalities.

Dusts or fumes that are irritating or corrosive can also injure lung tissue directly. This damage can range from mild to severe, depending on the amount inhaled and the corrosivity of the particles.

The small liquid droplets in mists are usually more toxic than the vapors of the liquids from which they are made because they deliver concentrated little drops to the lung tissue.

Mists are also more complicated than other air pollutants because they can be both pure liquid droplets and liquid droplets that contain other chemicals. For example, a mist of pure solvent, such as a spray of alcohol, will only evaporate in the air to form a vapor.

A paint spray mist, on the other hand, contains solvents like alcohol, as well as solid materials, such as pigments and paint solids. When these droplets are suspended in the air, they deliver the whole paint mixture to your lungs. Paint mist that doesn't land on the surface that is being painted (overspray) will float on air currents for a time. Then the liquid portion of the paint droplet will vaporize— convert to a vapor—and the solid part of the paint will float down onto surfaces and settle as a dust particle. Both the vapor and the dust from paint mists can be inhaled as well.

Some chemicals are toxic by merely getting on the skin. For example, the skin's protective barrier of waxes, oils, and dead cells can be destroyed by chemicals such as acids, caustics, solvents, and the like. Once the skin's defenses are breached, some of these chemicals can damage the skin itself and the tissues beneath the skin or even enter the bloodstream, where they can be transported throughout the body, causing injury to other organs.

Anyone with cuts, abrasions, burns, rashes, and other violations of the skin's barrier should be aware that chemicals that get on this damaged skin can easily penetrate it and be transported throughout the body.

Yet even more curious are chemicals that can—without your knowing it—enter the blood through undamaged, healthy skin. Examples of these are wood alcohol (for example, from Sterno or certain shellacs) and toluene, a solvent found in some types of paint and paint strippers. The glycol ether cleaning solvents mentioned earlier are also absorbed through your skin and through your rubber gloves, without changing the appearance of either.

It is also now known that lead can be absorbed through the skin. This has been established in a number of studies.[1] Lead metal forms a layer of oxides and sulfides on its surface, which can be absorbed when lead metal is handled. Lead fumes and dust on the skin during work or from contaminated soil dust can penetrate the skin.

It was assumed by most toxicologists that lead was not absorbed through the skin until the first study in 1988 showed otherwise. Today it is assumed without any supporting data that most other metals do not penetrate through the skin. I don't think this is a viable assumption. In fact, the German occupational standard for cadmium (the standard accepted by many European Union countries) includes a notation that this metal is absorbed through the skin.

I think it is wise to limit skin contact with metal dusts and fumes in particular. Highly toxic metals in solid form such as lead, cadmium, and antimony (which may be found in certain solders or lead printing type) should be handled with gloves if they are to be used regularly in your work or hobbies.

Accidental ingestion of small amounts of substances can occur when people use toxic materials while they eat, smoke, or drink or when they point brushes with their lips, touch soiled hands to their mouths, bite their nails, and engage in similar habits. Large numbers of ingestion accidents occur every year when children or adults pour chemicals into paper cups or glasses and later mistake them for beverages.

Yet air-polluting chemicals are also ingested when the lungs' mucus traps dust or mists and removes them by transporting them to your throat, where they are swallowed. Particles in the air can also settle out of the air to contaminate the surfaces of food or other places where they are transferred to people's hands and ingested when the hands touch the mouth or when food is eaten.

Some substances are highly toxic by one route and perfectly safe by another. For example, you can ingest large amounts of mineral oil as a laxative. Yet inhaling small amounts of it can cause serious lung damage, which may even be fatal. This is why there is no longer mineral oil in nose drops. In the distant past, mineral oil–based nose drops were sometimes accidentally inhaled into the lungs, where they caused life-threatening lipoid pneumonia in certain victims.

Yet you have probably inhaled mineral oil if you ever attended a concert or a theatrical event where the lights onstage appeared to "beam" from floor to ceiling. This occurs because light is bouncing off tiny mist particles that are usually made from mineral oil and are only about one micron in diameter (glycols can also be used, see chapter 7). The special effects people who generate this mist during the event are told this is safe because it is food-grade mineral oil. Yet this mineral oil is not ingested, it is inhaled. And the mist particles are so small that we really don't know what it does to people in the long term. Here again, you are the guinea pig.

Titanium dioxide has been a white pigment in makeup for decades, and it appears on tests to be very safe by skin contact. There are even some European tests of nanoparticle-size titanium dioxide, and it doesn't seem to penetrate through normal skin and into the bloodstream, as was feared. So these nanoparticle titanium dioxide makeup products may be safe by skin contact. (Yet at the time I am writing this book, there have been no studies of titanium dioxide makeup nanoparticles on people with acne, dermatitis, birth marks, scars, or other skin abnormalities that may make skin more penetrable.)

Recently, some creative people decided it would be a good idea to apply makeup by airbrush for a nice smooth effect. This creates very fine particles that can be inhaled deep into the lungs, and titanium dioxide is listed by the International Agency for Research on Cancer as a carcinogen by inhalation. All of these types of airbrush makeup are technically illegal, because *none* of the FDA-approved makeup ingredients have been approved for inhalation.

Mineral oil and titanium dioxide are two examples of substances that may be very safe by one route of entry (ingestion or skin contact) but are hazardous by another (inhalation). Always consider the way in which a substance enters the body before you decide whether it is safe or harmful.

Now let's apply all of the information we have about air pollutants and toxicity to the problem of selecting an air purifier. We can prevent exposure to toxins by getting rid of all of these gases, vapors, fumes, dusts, and mists by installing an air purifier, right? Wrong.

You especially don't want to buy some of those air purifiers demonstrated on late-night TV. The advertisers really count on your not knowing about gases, vapors, fumes, dusts, and mists when they pitch their products. You can see through their pitches if you apply what you have learned about air pollutants.

We know that gases and vapors are molecules flying around in the air. What kind of filter can capture these? Gases and vapor will go right through the best-quality high-efficiency particulate air (HEPA) filter that is advertised. To capture a gas or a vapor with a mechanical filter would require a filter with holes smaller than a molecule in diameter—and this would mean that even air would have a tough time getting through that filter!

HEPA filters are only for particles such as fumes, dusts, and mists. It is unlikely that HEPA filters can control some of the nanoparticles. And the regular filters in most shop and home vacuum cleaners can capture only the larger inhalable dusts (10 to 100 microns), not the very fine respirable ones (10 to 0.1 microns).

There are even some vacuum cleaners on the market that don't capture fine particles at all. These are the machines that capture particles by centrifugal force and are touted as "never losing power." They maintain their efficiency because they don't have a filter at all. They collect only large particles by centrifugal force (spinning the dust around).

Whenever you purchase an item that is supposed to capture dust, you want the salespeople to provide you with two numbers:

1. The particle size that the cleaner or the filter is designed to capture; and
2. The percent efficiency at that particle size.

For example, a true HEPA filter can capture particles that are 0.3 micron in size at 99.97 percent efficiency. This way, you know that fine dusts and fumes will be captured. Unless the seller provides documentation supporting the particle size and the percent capture of the filter, he or she is probably lying to you. After all, even the worst air filter in the world will capture 100 percent of marbles.

Be sure the air actually goes through the filter. Some machines that were designed to have HEPA filters lost power too quickly as the filter filled up, so unscrupulous manufacturers added a way for a significant portion of the air to bypass the filter, which renders the machine highly inefficient. You want to see diagrams of how the machine works and ask the hard questions. Good manufacturers have good answers and are proud to answer your questions. Also, check the manufacturer out with the Better Business Bureau and *Consumer Reports*, and look at the Consumer Product Safety Commission's list of recalled products to make sure the item you want is not listed.

If the pollution in your home or workplace is in the form of a gas or a vapor, a good HEPA filter system will not help. Instead, some gases and vapors can be captured by chemical filter mediums, such as activated charcoal. Yet the charcoal does not permanently trap or react with the gas or vapor molecule.

For example, if a charcoal filter is used to capture solvent vapors from paints you use in your home or workshop, it will stop collecting fairly soon because only a small amount can be absorbed by the charcoal. Then if the humidity rises, the charcoal filter prefers the water vapor in the air. It will absorb the water vapor and release the solvent vapors back into your air.

Charcoal filters are also used in air-purifying respirators to protect against gases and vapors. The practice in industry is to use these cartridges only for one eight-hour day because they can be spent (filled up) so quickly. In addition, the right cartridge must be chosen for the air contaminant. The cartridge that is designed to capture formaldehyde will not be very helpful with solvent vapors. The cartridge for solvent vapors will not be effective against acid gases or ammonia, and so on. There are many gases and vapors, such as ozone or propane gas, for which there are no approved cartridges.

The charcoal used in home air purifiers is not specific for any single contaminant, so it can be expected to capture even less of the diverse amounts of gases and vapors in your home. Honest manufacturers should tell you that these activated charcoal filters are only for "odor" control and not for handling significant amounts of toxic gases and vapors. For example, you should not use a charcoal filter unit to protect yourself from solvent vapors when you paint your walls—even with water-based paints. Even though these paints contain a small quantity (usually less than 10 percent) of solvents, this amount can become significant when the paint evaporates from a large surface area like your wall.

Instead, ventilation should be used for processes in which significant amounts of gases and vapors are released. One ventilation system that works for painting a room it to open a window on one side of the room to allow fresh air to enter, while blowing contaminated air out the other side of the room with a window exhaust fan.

One type of air purifier you can definitely cross off your list is the kind that produces ozone. Ozone is a gas that is high up in the stratosphere and should be in a layer thick enough to deflect the sun's ultraviolet rays and reduce our risk of developing skin cancer. Down here where we breathe, however, ozone is toxic. Down here, ozone is pollution.

The plain fact is that we get too much ozone exposure from pollution alone. We don't need to add any ozone to our air with an air purifier.

Ozone is one of the chemicals that is created when emissions from our cars and factories react with sunlight to form smog. Ozone is also created as a by-product of various electrical processes, being produced by electric generators and motors, copy machines and laser printers, and, yes, several types of so-called air purifiers, such as negative ion generators, ozone generators, and electrostatic precipitators.

In addition, ozone is created when lightning flashes through air. We recognize the "fresh air" odor of ozone after a storm. Ozone's pleasant odor makes it easy for charlatans to sell ozone-producing air purifiers that cause the air to smell clean and fresh. They can claim that the machines are good for your health, whereas the ozone they produce actually makes the air more hazardous.

Sellers of certain ozone generators point out that ozone can kill mold and deodorize air (break down odorous chemicals). It can—but the concentration in air at which ozone kills mold and deodorizes significant amounts of chemicals is far too toxic for you to breathe safely.

Ozone's toxicity lies in its very simple structure. When air is subjected to an electrical charge, some of the normal oxygen (O_2) converts to ozone (O_3). Ozone, in turn, breaks back down to normal oxygen (O_2) and releases a negative oxygen radical (O^-).

The negative oxygen radical is highly toxic and can kill just about anything it has intimate contact with. Ozone will kill growing mold organisms, destroy bacteria when it's used in water-purifying systems or pools, or decimate the cells in the tissues in our lungs. In fact, the

Occupational Safety and Health Administration sets the same workplace air quality level for ozone as that set for phosgene, which is a chemical warfare gas.

The EPA also sets air quality indexes (AQI) for ozone.

The AQI standards for ozone exposure published on March 27, 2008, are shown in the following list.

Description	8-Hour Limit in Parts per Million
Good air quality	0–0.059
Moderate	0.06–0.075
Unhealthy for sensitive people	0.076–0.095
Unhealthy and very unhealthy	0.096–0.375

It doesn't take much ozone to make air unhealthy. In fact, the lower the ozone in the air, the better the air quality. The best air would have no ozone at all. The EPA sets the ozone limits to designate when pollution levels of ozone are becoming dangerous and people are developing symptoms. Typically, ozone is associated with lung and eye irritation, which can lead to increased incidents of colds and respiratory infections. These symptoms can progress in some people to chronic lung problems, such as bronchitis and asthma. An article in the June 2006 issue of *Environmental Health Perspectives* showed that levels of ozone in the air that averaged 0.054 ppm, with peak measurements averaging 0.061 ppm, were associated with greater breathing problems in normal babies born to mothers who have asthma.[2] So these EPA levels may not be protective for people who have a propensity for respiratory problems.

Nothing seems to discourage the sellers of these ozone-creating devices. A pair of ozone touters, Kenneth Thiefault and his wife, Mardel Barber, were ordered in 1990 to stop claiming that ozone could treat diseases. The couple ignored the order. In March 1999, Thiefault and his wife were sentenced in a U.S. district court in Florida to prison terms that together totaled longer than eight years and fines adding up to more than $100,000.[3]

Another manufacturer has been fined repeatedly. In 1992, a Minnesota court of appeals found William J. Converse guilty of fraud for claiming that his ozone generators could improve health. The court ordered him to pay $70,000 in civil penalties and $104,105 in attorney's fees.[4] At that time, Converse was president of Alpine Air

Products, and he sold the company to a buyer who renamed it Alpine Industries and kept right on selling the machines!

In April 2001, Alpine Industries, Inc., and its once-again president William J. Converse were ordered by a federal judge to pay a civil penalty of $1.49 million, plus interest and costs. The judge also issued an injunction barring Alpine and Converse from making any claims that the "air purifiers" sold by the company are able to remove any indoor air pollutant except for visible tobacco smoke and some odors. Converse was also prohibited from making any health claims for the machines and from telling people that sensors in the generators can control ozone levels in rooms.[5]

In 2003, *Consumer Reports* magazine warned readers that Ionic Breeze and other ionic cleaners do a poor job of cleaning the air and they also emit ozone, a dangerous gas. Sharper Image, a manufacturer of these devices, filed suit in California against *Consumer Reports* for saying that its Ionic Breeze was "ineffective" and produced "almost no measurable reduction in airborne particles." The court looked at the science and dismissed the lawsuit.[6]

Then a consumer named Michael Figueroa filled a class action lawsuit on behalf of himself and 3.2 million other consumers. A settlement was reached between the parties in 2007 in which Sharper Image was to provide about $60 million in the form of $19 merchandise credits to each person who bought one of its Ionic Breeze purifiers since May 6, 1999. This same group of consumers would also have been able to buy, at cost, a grille attachment for the Ionic Breeze for $7 that Sharper Image said would reduce the toxic ozone emissions from the device. But a federal judge ruled that the settlement was unfair. The judge objected to giving $19 coupons to consumers who paid between $300 and $499 for the devices. This ruling opens the way for a competing class-action lawsuit initiated in San Francisco that seeks full refunds for the Ionic Breeze buyers. However, don't hold your breath waiting for the money. Sharper Image filed for Chapter 11 bankruptcy protection in 2008.[7]

I don't know whether you've ever seen an Ionic Breeze cleaned, but the amount of dirt it removes from the air looks similar to that collected on the glass front of your old TV screen. I suggest buying a digital converter box and a secondhand TV instead.

CHAPTER 9

Silver Socks Rocked by Toxic Shocker!

Our Weak Worker and Consumer Protection Laws

B eware of your socks, shirts, and underwear. These items are now often impregnated with wrinkle- and odor-fighting silver nanoparticles. Do these affect people in some way? Manufacturers don't think so, but they don't know. And do the nanoparticles of silver stay forever in the socks? Apparently not. A study in 2008 showed that plain old water washing releases the silver to the environment. Well, duh!

Troy M. Benn, a graduate student at Arizona State University, presented the results of the washing study to the Division of Environmental Chemistry at the American Chemical Society's national meeting in April 2008 in New Orleans.[1] Benn and an ASU professor of civil and environmental engineering, Paul Westerhoff, carried out the study.

The researchers shook each of six brands of socks in one-half liter of distilled water with no detergent for one hour and then analyzed the effluent with electron microscopy. The socks contained up to 1,360 micrograms (μg) of silver per gram of sock and released as much as 650 μg of silver in both ionic and colloidal forms. So, some socks released almost half of their load of silver in a soap-free water wash!

The study showed that silver is released in amounts that varied widely. The researchers assumed that this variability in silver release is related to the different manufacturing processes that were used to deposit silver onto textiles, but they don't know. The effects of detergents and bleaches on the nanosilver were not studied either.

Then, in September 2009, a second, Swiss, study was published in *Environmental Science and Technology*.[2] The Swiss researchers looked at the effects of detergents and bleaches on the release of silver. They found that bleaching agents can greatly accelerate the release of silver. The percentage of the total silver emitted by the nine fabrics they tested under various conditions ranged from 1 to 45 percent.

Both studies' findings are of concern because dissolved (ionic) silver and nanosilver particles are released from the socks. Silver is known to exhibit adverse effects on aquatic organisms in the environment. Wash water containing silver will be washed down the drains and the mains to the local water-treatment plant, and most of the silver is expected to be trapped in the solid waste material created by these plants.

The silver that is not captured by waste treatment will be released directly into the environment. The EPA regulates this silver under the Resource Conservation and Recovery Act (RCRA) because it is highly toxic to waterborne microorganisms, including the bacteria that digest the waste in the treatment plant.

Yet the bulk of the silver is captured in the solid waste created by water-treatment plants. The EPA doesn't regulate silver levels in the solid waste from wastewater treatment facilities. Most treatment facilities sell or give away the solid waste from treatment to be used as fertilizer, but solid waste laced with silver is not suitable for use in agriculture.

As a strategy to provide some sort of check on the use of silver, EPA officials announced in 2006 that they would begin to regulate the silver ions that are intended to kill bacteria in textiles under the EPA's pesticide regulations. On June 24, 2009, the EPA published in the *Federal Register* the establishment of a pesticide review docket for silver and compounds.[3] Manufacturers that make claims that nanosilver kills bacteria in your clothes will soon have to provide a list of current product registrations, a risk assessment, and other documentation. If manufacturers drop their antibacterial claim, however, and advertise only their products' ability to reduce wrinkles, they will be out of the EPA's jurisdiction to regulate.

It is also important to note that the first study was done at a university (Arizona State University) and the second by a Swiss federal laboratory. As citizens, we should ask why the textile industry wasn't required to study the release of environmentally damaging substances under normal use *before* it put the products containing them on the market.

On top of the multitude of untested chemicals we use, industry is now chopping up or reconfiguring some of our old and tested chemicals into itsy-bitsy "nanoparticles." Tens of thousands of these nanoparticles can fit on the tip of a needle. These particles are so small, they begin to act like gases, and some can penetrate skin, nasal passages, and lungs with ease. Scientists are now finding that chemicals in nanoparticle size can exhibit toxic characteristics that are very different from larger particles of the same substance.

We may also find that our American Conference of Governmental Industrial Hygienists (ACGIH) air-quality standards will not provide adequate protection from nanoparticles because particle size is a factor in toxicity. For example, particles that are smaller than 10 microns in diameter are likely to be deposited deep in the lungs' air sacs (alveoli) and may be more damaging. The threshold limit values for dusts and fumes whose particles' sizes are less than 10 microns in diameter are designated as "respirable" and usually have more restrictive limits, due to their greater toxicity.

The EPA regulates outdoor air pollutants by their size as well. There are two sets of standards for outdoor dust and particles. One set of standards is for PM_{10}, meaning particulate matter that is 10 microns in diameter and smaller (down to 2.5 microns). Another set of standards is for $PM_{2.5}$, meaning particulate matter that is 2.5 microns in diameter and smaller—these being the most toxic. The latter particles are associated with asthma, stroke, heart attacks, and other health problems. The EPA has documented that these toxic effects are related to particle size and, accordingly, has set more restrictive standards for the $PM_{2.5}$ particles in outdoor air.

Although only a handful of the nanoparticles have been tested for toxicity in animals, some have demonstrated unexpected results. For example, manganese nanoparticles have been shown in animal tests to penetrate the nasal mucosa (sinuses) and travel directly to the brain.[4] Manganese nanoparticles also occur in welding fumes, and these animal data may explain the higher rates of manganese-induced Parkinson's disease that are seen in welders.

Plain old carbon, which is nontoxic in its ordinary forms, changes when it is reconfigured into tiny long carbon nanotubes. Animal tests show that the carbon nanotubes can cause the same kinds of cancer that asbestos does.

All of our protective gear, such as respirators and special air filters known as high-efficiency particulate air or HEPA filters, are designed to deal with micron-size particles. For example, HEPA filters should capture 99.97 percent of particles that are 0.3 micron in size. Converted to nanometers, 0.3 micron is 300 nanometers. Yet ingredients in many products, such as those in the new cosmetics women may be wearing, are in the range of 5 to 30 nanometers. Even smaller particles are being created and used in industrial applications.

Tests show that certain types of particles in the range of 50 to 300 nanometers are well captured by the electrostatic forces on HEPA filters. Other types of nanoparticles in this size range, however, may not be attracted by these electrostatic forces. I couldn't find filter data on the very fine particles in the 5- to 50-micron range.

The dirty secret of the burgeoning nanotechnology industry is that there are no data on how to reliably protect the workers, the consumers, the public, or the environment from exposure to the smaller-size nanoparticles once these are loose in the air or the water.

As usual, manufacturers put products containing the nanoparticles in our hands without testing them or providing a way for us to protect ourselves. Products already on the market include a special self-cleaning glass surface, wrinkle- and stain-resistant fabrics, scratch-free paint, cosmetic and sunscreen ingredients, the carbon nanotubes in automobile tires, silver nanoparticles in textiles to control body odors, nanoparticle clay filler in a tennis ball's polymers, and paint pigments. More uses for nanoparticles are being found every day.

The general population is now exposed to nanoparticles of titanium dioxide (a lung carcinogen), zinc oxide, and other ingredients in makeup and sunscreens. Many experts recommended testing first, but it's too late; the products are already out there.

Linda M. Katz, the director of the FDA's Office of Cosmetics and Colors, said the agency is examining the issue, but Katz admits that the FDA doesn't even have a list of the cosmetics that contain nanoparticles, and product labels do not reveal whether cosmetics ingredients are nanosize.

Questions that need to be answered about cosmetic nanoparticles include

1. What percentage of each of the various types of nanoparticles penetrate the skin, rather than ride on its surface?
2. How are these percentages affected by the type of makeup base in which the particles are suspended?
3. How deep into the skin or the body do these particles penetrate through both normal skin and skin damaged by dermatitis, acne, and the like?
4. What is the fate of the particles once they're in the body (e.g., where do they go and how long do they remain)?
5. Which particles can cause pathology and of what types?

Now we will have to add another whole series of questions about the inhalation of nanoparticles because manufacturers are selling cosmetics in airbrush and aerosol-spray forms. In the United States, this may be technically illegal, since the FDA does not approve any cosmetic ingredients for inhalation (see chapter 4 for more information about this problem). Yet the products are on the market anyway.

We have been told, and we want to believe, that our worker and consumer protection regulations are the best in the world. Actually, the laws protecting us from chemical exposures—from nanoparticles or regular ones—are just about the most pathetic anywhere. They are far weaker than the laws in the European Union. But you shouldn't take my word for this. I will support this view with a synopsis of the history of these regulations and some technical concepts. These concepts are important to all of us, whether we have jobs in a workplace or spend our days at home working or taking care of children.

Let's start with the Occupational Safety and Health Administration (OSHA). Surely, workers are protected from chemical exposure on the job today. After all, doesn't every employer fear the OSHA inspector who can show up and shut down his or her business? So employers must protect workers from chemical exposures on the job, right? Well, if you've read this far, you know better than to assume this is the case.

To understand why OSHA's chemical and air-quality laws are so weak, we have to begin with another organization called the National Conference of Governmental Industrial Hygienists. It convened its first conference in 1938. The membership of this organization was limited to two professional representatives from each governmental agency: two from the U.S. Public Health Service, two from the U.S. Bureau of Mines, and so on.

In 1941, this organization formed a committee to set guidelines to limit the concentrations of chemicals in workplace air to levels that would maintain the health of the workers. The committee was charged with investigating, recommending, and annually reviewing these exposure limits.

Then in 1946, this organization changed its name to the American Conference of Governmental Industrial Hygienists, the name it bears today. The ACGIH offered full membership to all industrial hygiene personnel with U.S. governmental agencies, as well as to those in other countries. (Today, membership is open to all practitioners in industrial hygiene, occupational health, and environmental health and safety, domestically and abroad. I joined the ACGIH as an associate member in 2000.) Also in 1946, the ACGIH adopted its first list of 148 exposure limits, then referred to as maximum allowable concentrations. In 1956, the name of these limits was changed to threshold limit values (TLVs). The United States was the first country to set workplace air-quality guidelines. So, by default, these TLVs were the best standards in the world. In the 1940s and the 1950s, there were very few studies on which to base the TLVs. To their credit, the early governmental professionals did the best they could with the limited information. But we now know that these old TLVs recommended airborne limits for chemicals that were far too high and that exposed workers to hazardous amounts of chemicals. For example, in 1946, benzene, then a common household and industrial solvent, was assigned a TLV of 100 parts per million—two hundred times higher than the TLV it is assigned today! The histories of many other chemicals are similar, with the ACGIH repeatedly lowering the TLVs over the years as more data became available.

Despite their shortcomings, however, the 1946 TLVs put the United States ahead of the rest of the world with respect to recommended guidelines for worker safety. Soon other countries began to set up their own versions of the TLVs, such as the Canadian and British occupational exposures limits (OELs).

TLVs are the amounts of chemicals in the air that almost all healthy adult workers are predicted to be able to tolerate without suffering significant adverse effects. So TLVs are not "safe" limits. Even *a few* healthy adult workers will be unable to tolerate these concentrations without some degree of harm. TLVs also do not apply to people with certain health problems, such as allergies or asthma, and may not protect people taking various medications or drugs. In addition, they should never be applied to children or pregnant women.

According to the ACGIH, you are not supposed to use TLVs if you are not a professional industrial hygienist. Yet you can deduce that you should be breathing fewer substances that have low TLVs! On this basis, you can choose safer substitutes by selecting products that have higher TLVs. The following list of 2009 TLVs for common chemicals should illustrate my point.

Gas or Vapor (vapor = gaseous form of liquids that evaporate)	TLV-TWA (ppm)
Carbon dioxide	5,000
Acetone (a type of nail polish remover)	500
Ethyl acetate (another type of nail polish remover)	400
Mineral spirits, paint thinner, etc.	100
Turpentine	20
2-butoxyethanol (the solvent in most fast household cleaners)	20
Phosgene (chemical warfare gas)	0.1
Ozone (from ozone generators and negative ion air purifiers)	0.1

(continued)

Dusts and Fumes (solid particles)	TLV-TWA (mg/m³)
Nuisance dusts (e.g., plaster or starch)	10
Graphite, talcum powder	2
Lead (e.g., from lead paint dust or fumes from lead solder)	0.05
Silica (e.g., from finely powdered sand, from granite or other stones, etc.)	0.025
Cadmium (e.g., cadmium pigments; very small particles)	0.002

The choices are more complicated when you want to select a chemical for a particular task or product. Then you might want some professional advice, because you need to look at other factors, such as how fast it evaporates, whether it is a fire hazard, the health effects the TLV was set to protect against, and more.

As an example, imagine that you are employed in a nail salon and want to make an informed choice between two nail polish removers, one of which is primarily acetone and one that is proudly marketed as "acetone free" and is actually ethyl acetate. (When activists pressured the nail polish manufacturers to replace acetone, manufacturers usually substituted it with ethyl acetate.)

Choosing between acetone and ethyl acetate is more difficult because the two substances have somewhat similar TLVs. Acetone looks a little safer because it has a higher TLV. Yet acetone evaporates a little faster than ethyl acetate does, so exposure during use could be higher. Also, acetone is a greater fire risk than ethyl acetate is. Both TLVs were set primarily to avoid upper respiratory tract and eye irritation, so there is not much difference between their primary effects.

In order to choose, you or your professional adviser needs to look at all of these factors. If you do, you will notice that the consumer activists who pressured the nail polish manufacturers to get rid of acetone and replace it with ethyl acetate may have slightly increased the toxicity of these products and only lessened the fire hazard somewhat.

. . .

The ACGIH TLVs are only recommendations. Employers could ignore them without penalty. Until the early 1970s, there was no organized body of regulations in the United States to protect workers from chemicals or accidents.

Then in 1970, the Occupational Safety and Health Act was passed to protect workers from harm on the job. Secretary of Labor James Hodgson, who had helped shape the law, established the Occupational Safety and Health Agency (OSHA) within the Department of Labor, effective April 28, 1971. Fine, so far. But now the new agency would have to create from scratch programs that would meet the intent of the act, that is, to protect workers.

To protect workers from excessive chemical exposures on the job, the new OSHA incorporated the roughly 470 TLVs published by the ACGIH in 1968 and made them law. OSHA renamed these TLVs permissible exposure limits (PELs) and made them enforceable. For a time, we were leading the world in providing safer workplaces—but industry was not about to let something like this happen again. Its strategy was two-pronged: (1) to influence the setting of TLVs, and (2) to hamstring OSHA's standard-setting process.

Even in the 1940s, the TLV committee often considered input from industrial interests, such as the Manufacturing Chemists' Association, but once chemical manufacturers saw that the TLVs would be adopted by OSHA, they got seriously involved. The first industry representation on the ACGIH TLV committee began in 1970 with the addition of two Dow Chemical representatives as non-voting, liaison members. These two men were assigned the responsibility for developing the documentation on which new or revised TLVs would be based. Then in 1972, an industrial hygienist from DuPont joined the committee, and the door was opened to others. It is estimated that corporate representatives were given primary responsibility for developing TLV documentation on more than a hundred substances between 1970 and 1988.[5]

As a result, some TLVs were set with industry's influence. That influence generally was used to keep the exposure levels high so that manufacturers would be spared the expense of providing costly ventilation, respiratory protection, or other precautions for workers.

The second strategy used by industry was to keep the old, outdated standards in place by using some of the steps in the regulatory process to its advantage. To illustrate: when OSHA wants to set a new air-quality PEL or upgrade an existing one, it must publish the proposed limit in the *Federal Register* and provide a period of time during which interested parties can comment. During this comment period, it is common for industry spokespersons to challenge OSHA's scientific data, claim economic hardship if they have to meet the new lower standard, or state that adhering to the lower standard is technically not feasible. OSHA then must research all of these claims and respond with data to refute them. Industry can respond again, and so on. In this way, new PELs usually take years to institute.

If OSHA manages to get through this process and actually set a new PEL, industry then may sue OSHA. In court, the level of proof needed by OSHA is even higher. In fact, with the limited test data on chemicals, it is rare that you can establish clear and convincing evidence that the difference between two levels of protection would prevent significant numbers of people from becoming ill or dying. At the very least, the case can drag on for another couple of years to slow the institution of the new PEL.

As a result, only a handful of new standards have been set, and the vast majority of the PELs remain at the old, outdated 1968 limits and will not protect your health in the workplace.

When OSHA set those original standards in 1968, there were only about 470 TLVs to adopt. In the following years, the ACGIH has continued to review its TLVs to revise old ones and set new ones for chemicals that previously had none. Today, there are 642 TLVs. This means that more than a hundred chemicals have been documented to be toxic to workers when the ACGIH set TLVs for them, but there are no OSHA PEL standards to protect workers from these chemicals.

By 1980, it was clear that industry's regulatory foot-dragging and lawsuits had left OSHA with grossly outdated worker-protection standards. So OSHA devised a plan to update the PELs en masse. It published a proposed rule in the *Federal Register* that would revise or set anew 428 PELs.[6] Then OSHA provided industry with the required comment period and answered its comments. On the basis of these comments, OSHA changed a couple of PELs, including those for wood dust, acetone, and styrene. Then in 1989, OSHA published its spanking-new set of PELs in the *Federal Register* as a final rule, with which all employers would have to comply.[7] This was the first major update since OSHA was established in 1970. Most professionals in health and safety, myself included, dearly hoped that we wouldn't have to wait almost twenty years for another updating. We were all dreaming. We were not even going to see these PELs enforced.

Coalitions of industries formed and took OSHA to court. On July 10, 1992, the U.S. Court of Appeals for the Eleventh Circuit vacated the whole OSHA 1989 air contaminants standard. The judges' decision states in part that OSHA failed to establish that existing PELs present a significant risk of material health impairment and that the new standards eliminate or substantially reduce the risk, plus, OSHA did not meet its burden of establishing that its 428 new PELs were either economically or technologically feasible.

Actually, OSHA provided risk assessments for each of the new standards as part of its documentation, but the plaintiffs prevailed in their claim that these were not sufficient and OSHA needed to do much more in order to change its rules. In other words, OSHA was condemned from this point forward to

1. Develop a detailed risk assessment for each of the old PELs sufficient to prove that a "material health impairment" would be caused at these old levels;
2. Provide a detailed assessment of each of the 428 new PELs to prove that there would be a "substantially reduced risk" produced by the new standards;
3. Research state-of-the-art air-monitoring techniques, ventilation systems, protective equipment, and respiratory-protection devices and prove that it would be technically feasible for each industry to monitor their use to keep the exposure below the PEL; and
4. Survey all of the industries that use each of the 428 chemicals and provide an economic impact study for each one showing that these industries could afford to meet the new standard.

I submit that there are not enough trees on the planet for the paper it would take to write these assessments for 428 PELs, and it would require all of OSHA's personnel and resources full-time for the next twenty years to accomplish this, by which time, these new PELs would also be outdated!

Note that OSHA is prohibited from changing any rule that would protect only a few workers, because the old standards must cause a "material health impairment" and the new standard must produce a "substantially reduced risk." In other words, harming a few workers is just fine with the courts.

Worse, the court decision clearly establishes that OSHA can set no standard that would provide a negative financial impact on any industry that uses the chemical. In other words, if an industry derives a profit from a chemical-manufacturing process that harms its workers, the industry can continue to do so unless OSHA can come up with an inexpensive method to control the hazard!

As a result, OSHA now had to enforce the outdated PELs for 212 substances and was left with no standards at all for another 164 toxic substances. OSHA published the list of the old, reinstated PELs but stated that it

> believe[s] that many of the old limits which [OSHA] will now be enforcing are out of date (they predate 1968) and not sufficiently protective of employee health based on current scientific information and expert recommendations. In addition, many of the substances for which OSHA has no PELs present serious health hazards to employees.[8]

This is an important statement because it makes perfectly clear that OSHA does not approve of its own PEL standards. In the 1989 comments that accompany the revised PELs, OSHA concluded that its new air contaminants rule in general industry would result in a reduction of approximately 700 deaths, 55,000 illnesses, and more than 23,300 lost-workday illnesses annually. These benefits are now lost to U.S. workers.

Industry has won this battle completely. Today, most of the PELs that protect U.S. workers are still at 1968 levels, there are more than a hundred chemicals that are known to be toxic and for which there are no PELs, and there is no way OSHA can update the PELs under the current system. Our OSHA standards are a bad joke all over the world.

Some industries were not satisfied by merely having corporate members on the TLV committee to influence the ACGIH. They tried to use the courts to control the ACGIH's TLV process.

For example, in December 2000, the ACGIH was served with three lawsuits, all relating to the TLVs. These lawsuits were costly. I became a member of the ACGIH only to be assessed almost immediately, as were all other members, an additional $200 to help defray the legal costs.

One of these three lawsuits was particularly noxious. At issue was the new TLV for a substance called refractory ceramic fibers (RCFs). This stuff is a fine fibrous material that is spun from high-temperature ceramic materials and is used as a substitute for asbestos. Like asbestos, it is a good insulator for high-temperature equipment such as kilns for ceramics, furnaces for glassblowing, and other high-heat applications.

If you have children in school at any level, from elementary school to college, there is a good chance that a ceramic kiln somewhere in that school is insulated with RCF. RCF looks like asbestos, insulates like asbestos, and causes the same kinds of cancers that asbestos does in animal tests. Based on these tests, the National Toxicology Program had listed RCF as "reasonably anticipated to be a human carcinogen." In 1993, the EPA summed up the animal studies and the data on RCF as follows:

> Several studies show that RCFs are an animal carcinogen, and EPA has classified RCF as a probable human carcinogen. A major animal inhalation study . . . has shown a positive tumorigenic response in rats and hamsters, with 35 percent of the hamsters exposed . . . developing pleural mesothelioma and 13 percent of the rats exposed to kaolin RCFs developing adenoma-carcinomas.[9]

The RCF animal tests are so definitive that even the manufacturers realized they would need to set some kind of air-quality guideline for the substance. (Clearly, OSHA couldn't set one for this new material.) The manufacturers set a recommended limit of 0.5 fiber/cubic centimeter (f/cc). This is five times higher than the 0.1 f/cc ACGIH and OSHA limits for asbestos.

The ACGIH looked at the same data and set a more restrictive guideline than the coalition of manufacturers had. Its TLV was

0.2 f/cc for refractory ceramic fiber—only twice as high as the asbestos limit.

The RCF manufacturers didn't like the implication that their product was almost as hazardous as asbestos. They took ACGIH to court. The plaintiffs were the Refractory Ceramic Fibers Coalition, Thermal Ceramics, Inc., Unifrax Corporation, and Vesuvius U.S.A. Corporation. These plaintiffs asserted in part: (1) that the ACGIH's research regarding the TLVs for RCFs is flawed and (2) that the ACGIH has a conflict of interest, because many of its members are federal and labor union employees. Let's look at these two arguments.

First, the ACGIH had highly qualified industrial hygienists and toxicologists on the TLV committee. The Refractory Ceramic Fibers Coalition is made up of five manufacturers that would have a hard time comparing the credentials of their hired toxicologists and industrial hygienists with those of the experts on the committee.

Second, by filing a brief charging bias, the Refractory Ceramic Fibers Coalition called attention to the fact that its own recommended exposure guideline was set by its members, *all* of whom are RCF manufacturers with obvious conflicts of interest!

On January 12, 2001, the United States District Court in Atlanta held a hearing on the Refractory Ceramic Fibers Coalition's request for a temporary restraining order enjoining the ACGIH from publishing the new TLV. After reviewing the legal briefs filed by both parties and listening to both counsels, the court denied the coalition's request, and the ACGIH was free to publish the TLV for RCF. Later, the case was thrown out of court.

Did this end the lawsuits? No. Instead, industry found that it could delay standards and cost the ACGIH large sums for defense—money that exceeded the ACGIH's small treasury and caused the organization to assess its members. Whether it was their motive or not, this coalition of industries saw that its lawsuits could bleed the ACGIH.

It happened again in 2004. In the fall of that year, the International Brominated Solvents Association, the National Mining Association, and Aerosafe Products, Inc., claimed that the ACGIH is a government advisory group whose proposed TLVs for some of their pet chemicals were too restrictive. These were 1-bromopropane, copper, silica, and diesel exhaust. The plaintiffs claimed that these lower TLVs constituted false and misleading information that interfered with their business. They filed a restraining order to enjoin the ACGIH from taking any action on these TLVs, but a U.S. District Court judge in Macon, Georgia, ruled that

- The plaintiffs do not have standing to bring this action under the Federal Advisory Committee Act (the ACGIH is *not* a governmental agency);
- An injunction would constitute restraint on free speech; and
- TLVs are not commercial speech and the ACGIH is fully protected by the First Amendment.[10]

So the ACGIH survived another set of challenges. But the next time someone tells you that personal injury lawyers file all kinds of frivolous lawsuits, you tell them to compare the suits to those that industry files.

Couldn't the United States simply find some way to adopt the ACGIH guidelines, as some states have done, and then we would all be safe? Despite the influence of industry on the AGCIH TLVs, that would be better than the OSHA standard we have now. Unfortunately, however, this would not be enough. It would not address the two massive problems underlying the setting of chemical safety limits, which are (1) the sheer number of chemicals, and (2) how few chemicals have ever been tested for their toxic effects.

On September 7, 2009, the Chemical Abstract Service (CAS), an agency that registers every new chemical as it is invented or discovered, assigned a registry number to the fifty-millionth chemical. The CAS began to register chemicals in 1956, and it took thirty-three years to register the first ten million new chemicals. The CAS identified these chemicals primarily from research papers it accumulated from worldwide sources.

Yet the last ten million chemicals were registered in nine months at the rate of twenty-five per minute! Even more important, the CAS's primary source for identifying these chemicals was not research papers. Instead, 60 percent were from major patent offices worldwide. The next significant category included chemicals that were currently available in chemical catalogs![11] In other words, these chemicals are already out of the box and in the marketplace.

Has anyone ever tried to convince you that we're a lot smarter and safer now than we were back when we used to do anything we wanted with asbestos, lead, DDT, and so forth? Now that you know about these dangerous substances, you have the choice between laughing at this deluded person and sadly shaking your head.

Of the fifty million chemicals that are registered, there are various estimates of the total number of chemicals in commercial use. The number used by most people in the United States is now a hundred thousand, based on EPA estimates (visit www.epa.gov/grtlakes/ toxteam.pbtrept/pbtreport.htm for more information). This is probably a low estimate, because the European Union has now registered 143,000 and at this moment is still registering more.

If we restrict our concerns to the estimated 100,000-plus chemicals currently in commercial use, it is absolutely frightening that only 642 of these have been studied sufficiently for the ACGIH to set workplace air-quality guidelines for them. As for long-term testing, only about 900 chemicals have been studied for cancer effects with enough depth to be assessed by the main cancer research agencies, and about 300 chemicals have been assessed for reproductive and developmental effects and birth defects. The following table summarizes these

Quick Statistics: Chemicals vs. Data Available

Number of Chemicals	Information Available
50,000,000 and rising fast	Registered by the Chemical Abstract Service
140,000 and rising	Chemicals in commerce registered by the European Union
Approximately 900 chemicals and biological substances (viruses, toxins from molds, etc.)	Studied and evaluated for cancer effects
642 chemicals	Have air-quality standards set by the ACGIH
Approximately 300 chemicals and biological substances	Studied and evaluated for potential reproductive and developmental effects and birth defects

data so that the disparity between the number of chemicals in use today and the numbers of chemicals that have been studied for toxic effects can be clearly seen.

Obviously, we can't assume that a majority of the 143,000 or even the 50 million chemicals are nontoxic. There could be 143,000 surprises out there waiting for us. And since cancer tests require two years to perform, just how will we catch up when new chemicals are being discovered or synthesized at a rate of 25 per minute? We are clearly clueless about this swamp of chemicals through which we slog.

The advertising from most manufacturers leaves consumers with the assumption that all of the ingredients they use in their products have been tested for every kind of toxic effect, including cancer. If you want to know how they actually test these substances, look at their lab rats. There's one in your mirror.

The U.S. industry practice of creating chemicals and putting them into commerce without testing has been observed critically by the rest of the world and particularly by the European Union (EU). It did not want to operate on the faulty U.S. principle that chemicals are "innocent until proven guilty."

The European Union chose to frame its approach to this problem in the reverse. Its position is that chemicals should be "suspect until proven innocent." In essence, its regulations say to industry, "If you can't prove your chemicals are safe, you can't put them on our market."

This is called the precautionary principle. It states that in the absence of test data, you cannot assume a chemical is safe, and precautions should be instituted as if the chemical were toxic unless the manufacturer proves otherwise. This simple principle forms the basis for EU regulatory programs.

First on the European Union's agenda is getting the testing done. It understood the absurdity of trying to set safety and environmental policies in the absence of toxicity data. The Union passed regulations that require physiochemical, toxicological, and ecotoxicological testing of "all substances manufactured or imported in quantities of 1000 tonnes or more"[12] per year. It is estimated that there are more than thirty thousand of these large-volume commercial chemicals on which almost no data exist. There are even more smaller-volume chemicals for which testing will have to wait. In fact, chemicals manufactured in amounts of less than a ton a year do not have to be registered at all.

This means small amounts of low-production-volume chemicals can still be used in European products without being registered or tested.

The program under which the European Union requires this chemical testing is called REACH (Registration, Evaluation, Authorization [and Restriction] of Chemical Substances). Now REACH requires each industry to submit the basic test data or else the manufacturer will not be allowed to import or sell either the chemical or the products containing the chemical anywhere in the European Union.

The first REACH report of chemical test data is scheduled for 2012. By that time, industry will have invented millions of new chemicals, so it's still a race in which industry is winning. But the EU regulations are at least making it a race, rather than the compete rout that we see here in the United States.

The Bush administration's response to REACH was predictable. First, emissaries were sent to the European Union when the new law was being promulgated to lobby against it. When that failed, the administration fought against any similar proposals for chemical testing introduced in the U.S. legislature, such as the Kid-Safe Chemical Act introduced in July 2004 by senators James Jeffords (I-VT) and Frank Lautenberg (D-NJ). (As this book goes to press, a 2010 version of this bill, called the Safe Chemicals Act, was introduced in the House. Six congressional hearings and ten stakeholder meetings later, it appears dead. Lautenberg vows to introduce another next session.)

The Kid-Safe Chemical Act addressed the regulation that is at the heart of our failure to test chemicals, that is, the U.S. Toxic Substance Control Act (TSCA). This act is enforced by the EPA. In 1976, when the TSCA was instituted, the EPA was charged with trying to "compile, keep current, and publish a list of each chemical substance that is manufactured or processed in the United States." The TSCA gives the EPA the authority to review and evaluate new chemicals. In general, if there is reason to suspect by virtue of the chemical's class or structure that it could be potentially toxic, testing is required and precautions are instituted during manufacture.

Yet this applies only to new chemicals. Similar to the FDA regulations discussed in chapter 1, the TSCA limits the EPA's authority to address the roughly sixty thousand chemicals that were already in production when the act became law in 1976.

Today, there are somewhere between eighty-two thousand and eighty-three thousand chemical substances on the TSCA's list, depending on which agency you ask. These substances are organic, inorganic, polymers, and "chemical substances of Unknown, or Variable composition, Complex reaction products, and Biological materials." The TSCA's list has only about eighty-three thousand entries because it does not include any chemical substances that are subject to other U.S. statutes, such as foods, food additives, pesticides, drugs, cosmetics, tobacco, nuclear material, or munitions.

The limits of the TSCA are well understood in Washington. The Government Accountability Office (GAO), in a report dated July 13, 2004, described the regulatory hurdles it poses. To control or ban any of these chemicals, the EPA must first prove that the chemical poses an "unreasonable risk." Once this is proved with chemical testing, the GAO notes that the EPA must then apply the "least burdensome requirement," meaning the cheapest method, to protect the public or the environment, and must "prove that no other federal law can address the health or environmental risk."

The GAO adds that the EPA "has found it difficult to meet all of these requirements for rulemaking." The GAO estimated that issuing rules to obtain toxicity and exposure information about chemicals can take from two to ten years and is incredibly labor-intensive. "Given the time and resources required, the agency has issued rules requiring testing for only 185 of the approximately 82,000 chemicals in the TSCA inventory," the GAO said. Only 169 of these 185 have actually been tested![13]

Even if the EPA has information showing that a chemical can be harmful, industry can always take the EPA to court as it does with other agencies. For example, based on substantial scientific data about the cancer-causing effects of asbestos, the EPA banned the substance in 1989. The asbestos industry took the EPA to court, and the rule banning asbestos was overturned in 1991 by the U.S. Court of Appeals for the Fifth Circuit. The court ruled that the EPA failed to meet TSCA requirements for proving a ban was necessary because it poses a substantial risk.[14]

If asbestos is found not to pose a "substantial risk," as required under the TSCA, then clearly the EPA's attempts to ban substances will be another blind alley like those faced by OSHA. Industry wins again.

One of the actions the GAO suggested to improve this situation was to have Congress give the EPA the authority to require chemical substance manufacturers and processors to test their chemicals. Does that sound familiar? That is exactly what REACH did—and it is what we need to do in the United States.

During the Bush administration, the EPA was headed by Christine Whitman. The Whitman EPA said it didn't need the authority to require industry to test and that it would, instead, institute a better program than REACH. This program is the EPA's Chemical Assessment and Management Program (ChAMP), a primarily voluntary industry program meant to address chemicals manufactured in amounts greater than *twenty-five thousand* pounds per year. The deadline to produce the information is 2012, the same as the REACH deadline. Yet the EPA can only ask industries to voluntarily adopt standards and provide the testing and/or to produce their hitherto unpublished (and secret) industry studies.

I could be wrong, but it sounds like Whitman and her EPA cohorts actually may have been naive enough to think that chemical manufacturers were good stewards and were secretly safety-testing their hundred thousand chemicals before unleashing them on the public. The ChAMP challenge, however, has managed to flush out only around eighty-one hundred previously unpublished studies on the eighty-three thousand chemicals. These studies were, of course, done by and for industry without external auditing and may not be worth much.

In 2012, REACH's studies, conducted under the strict scientific protocol procedures required by the European Union, will be made public. That same year, the EPA will probably release some or all of the eighty-one hundred U.S. industry studies. By now, I think you can also predict what will happen with the two sets of data. U.S. industry will have its own less disciplined studies as fodder for numerous court fights that place highly paid industry experts against governmental experts, and decades more will be lost to this nonsense.

The European regulations already "reach" right into our own back pockets. For example, the United States can no longer export lead-laden computers and electronic equipment to the European Union. Meeting the EU requirements for electronic equipment has forced our industry to reduce the use of lead in our own manufacturing procedures.

Lead-free solders for electronic components have been available in the United States for more than fifteen years, but the electronics industry preferred to use the cheaper and more toxic lead solders. Now, the European Union is forcing it to switch to the safer solders that reduce the electronic industry's damage to the environment and provide a safer workplace for our workers. We should have done this fifteen years earlier because it was the right thing to do. (It appears that the lead-free computers are made for the EU market, and some of the computers we buy are still soldered with lead.)

Two other, more complex, EU rules are a good illustration of how the European Union will force us to change our manufacturing processes. These rules will also affect the types of textile and jewelry products you find on the market and how our textile and jewelry artists and craftspeople will have to work. These rules are the EU Dye Directive and the Nickel Directive.

Only a handful of commercially available dyes have ever been tested for long-term toxicity, such as cancer and reproductive effects. Those few that have been tested were often found to be carcinogens. Dyes in general are in potentially toxic classes. It is no accident that among the roughly two thousand commercial synthetic dyes, only six are approved for use in food.

It would be prohibitively expensive to require the time-consuming (two-year, two-species) cancer tests for every one of those two thousand dyes. Yet there is a better way for at least one type of dyes, and the European Union found it. It is based on a simple understanding of the fact that when a dye fades or is bleached and becomes colorless, the dye does not simply disappear. Instead, it breaks down into its colorless component parts. Often, these colorless compounds are even more toxic than the dye itself.

It was German chemists who crafted the early versions of the Dye Directive. They decided to take on one of the biggest and baddest chemical classes of commercial dyes, that is, the "azo" dyes. An azo dye molecule contains an azo unit, consisting of two double-bonded nitrogen atoms in a configuration that is inherently weak. Any chemist with experience can look at the structure of an azo dye and assume that the dye molecule will cleave into parts when the azo bonds break. Then it is easy to see the pieces of molecules that result to figure out what is created when the dye fades, is bleached, or is metabolized in the human body or the environment. The new EU rule regulates dyes that would break down to release any of twenty-two chemicals that are known or suspected carcinogens.

In other words, for an initial evaluation, expensive testing is not needed. If the dye is known to release chemicals that are carcinogens, the dye itself is considered a carcinogen. It's simple and elegant.

The Dye Directive also regulates recycled textile and fiber products, but since recycled products are likely to be made from old materials manufactured before the regulations were in effect, they will probably contain these cancer-causing dyes at higher levels. As a concession to recyclers, the test for recycled products allows a greater amount of cancer-causing substances to be released (concentrations below 70 ppm). This illustrates another point that consumers should remember: recycled products usually contain more toxic contaminants than freshly made products do.

The directive testing protocols effectively ban hundreds of dyes for use on products that will contact the skin. Major manufacturers are probably complying with the Dye Directive, but many small producers do not know how to evaluate their dye chemicals to figure out whether these release carcinogens. In fact, most U.S. art and craft dyers don't even know the chemical names of their dyes. Fundamental changes will have to be made for our industries, big and small, to catch up to the European Union on dye regulations.

Nickel is a nasty metal. It can cause cancer and is also a powerful allergen that produces skin rashes on contact and respiratory allergies when inhaled.

Nickel-containing alloys are still used in the United States for making jewelry. In fact, many high school, college, and university art programs teach the casting of nickel-silver alloys (sometimes called Monel metal). Casting releases cancer-causing nickel fumes that students can inhale. They can also breathe in the nickel-containing dusts when the jewelry is cut or polished. Schools that use nickel-containing metals are teaching students to create jewelry items that are banned in the European Union and dangerous for people to wear. This is not a good use of your tuition dollars.

The sensitization caused by nickel was especially evident in the United States at the beginning of the body-piercing craze. One typical article on the subject was published by the New York Times in 1998.[15] The reporter interviewed Dr. David Cohen, a New York University dermatologist and an expert on contact dermatitis. He explained that a large number of his patients were fans of body piercing and that most of these pierced patients were allergic to their jewelry, specifically to the nickel found in costume jewelry.

During the decade from 1988 to 1998, the percentage of Americans who are sensitive to nickel rose from 10.5 percent to 14.3 percent. Dr. Cohen and other experts think the increase is linked to the body-piercing craze, because newly pierced skin is most likely to react to nickel.

Often, people with this allergy are not aware they have it because there typically is a time lag between wearing the jewelry and breaking out in a rash. "You might wear it on Friday night, and you start itching on Tuesday," Dr. Cohen said. Then the rash can persist for weeks, and it is easily mistaken for an infection. Or the fluid-weeping rash may actually become infected after a time.

To prevent these allergies, the EU regulations do not allow nickel and its compounds to be used in jewelry that is inserted into pierced ears or other parts of the body unless they have been tested and proved not to release nickel in amounts greater than 0.2 microgram per centimeter square per week.

Jewelry and other metal items that contact but do not pierce the skin also must be tested, but the level of nickel released may be higher (less than 0.5 microgram per square centimeter per week). Covered under this provision are articles that come into prolonged or direct contact with the skin, including earrings, necklaces, bracelets and chains, anklets, finger rings, wrist watch cases, watch straps and tighteners, rivet buttons, tighteners, rivets, and zippers.

In case manufacturers think they can put paint or a plated metal over the nickel items so that they will pass the test, the European

Union is way ahead of them. Testing must also be done for all articles that contain nickel that has been covered with a nonnickel protective coating. These are the most expensive tests because they must show that the item does not release nickel after at least two years of normal use, which might wear down the coating.[16]

The tests for the nickel release are specified in the regulation as well. These tests would be prohibitively expensive for small-business craftspeople who are currently using the cheaper silver/nickel alloys. In the United States, that economic fact probably would make the law indefensible in court! In the European Union, however, it's tough noogies for the small-business jewelry makers. They will simply have to make jewelry out of metal alloys that don't contain nickel, such as sterling, gold, copper, steel, and the like.

If our craftspeople want to sell their wares in the European Union, they will have to either send documentation of these tests from a certified lab or use alloys that don't contain nickel. The United States should have done this as soon as we knew that nickel was a carcinogen and that serious allergies from nickel were on the rise. It was the right thing to do. Certainly, we shouldn't still be using nickel in our high school and college art programs.

The new European regulations limit or ban many other chemicals. For example, the EU regulations effectively ban asbestos, something our EPA was unable to do. And the EU regulations list refractory ceramic fiber as a carcinogen, which under its laws means that industry must protect workers with the most advanced technology—regardless of the cost—to keep exposure as low as is technically feasible. On January 14, 2010, the European Chemicals Agency added fourteen chemical substances to the Candidate List of Substances of Very High Concern (SVHC), two of which were types of refractory ceramic fiber. Here in the United States, however, OSHA has no permissible limit for the fibers at all to protect workers.

Our workplace and environmental chemical exposure standards, such as OSHA workplace air-quality standards, have not essentially improved since 1968. Unfortunately, independent health agencies like the ACGIH and governmental agencies, such as OSHA and the EPA, are powerless in the face of industry's ability to use the regulatory process and the courts to make every improvement in the rules take decades to accomplish, if not to stop progress completely.

Rendering private and governmental agencies ineffective has left industry free to continue what it started in the 1800s, that is, create and discover tens of thousands of chemicals, put these into production in factories without testing, expose its workers to essentially untested chemicals, and make the chemicals into products that are sold to the public without safety or environmental testing. Today, the manufacture of common chemicals in nanoparticle sizes provides another arsenal of unregulated, potentially toxic chemicals in our home and workplace environments.

Of the 100,000 or more chemicals in commerce, the EPA has jurisdiction over about 83,000 and has managed to require and obtain testing of 169. The ACGIH has set workplace air-quality limits for only 642 chemicals, and about 470 of these same chemicals also have OSHA permissible exposure limits, most of which are still at 1968 levels. Only about 900 chemicals, some of these the same ones for which there are OSHA and ACGIH limits, have been evaluated for their cancer potential. This still means there are 100,000 or more potentially rude shocks out there waiting for us.

And we, the chemical industry's lab rats, will eagerly buy the new nanoparticle-containing socks and cosmetics, the clothes colored with untested dyes, the jewelry made with cancer-causing nickel, and thousands of other potentially toxic products. If it turns out that these and the many other chemicals in products we've been sold cause cancer, reproductive damage, or other harm that takes years to develop, we will not be able to prove conclusively to any court that a particular chemical caused us harm. Studies comparing our fate to that of people who were not exposed to all of these pollutants cannot be conducted because there is no group of people left on the planet whose bodies are free of hundreds of these toxic substances.

One hope lies in the EU regulations that will indirectly force U.S. manufacturers to test various chemicals if they intend to sell their products in the European countries. Later in the book, you will learn that these EU regulations are not perfect either, but at least there is a sliver of light breaking on our eastern horizon. It's called the precautionary principle, the revolutionary principle that does not assume chemicals are innocent until proven guilty.

Another glimmer of hope for U.S. workers is seen emanating from the new assistant secretary of labor for OSHA, David Michaels. He gets it. A week after he was sworn in as the new OSHA director, Michaels spoke at a Going Green Workshop held by the National Institute for Occupational Safety and Health:

> Today we suspect that at least a couple of thousand high-use chemicals out there may present some threat to worker health. Yet, OSHA currently regulates about 500 chemicals, based mostly on science from the 1950s and 1960s. How many chemical standards has OSHA issued in the past 12 years? Two—and one of these two only came about because of a court order! We haven't been keeping up with the science.[17]

Let's hope Mr. Michaels can make a difference.

CHAPTER 10

Chemicals Known to the State of California

A Political Action Plan

Despite everything you've read, I'm still optimistic that we can make changes, because I personally know it is possible. I was part of a small group of activists that got the Federal Hazardous Substances Act amended, although it took about eight years' worth of effort. Our aim was to stop manufacturers of art materials from labeling products "nontoxic" if they contained known carcinogens and other highly toxic ingredients. Manufacturers could do this legally because the only toxicity tests required by the Federal Hazardous Substances Act were limited to acute toxicity tests that are incapable of detecting cancer or other long-term effects.

We accomplished this change between 1979 and 1988 with a handful of activists, the Public Interest Research Groups, and a few other organized consumer groups. Yet when we first began this effort in 1979, we had easier access to the regulatory process than people do today. This access was through a governmental program called Compensation for Testimony.

Compensation for Testimony worked like this: If a particular governmental agency was planning to change a regulation or institute a new one, the agency could use a special fund designed to obtain the opinion of experts or organizations that had specific knowledge or expertise about the proposed changes. Take it from someone who was paid this compensation in the late 1970s: it was not much money. Yet it reimbursed our nonprofit organization for our time to do the research, for our copying costs, and for the trip to Washington to testify. And, in fact, a portion of the research that we compiled for the September 1980 congressional hearing where some of us testified was financed this way.

This whole program was ended by a stroke of Ronald Reagan's pen shortly after he was elected in 1981. The moment Reagan eliminated compensation for testimony, the comments on new regulations in the *Federal Register* instantly changed. After 1981, the comments in the *Federal Register* were almost exclusively from industry—the entities with the money, the time, and the financial incentive to present their positions.

Despite the setback, we continued to fight to change the labeling regulations at a time when we had to do it all on our own dime and we were being told there were already too many regulations and government should get out of industry's business. (This is the same climate we face today.)

The nonprofit for which I worked, the state Public Interest Research Groups, and other organizations continued to press this issue. We developed a procedure. We got lists of art materials commonly purchased by public schools and investigated to find out which of them contained known carcinogens or other chronically toxic ingredients and had no warning labels. Reports were written with details of the findings and were provided to audiences at public hearings. The attendees could see the names of products that they knew their children were using in school and the many chronically toxic and cancer-causing substances these contained.

As a result, bills were introduced by 1981 at the state level, and by 1984, California passed the first of the Art Hazards Labeling bills. Three more states passed bills within a few months.

After that, the art materials' industry wanted a federal law because it had to design and print labels to meet different laws in each state. In 1988, six states had passed the bill, and the bill was being introduced in several more states. In October 1988, the Labeling of Hazardous Art Materials Act was passed by Congress.

The new labeling act would be enforced by the U.S. Consumer Product Safety Commission, which is charged with enforcing the Federal Hazardous Substances Act. Within a couple of years, the commission ruled that all consumer products that contain known carcinogens, not only art materials, should be labeled with warnings. Well, it was just common sense and about time!

Not long after that, the CPSC added labeling requirements for neurotoxicity (damage to the nervous system) and developmental toxicants, such as those that affected the reproductive capacities of men and women, caused fetal death, or produced functional deficiencies in offspring. The CPSC published its intent to add more categories, but as the deregulation craze mushroomed, the CPSC made no further changes. As it stands, manufacturers have to label products that contain chemicals known to cause cancer or developmental or nervous system damage. If a product can wreck your liver, shut down your kidneys, stop your heart, or cause any other organ damage, however, it still doesn't have to be labeled. And of course, there is no limit on untested chemicals, which many manufacturers even label "nontoxic" in the absence of any proof to the contrary.

So we didn't win the whole war, but our small-time fight ended up making major changes to the Federal Hazardous Substances Act.

Governmental regulations are not working. The manufacturers are not telling us what we need to know. Even if the manufacturers wanted to tell us whether the ingredients in their products were toxic, the fact is that these substances have not been studied and they can't tell you. It sounds pretty hopeless, but it's really not.

In fact, if you understand this much of the problem, you are already one part of the movement to change this. You will be someone who will vote on the right side of these issues because you understand. All that it takes is enough of us, and it will have to change. It has to, because the current path is folly.

There's no reason everyone shouldn't already know what you know. The facts and the issues I've discussed in this book are not hidden in some secret archives. They are out there for all of us to see. We simply didn't want to look.

We need to fix this by owning the fact that we let the corporations and the manufacturers introduce untested chemicals and provide misleading labeling. We let this happen because we collectively have an almost religious belief in free market capitalism. We bought the theory that if government regulators get out of the way, manufacturers will be free to create good products, make more profits, and provide us with more jobs, and all of that wealth the CEOs at the top make will trickle down to us. Only now are we learning that manufacturers discovered that they can make bigger profits by shipping our jobs to China. There, cheap products are made that repeatedly need replacing, so we spend more money buying new ones and jamming our landfills full. And that trickle down from the top is not money, it's pee. We also believed the corporate propaganda. We reasoned that companies wouldn't do these evil things because it would be bad for their image, and they might be sued for making hazardous products. In fact, though, CEOs are insulated from most product-liability lawsuits, and their corporations have resources and time on their side at trial. Chronic diseases take years to manifest themselves, and a long, long time is required to prove beyond doubt that a specific chemical has caused a particular individual's disease. Animal cancer tests take two years. Reproductive tests can run even longer. And memories are short.

Once all of those studies are done, industry will dispute them for years. It can point out that animals and people are different, and it will want proof that its chemical can actually affect people. Well, the only human proof is found in large epidemiological studies of people or workers who are exposed to the chemical. Often, it is difficult or even impossible to find a group of workers who were exposed to a single chemical. If researchers do find such a population to study, it is too late for the workers in that study. They may have contributed their lives or their health to provide those data.

If not the government, at least we can turn to the courts, right? Between Erin Brockovich in the movies and the cries for tort reform from the right, you could be forgiven for thinking that lawsuits might be the last, best resort.

Suppose *you* were one of the people who were made ill by a chemical *after* it had been studied in people and *after* the manufacturer knew it was hazardous. You should be able to easily recover damages, right? To do so, all you have to do is prove that this chemical was the primary cause of your cancer, kidney failure, or whatever disease you have. Unfortunately, it's often impossible to prove this because you have undoubtedly been exposed to other chemicals and have other risk factors that might also have caused or contributed to your illness. The manufacturer's legal team will pry into every corner of your life to find those factors. The lawyers will look into your lifestyle, every job you've held, everywhere you've lived, your parents' work and medical histories, hobby products you've used, products you used in household renovations, and more.

Then suppose, by some miracle, that your case begins to look better and better, but the opposing attorneys apply for postponement after postponement. And suppose you've managed to remain alive this long. Your money is almost depleted, your kids' needs are not being met, and you are hanging onto your home by a thread. About this time, the lawyers for the defendant will hold a meeting with you and your attorney. The opposing lawyers will let you know that they can probably delay trial for more years, and then even if you win at trial, they will appeal the verdict and use up a few more years of your life before you actually see any money. They have an answer for you: they will give you a reasonable settlement.

The number on the paper they put in front of you looks pretty good. It is not as high as what you would expect to get from a jury, but enough to get you out of the financial hole you are in and then some. There's only one little catch. You will have to sign a confidentiality agreement. You will not be able to talk about the settlement or any facts of the case.

Even your own lawyer may press you to take this settlement. After all, he took your case on contingency. He has made nothing so far, has spent a great deal of time preparing for the case, and has laid out the money to retain all of the experts you needed. He may be feeling the pinch as well.

At this point, most plaintiffs give up and take the settlement. Now your experience and the information that you and your attorney have compiled will not be available to help all of those other people who were injured by the same chemical. More important, there is nothing on the record to alert other consumers that this chemical is dangerous or that this corporation has produced a hazardous product.

There are many cases like this on which I have been retained as an expert. I cannot tell you about these cases, but they certainly color my view of big business. The real heroes here are the plaintiffs and the lawyers who persist to the end to make sure that the information becomes public knowledge. This small fraction of the lawsuits has changed the chemical and product regulations.

In the last four decades, lawsuits, not regulations, have been the impetus for changing laws. For example, when the tide turned against the entire tobacco industry, it was not due to any efforts on the part of the FDA or the EPA, although these agencies raised public consciousness and helped reveal the hazards of smoking. The piles of studies conducted during a forty-year period showing the death and the carnage produced by smoking didn't convince Philip Morris that tobacco causes lung cancer or didn't get legislators to change the tobacco regulations. Only after many detrimental and expensive lawsuits repeatedly dragged this issue before the courts and the public did cigarette companies admit that smoking is hazardous to your health.

These court battles were waged by the widows and the widowers of deceased smokers and by the states attempting to recoup taxpayer money that was spent providing medical care for smoking-related diseases. In addition, the states and the cities started to pass laws making certain areas smoke-free. Today you can go to the American Nonsmokers' Rights Foundation's Web site at www.no-smoke.org and keep up with the growing number of these laws. As of April 2010, there are 28 states that have smoke-free workplaces. In addition, 654 municipalities have passed smoke-free workplace laws, 660 cities ban smoking in restaurants, and 526 ban smoking in bars. This emphasizes what every politician knows: all politics is local.

Likewise, the asbestos industry was not reined in by OSHA and the EPA nor by the piles of studies clearly demonstrating the link between asbestos and cancer. In fact, the EPA banned asbestos, and the asbestos industry took the EPA to court and overturned its ban. Instead, the asbestos industry was tethered by lawsuits brought by victims of mesothelioma, lung cancer, and asbestosis against Johns Manville and other producers.

We need to rethink our prejudice against those annoying lawyers who advertise on TV, the ones who ask you to call if you or a loved one has mesothelioma or has been injured on the job. They are the heroes of this story. I am immensely proud of being an expert witness in the first successful mesothelioma lawsuit against R.T. Vanderbilt that resulted in the closing of its asbestos-contaminated talc mine.

Now the same pattern is seen in the cases of the butter flavoring called diacetyl. Although it's been nearly ten years since the first factory workers were diagnosed with lung disease linked to the flavoring used in microwave popcorn, OSHA still hasn't issued a worker-protection standard. Yet $100 million in court awards and settlements have convinced flavor manufacturers that they must address the problem.

We need to stop laughing at the lawyer jokes and send our brightest kids to law school. It is these personal injury lawyers who are a major part of the solution.

We also need to be wary of any move to reform the legal system. The supporters of these tort reform bills will say that they only want to eliminate the costly filing of frivolous lawsuits. Listen to their remedy, though: capping giant awards. How does keeping a big, guilty chemical company from having to pay out millions stop your neighbor from suing you for tripping on a crack on your sidewalk? I don't know; you tell me.

In fact, supposed reform advocates want to make it harder for you to take your issue to a jury. Instead, we should let the juries and the judges eliminate suits that are without merit. Never let any law further restrict your rights to sue when you are injured.

Another legal reform that corporations have repeatedly asked for is that businesses and corporations should be protected from litigation if it can be shown that they have complied with all of the regulations that apply to them. This sounds fair at first hearing, until you know how outdated, weak, ineffective, and noninclusive most of our regulations are.

From the manufacturers' point of view, the chemicals they sell us have never been studied for long-term health effects, so they have never *knowingly* harmed anyone. They are pretty confident that they will not be successfully sued, because the injured party has to prove that the manufacturers knew or should have known that their products would cause harm. So legally, they are not at fault.

Even if a chemical is subsequently proved to be harmful, the manufacturers can't be held fully accountable for deaths and injuries from exposures that occurred before this proof was available. Their consciences are untouched, and they can use the "Who knew?" justification.

Instead, we need to ask how manufacturers can justify exposing people to their chemicals without first assessing the safety of these substances. Do they really think they have a right to invent new chemicals at break neck speed and expect some government agency using our tax dollars to research the hazards for them? It's their job, and they need to do it.

As for your right to sue if their chemicals harm you, you have a far better chance of getting a fairer hearing from twelve ordinary people sitting in a jury box than you would get by appealing to big business. Don't let anyone take away this option with tort reform.

As effective as lawsuits have been, industry wins if we put all of our resources into pursuing justice for one plaintiff at a time or trying to ban one chemical at a time. Industry can counter these efforts by doing its own biased studies to support its view that the chemical is safe. Then the battle comes down to pitting one pile of studies against another.

The battle of the studies can drag out for years. Using the same example of smoking, it took forty years prove smoking was hazardous. It took forty years to prove asbestos was hazardous. The battle to get lead paints restricted was just about as long, and it has taken more than twenty years to ban six piddling phthalates from children's toys, when there are hundreds of other phthalate plasticizers, many untested, now in those toys.

When a chemical is finally banned or restricted, industry can then use a substitute for it. Often, the substitute is almost identical to the banned chemical. Its molecule may be only slightly modified, but now it is technically a new, untested chemical, and the studies have to start all over again from scratch. Because there are more than fifty million chemicals registered by the Chemical Abstract Service to choose from, the folly of testing chemical by chemical is clear.

. . .

We need to look at a whole new approach. To do this, we have to bring together the various activists who have separated themselves into diverse single-objective causes, such as getting the mercury out of vaccinations, keeping Alar banned from use on apples, blogging about the hazards of the various plastic bottle additives, taking acetone out of nail polish, and so on. We must also contact the "green" organizations that fight for specific organic food criteria, particular clean energy methods, or recycling issues. If each of these hundreds of organizations got its own limited agendas passed tomorrow, the corporations would still be winning the war.

The way it stands now, manufacturers have forced us to prove that their products are hazardous. And because they don't study their chemicals, there are no data with which to make our case. How sad it is that activists jump on a tiny additional amount of mercury or a particular pesticide as a cause of autism, asthma, or any other illness when we are exposed to thousands of other possible chemical causes every day. We don't know any more than industry does whether this is the real cause, despite our intuitions, hopes, pain, and belief.

Instead, we need to work together on the chemical problem as a whole. It would be better to coalesce around the main issue, which is to require testing of chemicals by accepted scientific protocols for short- and long-term hazards *before* they are allowed in the marketplace.

I'm optimistic because I've seen change happen before, but also because we have witnessed the European Union making progress, including the requirements for testing it has promulgated. Another reason I'm hopeful is that there are now many federal and state legislators who understand this issue. I feel as I felt then: that with a little help, it can become a movement.

For instance, debate on Senator Frank Lautenberg's ill-fated Kid-Safe Chemicals Act (in committee as I write this) at least brought the need to overhaul the 1976 Toxic Substances Control Act (TSCA) to the floor. The TSCA requires manufacturers to provide information on trade secret ingredients to the EPA, but prohibits the EPA from sharing

information on this with the public or even with state and local author-
ities. Now several states are on board and demanding that the law be
changed. At this time, thirteen states have presented Congress with
changes they want in this law: California, Connecticut, Illinois, Maine,
Maryland, Massachusetts, Michigan, New Hampshire, New Jersey,
New York, Oregon, Vermont, and Washington.

In particular, these states want a reevaluation of the restrictions
on the roughly seventeen thousand chemicals registered as trade
secrets under TSCA chemicals. They want industry to prove conclusively that it would really be an economic hardship to disclose the
identity of each chemical before it is granted a trade secret exemption. Applying for and being granted trade secret exemptions has
been almost automatic for years, and these states want citizens and
states to have a right to know what is in their chemical products and
what is known about their hazards.

Today, changing the laws could be done in a very similar fashion.
We simply need to shift our focus from the 1980 effort to inform consumers about *known* chronic hazards in their products to a 2010 effort
to inform consumers when their products contain chemicals that
have undergone no chronic testing at all!

We can employ the same strategy that we used in the 1980s. We
held "teach-ins" around the country to explain the issue to parents
and consumers. We made our point by revealing that common carcinogens such as asbestos and cadmium could be legally labeled
"nontoxic," and when we showed them products for children that
actually contained asbestos, cadmium, and other carcinogens as
major ingredients, our point was made.

For better or worse, we have equally outrageous issues to start the
discussion today. We can take common products that everyone uses
and tell people what is known *and what is not known* about the hazards of their ingredients. We can make our points most strongly when
we look at chemicals in classes in which other substances have been
found to be hazardous, while very similar chemicals in the same class
have not been tested and require no warnings. This book is full of
chemicals that would fit this requirement.

For example, we can show that after polychlorinated biphenyls
(PCBs) were finally banned as carcinogens and environmental toxicants, the chemical manufacturers replaced the chlorine molecule

with a bromine and stuck these in your plastics and textiles as fire retardants. Now the data appear to show that these substances have very similar hazards—something that should have been known *before* the manufacturers put them in our products and before most of us had them in our bloodstream.

We can show that after twenty years, we finally got six phthalate plasticizers banned from certain types of children's products. Yet hundreds more probably have similar hazards and have not been tested. We don't even know which phthalates are in the products because manufacturers consider them trade secrets. There are similar stories about the glycol ethers in all of our cleaning products, about dyes used in our clothing, and on and on.

People are just as capable of understanding and becoming outraged by this issue as they were by the issues in 1980. In fact, especially in the last few years, Americans have started to wonder about what gets into their bodies, with a resulting increase in more people buying organic food and BPA-free water bottles, undergoing detoxifying regimens (even if these aren't always a good idea), and taking other incremental steps in this direction.

It is easy to show people that there now are fifty million chemicals registered by the Chemical Abstract Service, from which manufacturers can choose the many more than a hundred thousand chemicals already in commerce in the United States. And only about nine hundred chemicals have been evaluated for cancer effects. Most people will realize that something needs to be done.

I know for certain that this issue is just as powerful as the non-toxic issue was in the 1980s, because I have presented this information in hundreds of lectures and OSHA training sessions. I've seen how people respond.

We need to get the message out that both the testing and the enforcement should cost taxpayers almost nothing.

Clearly, the cost of the testing should be borne primarily by industry. It should have been doing this all along. As with the European rules, we can specify the types of tests and the requirement that these be done in third party–certified laboratories to prevent the tests from being conducted by researchers with a built-in conflict of interest. The testing would use up only a tiny fraction of the profits that manufacturers can make on a chemical.

The cost of enforcing the requirements to provide proper labeling and disclosure of information on material safety data sheets can be pennies and can provide jobs for a lot of people if we follow another model law. This is the Safe Drinking Water and Toxic Enforcement Act of 1986 in California. It is more often referred to as Proposition 65.

Proposition 65 is one of the few environmental laws in the country that works, yet costs almost nothing to enforce. You have probably seen evidence of the existence of this law in products with warning labels such as "This product contains chemicals known to the State of California to cause cancer, birth defects or other developmental harm."

Not only does this law cost California very little to enforce, many activist and legal organizations support themselves on this law. Here's how it works.

Enforcement is carried out through civil lawsuits against Proposition 65 violators who don't properly label products that contain any of the chemicals on the Proposition 65 list of toxic substances. The lawsuits may be brought by the California attorney general, any district attorney, or certain city attorneys in cities with a population exceeding 750,000. Lawsuits may also be brought by private parties "acting in the public interest," but only after providing notice of the alleged violations to the attorney general, the appropriate district attorney, and the city attorney and after they conformed to all of the requirements of drafting a legal Proposition 65 Notice of Violation.

A private party may not pursue an enforcement action directly under Proposition 65 if one of the government officials chooses to initiate his or her own action within sixty days of the notice. Private enforcers must also serve a certificate of merit, which provides the qualifications of their experts who generated the reports, analyses, or statements that support the violation. This is necessary to prevent frivolous enforcement actions.

The paperwork is worth it because the lawsuits can be very lucrative. A business found to be in violation of Proposition 65 is subject to civil penalties of up to $2,500 per day for each violation.

The chemicals that are regulated by Proposition 65 are in a long list developed and updated regularly by the California State Health

Department. The list is made up of chemicals the health department has determined are capable of causing cancer, birth defects, or developmental damage in children. Anyone can do a Google search for this list and see the chemicals for him- or herself.

All manufacturers, importers, and suppliers of products in the United States damn well better know this Proposition 65 list and make sure that if their products contain any of these chemicals, their labels provide the mandated warning. Yes, I'm aware that this is a California state law, but it has the same effect as a federal law. This is an important fact, because it may be that we would need to get only one state to pass a new labeling and testing law to make it effective. The reason Proposition 65 operates as if it were a federal law is that if a manufacturer allows people from California to purchase the product, the manufacturer comes under the law! So unless products clearly say they are not available for purchase by residents of California, the manufacturer can be sued big-time in California.

Now let's see how this works. Suppose you and I live in California and are running a small, poorly funded nonprofit green activist organization. Suppose we have reason to suspect that a certain manufacturer or importer of consumer products is selling something that contains a chemical that is on the Proposition 65 list and is not providing the required label warning. All we have to do is take the product to a certified laboratory and get an analysis of the product to prove we are right.

This is so easy to do today that we can even rent a hand-held X-ray fluorescent gun (XRF analyzer), train some of our people to use it properly, and simply aim the analyzer at products in a store until we find some that flunk for lead, mercury, cadmium, chromium, or any other substance that we set the gun to quantify. So we would already know when we send the product out for confirmatory laboratory analysis that we will get the data we need to file suit.

Our next step is to provide the proper documentation for our legal Proposition 65 Notice of Violation and submit it to the attorney general in our district. Now we wait sixty days. If the attorney general's office decides that we have a great case and wants to sue the violator itself, we get a part of the award or the settlement after it wins. If the attorney general doesn't file in sixty days, we get to call our staff lawyer and file ourselves. How can we afford to go after some deep-pocket multinational? If we win, we get all of the money!

At the federal level, the U.S. Consumer Product Safety Commission watches all of these goings-on in California and often jumps into the fray. For example, when lead-containing children's jewelry was being imported in vast quantities from China, the CPSC started a national recall of this hazardous stuff. Lost in the newspaper notices and the articles about this recall was the fact that California activists were already suing some of these importers under Proposition 65 and had petitioned the CPSC to take these actions.

Remember, Proposition 65 doesn't ban chemicals. And citizens, groups suing manufacturers under Proposition 65 do not have to prove that anyone ever got sick or was harmed by the product. The single issue is failure to properly label the product with warnings. This violation carries a high penalty, high enough to have created roving bands of lawyers and bounty-hunting activists whose income is enhanced by Proposition 65 settlements.

I cannot tell you in mere words how much this law is hated by manufacturers. Yet the law is fair to manufacturers and importers. They either must make sure their products do not contain any of the chemicals on the Proposition 65 list, or they must provide warning labels if the products do. How hard is that to comply with?

The thing that makes Proposition 65 unique is its "citizen's enforcement clause." This clause enables anyone who generates the proper paperwork to file suit against a manufacturer or an importer. It also means the State of California doesn't need thousands of inspectors purchasing and testing products. The activists and the lawyers will do it for them.

California's Proposition 65 enforces drinking water and waste regulations with similar ferocity. To appreciate the rationale for this law, the following language amending the California Health and Safety Code, Proposition 65, was in the 1986 ballot initiative:

Section 1. The people of California find that hazardous chemicals pose a serious potential threat to their health and well-being, that state government agencies have failed to provide them with adequate protection, and that these failures have been serious enough to lead to investigations by federal agencies of the administration of California's toxic protection programs. The people therefore declare their rights:

(a) To protect themselves and the water they drink against chemicals that cause cancer, birth defects, or other reproductive harm.
(b) To be informed about exposures to chemicals that cause cancer, birth defects, or other reproductive harm.
(c) To secure strict enforcement of the laws controlling hazardous chemicals and deter actions that threaten public health and safety.
(d) To shift the cost of hazardous waste cleanups more onto offenders and less onto law-abiding citizens.

Isn't this what we all ask for: to declare our rights to protect ourselves, to be informed, to secure enforcement of our rights, and to shift the cost to the offenders? Think about it.

We want the enforcement of labeling laws and hazardous waste regulations to be borne by the violators, not by the citizens or the government agencies. Now if we could just do the same in the U.S. banking and financial industries! Or imagine that some of the workplace safety regulations had citizens' enforcement clauses, and all that workers would have to do is take a picture of the safety hazard and get a portion of the fine against the boss.

This citizen's enforcement clause could be used to require product labels to warn users that untested ingredients are present at the federal level. It means enforcement of such a labeling law wouldn't cost the federal government much, and, if the penalties are high enough, both the government and the private enforcers can make money on the violators.

Perhaps there would be an added benefit if some forward-thinking manufacturers actually were inspired to formulate products made from ingredients that had been tested.

In any case, if we are serious about enforcement, this is a model we need to consider. Perhaps this is the time to act while Nancy Pelosi, a Democrat from California, is speaker of the House and is fully aware of how Proposition 65 works.

The Proposition 65 citizen's rights concept could also be coupled with the model of another law that requires the complete disclosure of ingredients. The story of this law begins with the banning of phosphate detergents in the early 1970s. Again, this story is local, rather than federal. The state is New York.

New York State acted to solve the phosphate detergent problem in 1970 by passing legislation that ultimately banned phosphates and required labeling of any remaining phosphate contents of detergents and soaps until the ban was complete. Detergent companies were not happy about changing their formulas and claimed that it would be difficult to replace the phosphates quickly. One of the points in their discussions with legislators was that some of the replacement chemicals might even be more dangerous to people and the environment than phosphates.

That issue of phosphate substitutes being even more dangerous did not sit well with legislators. Actually, it sounded as if the manufacturers were threatening to use even more toxic substances if they were forced to give up their phosphates. So the legislators countered by amending the act to require complete disclosure of all ingredients in cleaning products and to permit the commissioner of the Department of Environmental Conservation (DEC) to evaluate any new chemicals in detergents and set further restrictions on any ingredients found to be harmful to human health and the environment. (I've included more about this in appendix C.)

The regulations went on to specify that reports must be filed with the commissioner semiannually and that they must include the following information about each cleaning product: the amount of phosphorus; a list naming each ingredient present in an amount greater than 5 percent in the product, plus the percentage of that ingredient in the total formula; and the names of any ingredients in the formula occurring in an amount of less than 5 percent, with the exception of ingredients that are present only in trace amounts. All ingredients must be identified by their generic chemical names, rather than by fanciful and confusing trade names.

Also required is the disclosure of any investigations or research performed by or for the manufacturer concerning the effects of a substance on human health or the environment. Long before the EPA called in 2008 for the release of unpublished industry studies of chemicals, this New York law did the same.

Even more useful, "Such manufacturers shall furnish this information semiannually or at such other times as required," and the information is on public record, available at the DEC offices in Albany, with the exception of legitimate trade secret ingredients. This is needed because manufacturers change their formulas as often as they change their clothes. The semiannual requirement would bring consumers up-to-date information about ingredients.

The DEC further amended its regulations in 1985 to ban a chemical solvent called nitroacetic acid, or NTA, that was shown to cause cancer in laboratory animals. It was limited to 0.1 percent or less in any cleaning product.

Unfortunately, the law was not well enforced. As the Ayn Rand age of deregulation came into full flower, the law languished. Detergent labels remained uninformative and confusing to consumers, and no ingredient reports were being collected and made available.

Yet the law was there, on the books, waiting for some enterprising person or organization to require its use. In 2008, a nonprofit environmental law firm called Earthjustice did just that. In September 2008, an attorney for Earthjustice, Keri Powell, contacted all of the major cleaning product manufacturers that sell products in New York, advised them of the law, and requested them to comply by providing their complete lists of ingredients to the Department of Environmental Conservation as required.

Several companies, such as Method, Prestige Brands, Seventh Generation, Sunshine Makers, and Weiman Products, filed reports with the DEC. I was fortunate enough to be in receipt of some of these reports and was amazed at the difference in certain products when I compared the entire list of ingredients as required by New York law with the lesser numbers of ingredients listed on the labels or the material safety data sheets of these products. It clearly showed me that we need a law that requires complete ingredient labeling.

Then Earthjustice, representing a coalition of plaintiffs that included the Sierra Club and the American Lung Association, filed suit against the companies that refused to file reports with the DEC. These included Church & Dwight, Colgate-Palmolive, and Procter & Gamble, as well as the British company Reckitt Benckiser.

The respondents are arguing that the regulatory text doesn't require them to file a report unless the commissioner tells them to do so. They say that the initial text of the regulation states that the commissioner can require such information as he wants in such form as he may require, and this shows that the entire reporting regime is dependent on the commissioner exercising his discretion and asking for the reports. Earthjustice is arguing that the regulations clearly require semiannual reporting and specify the minimum information that must be contained in those reports. Furthermore, Earthjustice says that although the commissioner may require a particular form, he doesn't have to do so. Finally, the fact that he can request more information doesn't mean that the minimum reporting requirements aren't mandatory.

On February 4, 2010, the case went to a hearing. On July 30, 2010, the Supreme Court dismissed the petition. The judge decided that "the rights of the general public should be protected by officials of the executive branch" instead of by nonprofit groups. Earthjustice planned to appeal, but it wasn't necessary. The executive branch, in the form of the DEC commissioner Pete Grannis, decided to protect the general public by requiring ingredient disclosure, thus enforcing the law.

For the purposes of this book, however, it is enough that we know that there is a template for a law that requires complete ingredient disclosure and that provides regulators with the ability to require informative product labeling and to restrict the use of risky ingredients. Like Proposition 65, any company selling nationally that can't find a way to ensure that New Yorkers can't purchase the product must comply with this law. So again, we see that a state law can have the effect of a federal one. In fact, today anyone can visit Albany, New York, to see the ingredient lists for those products that have been compiled and even publish this information. In other words, a state law might do the job.

If we want testing, what type of testing do we want? Because the United Nations and the European Union are busy globally harmonizing labeling and safety data sheets, we might as well look to the list of tests that will be required in these documents. We'll need to comply in the long run, anyway. These tests are listed in the CHS Purple Book at Annex 4, "Guidance on the Preparation of Safety Data Sheets (SDS)," under Section 11: Toxicological Information. They are

1. acute toxicity
2. skin corrosion/irritation
3. serious eye damage/irritation
4. respirator or skin sensitization
5. germ cell mutagenicity
6. carcinogenicity
7. reproductive toxicity
8. target organ system toxicity on a single exposure
9. target organ systemic toxicity on repeated exposures
10. aspiration hazard

These include both acute and chronic tests. The rules also specify the standard test methods and require certified laboratories to ensure that the tests are not devised and done by people who have a financial stake in the outcome of the tests.

At the end of the previous list of tests, there is this sentence: "If data for any of these hazards is not available, they should still be listed on the SDS with a statement that data is not available."

As a result, consumers could see at a glance which tests have not been performed. I know for a fact that people can easily understand the implications of the lack of testing because I train public-sector workers in New Jersey who have a unique awareness about the lack of chronic data.

Public-sector workers in New Jersey come under the Public Employees Occupational Safety and Health Administration, which is enforced primarily by the New Jersey Department of Health and Senior Services. Part of its program is to provide public-sector workers with technical information, in terms that all workers should be able to understand and with the training required for all workers. The information is provided in the form of Hazardous Substances Fact Sheets. Compiled by the health department, they indicate both what is known and *what is not known* about the toxicity of a chemical. Each Hazardous Substances Fact Sheet clearly tells readers whether studies for cancer, birth defects, or reproductive damage have been done.

I've trained public-sector workers and teachers in New Jersey with the aid of these data sheets. It works like a charm. I typically provide trainees with both a material safety data sheet on a chemical product and the Hazardous Substances Fact Sheet on one or more of the chemical ingredients in the product. The participants can see the duplicity of the manufacturer when they compare the two sources of information.

I'm just supposin' in this chapter. Yet I think you can see that we have not looked at all of the ways we could accomplish testing and better labeling without costing the taxpayer. We have models of laws that can accomplish our purpose. These laws should be used to accomplish the following:

1. **Global harmonization chemical testing.** We have to do this anyway, or we'll lose 450 million potential customers in the European Union. Our laws do not have to be the same as those in Europe, but the objective of our laws must be the same: acute and chronic toxicity testing for all potentially toxic chemicals in consumer products, starting with the high-volume production chemicals and eventually extending testing to all potentially toxic substances in commerce.
2. **Banning of chemicals that are highly toxic to people or damaging to the environment.** A regulatory avenue to ban chemicals more efficiently is needed. We should also consider procedures for banning chemicals by class without toxicity testing, as is done in the European Union for certain chemicals, such as those azo dyes that break down to release known carcinogens. Should a manufacturer disagree with the ban of a particular chemical in a banned class, it would be free to test the substance and prove that it is not toxic to animals or the environment, after which the manufacturer could use the chemical.
3. **Restricting the use of trade secret exemptions.** There are already bills before Congress to modernize the Toxic Substances Control Act trade secret provisions that would allow industry to use these provisions only if it can demonstrate that the use of the trade secret ingredient is unique and unknown to its competitors and that revealing the identity of the trade secret ingredient would cause significant financial loss to the manufacturer.
4. **Global harmonization of industrial labels and safety data sheets.** This is presently in the works. OSHA has already proposed globally harmonizing data sheets. Because we have to do

this for all of our exports anyway, we might as well provide our own citizens with the same information that the rest of the world gets. Most important, the safety data sheets should both indicate the results of any toxicity tests and clearly state when these tests have not been done.

5. **Label warnings when products contain untested substances.** If we allowed only tested and proven safe chemicals in our products tomorrow, the economy would grind to a halt, and our stores' shelves would be almost bare. So we need an interim strategy during the time that testing is catching up with production. That strategy is to require ingredient labels that clearly indicate whenever chemicals untested for chronic hazards are present.

I don't think this is merely dreaming. I think these ideas could work. It beats the hell out of having another generation of people docilely using products that expose us to hundreds, perhaps thousands, of untested and/or trade secret chemicals every day.

We at least need to try.

CHAPTER 11

Don't Drive Yourself Crazy

Thirteen Reasonable Ways to
Change Today

In this book, we've looked at the history of how we got to this point and considered taking political actions to improve product safety in the future. Yet the marketplace is full of untested and potentially toxic chemicals *right now*. What can we do immediately? What types of chemical products should we use?

You might want to follow the guidelines used by people who opt out of all commercial products. They wash with bar soap and mix their own household cleaning and laundry products from simple chemicals. Many of these people avoid toxic dyes, fire retardants, and other additives by wearing natural fabrics such as hemp, cotton from special cotton plants that produce colored fibers, and various naturally colored animal hair products from sheep and llamas. Often, women who live this way are also the ones whose beauty regimen consists of using olive oil to keep skin soft, aloe to moisturize, cucumber slices to reduce puffiness around the eyes, and so on.

Information and recipes for these homemade household and beauty products are easy to find in books and on the Internet. Most of them work. To the people who use these products, I say, "Bless you!" You are doing *exactly* the right thing. You are the only people on the planet who know what is in your products because you make most of them.

I make a few of my own products as well—that is, when I have time. Yet this chapter is dedicated to those of us who can't always mix up a batch of laundry soap from scratch or find our cosmetics at the farmer's market.

Plus, if your job requires, as mine does, that you show up wearing the right makeup and clothes, you need to buy them. Men don't have it any easier. They are often required to come to work in those environmentally disastrous "dry clean only" suits and ties. So we need advice that is a little different. I've put together some general principles to live by.

1. Don't Make Yourself Nuts

Do the best you can with the amount of time you have to devote to searching out safer products. If, occasionally, you have to close your eyes and grab something that's handy, don't beat yourself up.

When you have a free moment, research the ingredients in the products you use most often and select the safer ones. When you haven't time to do the research, use common sense to avoid products that make extravagant claims about their ingredients. Some examples might be a seller's statement that the product is so revolutionary that the government or other manufacturers are persecuting him or her or claims that the product is completely nontoxic to people and the environment. Nothing is completely nontoxic. Some sellers of "ionized water" say that it cleans as well as detergents do, without containing any ingredients at all. It's a nice fairy-tale with scientific language and pictures, but it won't win a Nobel Prize. Tests show that some water that is "electrified" with a current and used immediately (which is not something you can put in a bottle on a store shelf) is capable of killing certain microorganisms. This product may find use as a biocide rinse for vegetables and other produce in the food industry.

2. Buy Less

The best thing for the environment and for your health is to consume less. Now I know that suggesting that people stop purchasing things is more un-American than registering as a member of the Communist Party. Our country's answer to every disaster is: buy stuff!

I'm going to suggest that for your health, sanity, and bank account, get off this hamster wheel. You don't need eight different cleaners, one for windows, one for floors, one for rinsing out underclothes, one for heavy laundry loads, another for bathroom fixtures, and another, and another. Just look at that collection of cleaners under the sink and out in the garage!

You don't need to try every new war paint at the cosmetic counter, every new gadget at the hardware store, every new fad in toys or technology and, for gosh sakes, take a pledge never to purchase anything after 11 p.m. when the TV hucksters are loose.

In your heart, you know there are a lot of items in your house right now that you don't need, your family and kids don't need, and you wish you'd never bought.

3. Buy Simple

Everyone should have a stock of simple chemicals that can be used for many household purposes. Included are bar soap (for example, Murphy's Oil Soap or plain castile soap), washing soda, borax, sodium metasilicate (the substitute for trisodium phosphate), vinegar, ammonia, and bleach. Then you will actually have enough products to take care of all of your cleaning needs. Your problem will be finding the time to learn which combinations work best for the tasks at hand and adjusting them for the water quality in your area. For example, hard water usually requires more "softening" chemicals, such as washing soda. No one is standing over you, demanding that you switch to these products immediately. Simply get them into the house, and you can experiment when you have the opportunity.

Clothing that doesn't require special care, such as toxic dry cleaning chemicals, can also be purchased. Many natural and sustainable fabrics will launder well but may require ironing. Most of the really wrinkle-resistant fabrics are synthetics full of dyes, flame retardants, and additives. I personally have chosen to use a lot of these synthetics because I travel so often for work. My clothes must be crammed into a suitcase and come out wearable; preferably, they can be washed in a hotel tub, thrown over a shower curtain rod, and be dry and wrinkle-free by morning.

In other words, we may have to make some compromises along the way. The only time this will change is when people's cultures and styles change to reflect simpler and more sustainable design. And with idols like Lady Gaga, change appears a long way off.

4. Buy Products That List Their Ingredients

Check labels and material safety data sheets to see whether the manufacturers are listing all or most of their ingredients, as I have suggested. Try not to use products whose MSDSs or labels indicate that the products contain ingredients that are proprietary or trade secret. Whatever those secret ingredients are, you can get along without them.

I personally try to reject products from the manufacturers who refused to comply with Earthjustice's request to file complete ingredient lists for their products in New York. These are Procter & Gamble Company, Church & Dwight Company, Reckitt Benckiser, and Colgate-Palmolive.

On occasion, you will need to use products that do not disclose their ingredients. For example, the biggest manufacturers of household paints will not tell you about the many complex ingredients that are used to make their acrylic plastic emulsions. You really can't make good wall paints yourself, though. Because I work for a union whose members include set painters, I get a lot of feedback about paints. In general, they say that the paints from small "green" manufacturers do not work as reliably as those from the big companies, such as Behr, Sherman Williams, and Glidden. So you may need to buy the major brands of paint and take precautions to avoid exposure to their ingredients.

5. Practice Precautions

If you must use a paint, a cleaner, or any other product with potentially toxic ingredients, avoid exposure by every route of entry: skin contact, inhalation, and ingestion. Common sense will tell you that if the product lists solvents and fragrances or if a chemical smell is emanating from the product, you should use ventilation. If the product is in powdered form and creates a dust, find a way not to raise the dust while using it. You can wet it down or switch to a liquid form of the same product. Wear gloves and protective clothing if it is clearly going to get on your hands or body. Remember: no one was ever harmed by a chemical he or she used but wasn't exposed to.

If you need to paint rooms in your apartment or house, you might want to consider the procedure I use. First, I pick summertime to do the work. Then I put an exhaust fan in a window at one end of my apartment and open a window at the other end and keep the air roaring through the rooms. That prevents my excessive inhalation of the vapors emanating from the paint. Then I either wear gloves or keep paint off my hands as much as possible. It is also wise to spend the night elsewhere or keep the fans running.

Similar ventilation can be set up for any air pollution problem, such as those caused by major cleaning projects, flushing out smoke after a fire, or the use of pesticides if they are needed.

6. Apply Integrated Pest Management

Integrated pest management is a collection of strategies to control roaches, mice, and other household pests by the least toxic methods, which include cleaning so well that there are no food sources to attract them and caulking up any cracks and openings through which bugs and mice can enter. If all else fails, there are some promising safer pesticides. For example, a product that operates with dry ice is about to come on the market to deal with bedbug infestations. The carbon dioxide it releases is the same substance that you exhale and that guides bedbugs to you during the night. The product uses dry ice to lure them into a trap.

The best advice I can give you is to contact reputable and licensed pest control operators and tell them you want to deal with your problem with the least toxic of their methods.

7. Check Recalls

Before you buy any paint, household product, appliance, or toy, go to www.CPSC.gov, search for recalled products, and see whether the item has been listed. Recalled products have been sold at major chain and department stores, but they are most likely to be found at bargain and factory outlet stores, on the Internet, in thrift shops, and in secondhand stores. Also keep in mind that it is illegal for you to sell a recalled product. You can be held liable if you sell someone a defective recalled item, even in a garage sale on your own property. So take a look at that Web site first.

8. Buy American

To preserve our jobs, we need to look for products that are made in the United States. You will also reduce the likelihood of buying recalled items, because most of the products that have been recalled were imported, especially those from China.

I say this knowing full well that the "made in the USA" label can lie. For example, all of the ingredients or the components may be manufactured in China and Bangladesh, and the product is merely assembled and packaged here. Yet that still provides jobs in this country for a few people.

I personally purchase American union-made goods whenever I have a choice, because I believe that the only way workers can protect themselves is by organizing. It is my experience that a lone worker asking an employer for safer working conditions will soon be unemployed. Only when many workers speak as one does the power on each side of the negotiating table become more balanced.

9. Maybe Buy Green

Remember that "green" usually applies to the safety of the environment. I think that *your* safety comes first. Although substances such as turpentine and citrus oil are biodegradable and considered green, they are not safe for you. And labels that proudly announce the product is green because it contains no VOCs or low VOCs merely mean that few, if any, smog-causing solvents are present. All of those other solvents that don't react with sunlight to create smog or damage the ozone layer, some of which are very toxic, may still be in the product.

Check the ingredients of green products just as you would any other item, and avoid any that contain toxic substances or whose ingredients are not revealed. If two products are equally safe for you and one is "green," buy the green one.

10. Choose with Care Whom to Believe

The only person you can really trust is yourself. And you know damn well that you sometimes choose to believe and say things that are untrue, for one reason or another. We all do.

Be very discriminating about whose opinions get your ear, especially on the Internet. For example, never bother reading material from a Web site that both describes a disease and sells the cure for it, don't read papers about air pollution on a site that is also selling air purifiers, and so on.

Instead, try to get your facts and science from governmental or educational sites. Even then, check the names of the authors of any peer-reviewed scientific article. These studies list the names of the authors and their affiliations. Continue to be skeptical until you know who the author works for. Even this may not be enough. I know one author who truthfully lists his job title at a prestigious university, but, unknown to casual readers of his studies, he has other, much more lucrative, income from consulting for the manufacturers of the products he studies.

You should also be skeptical about what I have written. I invite you to check my facts. I make no secret of my bias in favor of workers, unions, and consumers. It should be clear that I hold manufacturers responsible for most of the mess we are in. You may have noticed that I have refrained from making direct product recommendations in this book, except for some personal information about products I use. If I promoted particular products, you rightfully should ask whether I receive any financial compensation for this. If you investigate my financial assets and style of life, it will be pretty clear that I don't!

11. Protect Your Air

Don't use products in your home that release toxic air pollutants, such as solvent vapors, gases like formaldehyde, or dusts. That means avoiding many of the products we have discussed, including solvent-containing products; vinyl plastics, such as those in decorative wallpaper or window blinds that release phthalates, formaldehyde-emitting products, for example, furniture made of wood composites joined with formaldehyde-containing resins; products with strong fragrances; spray-can products; or smoke from burning any substance, ranging from candles to food.

Once these pollutants are released into the air, it is either difficult or impossible to get them out. Your only good option is to blow them outdoors with an exhaust fan and start with fresh air. That's not energy-efficient or green, but it's safe.

If, instead, you try to use an air purifier, you will find that it provides very limited air cleaning. If the pollutant is in the form of a dust, a HEPA filter air purifier may help, but the filter can only act on air it can draw into itself, so you may need one for every room. Gases and vapors are not captured by HEPA filters at all. Even the charcoal filters that are sold for capturing gases and vapors will absorb only some of them for a short time before the filter is spent.

Never use any air purifier that releases toxic ozone, such as negative ion generators, electrostatic precipitators, or ozone generators. It is far easier to keep harmful substances out of the air than to try to filter it.

12. Don't Detoxify

Sadly, it is also difficult or impossible to get pollutants out of your body once they are absorbed. The truth is, once those 212 complex chemical pollutants under study by the Centers for Disease Control are in your blood and tissues, they are there to stay. Once the lead and other toxic metals are in your bones, it's pretty much a done deal. Trying to remove them usually makes things worse.

Most of the complex organic pollutants are deposited in your fat cells and organs. The body has methods for getting them out of your body, but these metabolic processes are agonizingly slow, ranging from months and years to never. The only way to significantly reduce your body burden of these fatty-tissue contaminants is to lose weight. And if you lose weight too fast, one of the many reasons you will feel lousy is that those chemicals will have nowhere to go except into your blood. Some will be redeposited in the fat you have left, and the rest will be eliminated by the liver and the kidneys. On their way out, the pollution chemicals can give your organs one more toxic whack.

The lead that deposits in your bones has a twenty-five-year half-life, meaning that twenty-five years from now, one-half of the dose of lead you got today in your food, air, and water will be gone from your body. So, most of the lead you have absorbed will still be in your bones after you no longer have any use for your bones. Today, the CDC does not recommend chelation, which involves taking a drug to remove lead from bones, except in children with high levels and in cases of acute poisoning in adults. The studies that followed children after they were chelated in the 1970s and the 1980s show that the treatment did not improve their IQs or provide any long-term benefits. The CDC thinks that moving the lead from the bones to the bloodstream might be even more harmful than leaving it in place.

What about those doctors, healers, and herbalists who claim to be able to detoxify you—that is, get all of the harmful chemicals out of your body? Detox gurus are everywhere today: on TV, in the health-food store, running a makeshift sweat lodge in the Arizona desert, and even in some supposedly legitimate medical clinics and hospitals. Whenever you see them, run in the opposite direction.

If you are smart enough not to want to use potentially toxic and untested chemicals in your home, for gosh sake, don't let anyone use untested therapies that involve putting chemicals, natural or synthetic, down your gullet in pills or potions, injecting them into your bloodstream, or shoving them up your nether regions.

A coffee enema will make you feel terrific, of course, because you've had a bowel movement, and caffeine is absorbed faster by your colon than by your stomach. Remember, though, just because you feel good afterward does not prove you've been detoxified. If that was the test, the best detoxifiers would be morphine, booze, and other assorted recreational neurotoxicants.

One reason we can be fooled by the theories behind these cleansing therapies is that many of them started out as legitimate healthy practices. For example, Native Americans, Finns, Russians, and many other people have found that steam baths will cure a hangover and make you feel great. Yet excessive use of heat can cause dehydration, heat stroke, and kidney damage. Moderation and listening to your body are required when using these practices. Like it or not, however, none of these wonderful traditional practices will appreciably reduce your body's burden of industrial chemicals.

Do, instead, the only thing that works: take good care of yourself. You already know how. Eat greens and other good foods—but not too much. Get enough sleep. Take a good daily multiple vitamin and some extra vitamin C. Find people to love, and get a job that you at least like. And don't neglect those medical screening tests—even the dreaded colonoscopy, a legitimate reason to provide doctors access to your nether regions.

As for the toxic substances in your body, accept the fact you and everyone you see, old and young, are carrying some of these industrial chemicals around. One day we will probably be able to prove that these harmful substances are the reason for the National Cancer Institute statistics that show two in every five of us will be diagnosed with some form of cancer during their lives. The best strategy is to stay healthy and get checkups so that cancer is diagnosed early.

I know I'm going to lose some good friends with this advice. I advise you not to repeat what I've said to anyone who regularly engages in alternative practices like detoxification. Many people believe in these therapies with the same fervor and conviction that others reserve for their religion. But if I've got only one shot at telling you the truth in print, I'm taking it.

13. Be an Activist, Not a Crazy Person

In order to change the current process of putting untested chemicals into commerce, we need to take on the chemical manufacturers. Crazy people who want to resort to violence or verbal abuse to make their point only destroy our credibility. Instead, we first need to understand the people who run these industries. They are not the devil incarnate. They do not wake up every morning excited by the prospect of killing off more of us with their chemicals.

The chemical industry CEOs see themselves as people who worked hard to build their empires and personal fortunes. Yet once they achieved this goal, they fell prey to the Horatio Alger myth. Most seem to believe that anyone who worked as hard as they did could have achieved the same success. Their belief is unshaken by the fact that there are millions of other people who destroy their health with hard work, yet can't provide decent lives for themselves or their families. Chemical industry CEOs certainly do not see any of this as their responsibility, even though their own companies' policies include keeping the wages of their workers as low as possible or shipping jobs overseas, where the companies can pay a few cents a day for work that is longer and harder than any toil the CEOs have ever known.

It is not in the American tradition for successful people to admit that a combination of privilege, race, and genetics has far more to do with their success than hard work does. The bigger the empire they have built, and the more isolated they are from the daily life of the average citizen, the more defensive and conservative they are likely to become. This is wrong, but it is not evil. It is human nature. We had better understand it.

The most defensive CEOs are those of companies that owe their success to the development of products that have sickened or killed thousands of people. Representatives of companies such as Johns Manville, W.R. Grace, Georgia Pacific, and R.T. Vanderbilt, whose products contained asbestos, are in court every day somewhere in the world, defending against lawsuits brought by the dying or the families of the dead. If you saw or read their testimonies, as I have, you would know that they don't feel as if they have done anything wrong.

Therefore, you certainly can expect that the manufacturers of products whose ingredients are untested and cannot be *proved* to be associated with a particular disease, as asbestos can, will feel even more self-righteous. They don't believe there is any connection between their products and the excessive rates of cancer, autism, asthma, and other scourges of today, even though certain chemicals can cause some of these effects in animals. The fact that some phthalates, PCBs, brominated fire retardants, and a number of the other chemicals in our blood are known to cause cancer is irrelevant to them. These manufacturers feel that it was their right to make us the unknowing and unwilling lab rats in their vast experiments.

It doesn't matter to them that you would prefer not to have all of these chemicals in your body. "After all," they reason, "isn't this a small price to pay for a booming economy and the great diversity of products we made available to you?" The fact that you and I entered into this bargain for new products without knowing we would absorb their chemicals doesn't strike them as unfair.

Try to understand how they think. They feel justified and righteous. Manufacturers will fight the testing of their chemicals tooth-and-nail because they see testing as unnecessary and as an impediment to their "progress." I predict that they will even get around the European Union's testing requirements for a decade by switching to substitute chemicals that are equally untested.

Don't waste time expecting scientific studies, the plight of the manufacturers' own workers, or the health effects caused by their products to convince them to change their policies. The only directives they heed come from the courts and from regulators. We need to support the legislators and the organizations that work for regulatory change and that file product lawsuits. We can support bills like Senator Frank Lautenberg's Safe Chemicals Act of 2010 that revamps the Toxic Substances Control Act. We can get behind effective activist organizations such as Earthjustice, the Environmental Defense Fund, the Center for Environmental Health, the Environmental Working Group, and the New York Law & Environmental Justice Project. There are others, but these are the ones I try to support. I'm not employed or compensated by any of them.

I urge you to support these kinds of organizations and legislation because we are in great need of better consumer protection and chemical safety regulations. And if you don't want to pay for a governmental agency big enough to effectively enforce the new rules, consider supporting bills that include citizens' enforcement provisions like the one in Proposition 65. Then we can enforce the regulations ourselves and derive a profit from our efforts—a profit taken directly from the lawbreakers instead of out of our taxes.

If these strategies are successful, it will be our children and our children's children who will benefit. We need to strive for a world in which children will not be taking toxic chemicals into their bodies from their home and school environments.

As for you and me, it is a little late. We simply have to play the smartest game we can with the marked cards we were dealt by those sharks. Good luck to us all.

ACKNOWLEDGMENTS

Most of the people who helped me with this book were not aware they were doing so. They provided the research for many years before the book was even a thought in my mind. These are colleagues and friends of many years, who regularly feed and water me with great ideas, research, and health oddities that amuse and interest us. So when this book was proposed, I knew the files I have amassed from correspondence with these people could be used for many of the facts and figures I would need.

First, there is the chemist and EPA environmental scientist Cate Jenkins, whose nurturing started in 1977 when, with Michael McCann, we founded the nonprofit Center for Occupational Hazards.

Next, there are two people who began working with me in the 1980s. Eric Gertner, a cofounder of my current nonprofit, left a successful career as a Broadway lighting designer to go back to school in industrial hygiene; he worked many years specializing in hospital safety and infection control until his death in 2009. And Diana Bryan, teacher, artist, and expert at sailing the Internet in search of odd and quirky health stories—her untimely death midway through the writing of this book left the world a smaller, duller place.

Three of my board members, Toby Zausner, Elizabeth Northrup, and Kathy Hulce, were also instrumental. Toby is an artist with several advanced degrees and the writer of an inspiring book on the

211

effects of serious illnesses on the creative work of a number of artists. Kathy Hulce is a parent-activist, who with a handful of other very smart moms influenced the asbestos control and remediation policies of her Connecticut school district.

I wouldn't be the same writer without years of sharing information with the brilliant toxicologist Brian E. Lee, who worked many years for the U.S. Consumer Product Safety Commission and now has his own consulting firm. Or David Gordon, who is an industrial hygienist, a judo teacher, and the best ventilation engineer I've ever planned a building with. In addition, long time friends Sharon Campbell and Pat Sheffield are always on the watch for articles that they know will be of interest.

Some credit must go to Leonard Lopate, whose regular interviews with me on WNYC Radio helped me find clear and simple ways to explain complex health issues.

These people are my collaborators and technical kinfolk. They contributed far more than mere facts to this book. They also provided their tough, no-nonsense, show-me-proof attitudes that I hope I can also pass on to readers.

Appendix A
DETERGENT ADDITIVES

This list includes hundreds of chemicals. The detergents, plus this soup of additives and all of their degradation products, can be floating about in our waste water. It is difficult to imagine how we will ever know the environmental fate of all of these chemicals or their toxicity to us, especially in combination with one another.

Acids and alkalies are used to adjust the pH to fit the detergent. Acidity is useful in removing mineral buildup; alkalinity helps remove acidic, fatty, and oily soils; and enzyme detergents require a more neutral pH. Examples: acetic acid, citric acid, ammonium hydroxide, and the ethanolamines. They can be corrosive or irritating to the skin or to the respiratory system.

Antimicrobial agents kill or inhibit the growth of microorganisms that cause disease or odor. Examples: pine oil, quaternary ammonium compounds, sodium hypochlorite, and powerful biocides such as triclocarban and triclosan. These are either corrosive or sensitizing or they are biocides that may be able to kill microorganisms in the environment as well.

Antiredeposition agents prevent soil from resettling on laundry and dishware during the wash. Examples: carboxymethylcellulose, polycarboxylates, polyethylene glycol, and sodium silicate.

These do not appear to be very toxic, but not much is known about the long-term effects of inhaling particles of polycarboxylates and polyethylene glycol.

Bleaches help whiten, brighten, and remove stains. Examples: sodium hypochlorite (chlorine bleach), sodium perborate, and sodium percarbonate (oxygen bleaches may be combined with an activator). The bleaches are corrosive.

Bleach activators enhance or activate bleaches; for example, the high-performance peroxygen bleach activator and nonanoylbenzene sulfonate. Not much is known about nonanoylbenzene sulfonate's toxicity.

Builders reduce water hardness to allow better surfactant performance. Examples: sodium tripolyphosphate (yes, some products still contain sources of phosphates), sodium citrate, sodium carbonate, and zeolite. These do not appear to be toxic, but some mineral sources of zeolite are contaminated with fibrous minerals, such as asbestos.

Corrosion inhibitors protect metal machine parts and utensils. Example: sodium silicate. They are not considered to be toxic.

Dye transfer inhibitors keep fabrics from bleeding color onto one another. These are complex organic chemicals called ligands that have a metal ion, such as manganese, in the center. Most dyes are in chemical classes of concern, and manganese is a neurotoxic metal.

Enzymes catalyze the destruction of specific types of soil for removal by detergent. Enzymes are a unique class of proteins formed in living cells. These very large molecules (with molecular weights of ten thousand to a million or more) are capable of breaking down certain substances, such as fats, blood, and starch. They are also able to help break down the detergent itself to make the product more biodegradable. Examples: amylase, lipase, protease, and cellulase. They are associated with allergic reactions of the skin and the respiratory system.

A fabric shape-retention aid (introduced in 2003) called Fiberflex is a novel cationic aminosilicone that deposits on fabric even in the presence of high levels of surfactant. Nothing could be found on the toxicity of this chemical.

Fabric-softening agents soften and control static electricity in fabric. Example: quaternary ammonium compounds. Most quaternary ammonium compounds appear to be sensitizers.

Fluorescent whitening agents and optical brighteners attach to the fabric to enhance brightness in bright light. Examples: stilbene disulfonates and coumarin derivatives. The stilbene disulfonates and the coumarin derivatives function as fluorescent dyes by changing ultraviolet light to blue-white light to make the wash look whiter. Yet their toxicity has been insufficiently studied.

Fragrances mask odors of other ingredients and provide brand identity and a fresh scent to laundry. Fragrances are well known to cause allergies and sensitization in many people.

Hydrotropes ensure product homogeneity by preventing liquids from separating. Examples: cumene sulfonates, ethanol, toluene sulfonates, and xylene sulfonates. Ethanol is one of the least toxic of the solvents. Not much could be found on the toxicity of the other chemicals.

Preservatives protect the product from oxidation, discoloration, and bacterial attack. Examples: butylated hydroxytoluene, ethylenediaminetetraacetic acid (EDTA), formaldehyde, and glutaraldehyde. Formaldehyde and glutaraldehyde are sensitizers and irritants, and formaldehyde is a carcinogen. EDTA has caused allergies.

Solvents prevent separation or deterioration in liquids and dissolve organic soils. Examples: ethanol, isopropyl alcohol, and propylene glycol. All solvents are toxic, but these are some of the least toxic.

Suds-control agents stabilize or suppress sudsing. Examples of stabilizers: alkanolamides and alkylamine oxides. Examples of suppressors: alkyl phosphates, silicones, and soap. These are classes of chemicals with many members. Without more specificity, not much can be said.

Appendix B

EVALUATING THE MATERIAL
SAFETY DATA SHEET

Once you have the MSDS and know whether the product is a single component or a mixture, you are ready to go through the MSDS critically. Following is a summary of the basic items that either are required or should be present on the MSDS. I have organized the information as it would be found on the most common MSDS form, but the information could be presented in a different order. The more items in the following list that you find on the MSDS you are evaluating, usually the better it is.

Section I: Product and Company Identification

Identity of the product. The identifying chemical name or product name should be the same as that on the container label.

Emergency and technical information telephone number(s). A twenty-four-hour U.S. phone number must be included for emergencies. It does not need to be toll-free. Good manufacturers also provide a number you can call to get answers to your technical questions about the product.

Name/address of manufacturer or importer. Be sure that this name is exactly the same as the name of the manufacturer listed on the product label. Be sure the address is a U.S. address and is complete, that is, one at which you could reach the manufacturer.

Date prepared and name of the preparer. The date the MSDS was prepared and any later revision date need to be listed. MSDSs are invalid in Canada if they are more than three years old, but U.S. MSDSs can be ancient. The signature of the preparer is optional.

Section II: Hazardous Ingredients/Identity Data

Specific chemical name/identity. If the product is a single chemical, the name should be the same as in section I.

Common name(s). The product's common name, synonyms, and chemical class should be included, if it has the latter.

CAS number (Chemical Abstracts Service registry number). This is optional, but good MSDSs provide them.

Chemicals in products that are mixtures. Any chemical for which there is even one study that shows it may be capable of causing harm should be listed. Toxic chemicals that make up more than 1 percent of the product by weight must be listed. Cancer-causing chemicals that consist of 0.1 percent or more by weight of the product must be listed.

It is unacceptable to refuse to list ingredients either by citing a review of a toxicologist as required by ASTM D 4236 (see chapter 2), or by stating that none of the ingredients have OSHA standards. Many toxic substances do not have OSHA standards.

Trade secret exemptions. The identities of ingredients can be withheld by the manufacturer if they are trade secrets or proprietary. I do not recommend using products that are trade secrets in the home or with children.

Air-quality standards. If there are any OSHA permissible exposure limits (PELs) or American Conference of Governmental Industrial Hygienists (ACGIH) limits (TLVs), they should be listed here. (See chapter 9 for more information.) If none of these limits are listed, there are not enough data on inhalation exposure for these agencies to set one. You should avoid inhaling the substance.

Good manufacturers will list other limits here, such as the MAKs (Federal Republic of Germany Maximum Concentration Values).

Odor threshold (optional). The odor threshold (OT) is the concentration in air at which the chemical can be detected by odor. It is required on Canadian MSDSs when it is known.

Percent (optional). The percentages of each ingredient may be listed.

Section III: Physical/Chemical Characteristics

Boiling point (BP). The BP is the temperature at which the substance changes rapidly, usually with bubbling, from a liquid to a vapor.

Melting point (MP). This is applicable only to solid materials. The MP is the temperature at which a solid changes to a liquid.

Vapor pressure (VP) (mm Hg). The VP is the pressure exerted by a saturated vapor above its own liquid in a closed container. With a little training, workers can learn to use the VPs to determine how quickly the material becomes airborne.

Vapor density (VD) (Air = 1). The VD is the weight of a vapor or a gas compared to an equal volume of air. Materials with a VD of less than 1.0 are lighter than air. Materials with a VD that is greater than 1.0 are heavier than air. Flammable vapors that are heavier than air can spread to sources of ignition and flash back to the source.

Solubility in water. This term represents the amount by weight that will dissolve in water at ambient temperatures. Solubility is important in determining suitable cleanup and extinguishing methods.

Appearance and odor. Comparing this description to the actual product is a way to be sure the right MSDS has been obtained.

Specific gravity (SG). The SG describes the heaviness of a material compared to a reference substance. When the reference substance is water ($H_2O = 1$), it indicates whether the material will float or sink in water.

Evaporation rate. This is the rate at which a material will vaporize (volatilize, evaporate) from the liquid or solid state when compared to another material.

Section IV: Fire and Explosion Hazard Data

Flash point. This is the lowest temperature at which a flammable liquid gives off sufficient vapor to form an ignitable mixture with air near its surface or within a vessel. If the flash point temperature is 100 degrees Fahrenheit or lower, the material is flammable and a fire hazard. Flashpoints above 100 degrees are still combustible and a hazard.

Flammable limits. Only applicable to flammable liquids and gases, these are the minimum and maximum concentrations in air between which ignition can occur.

Extinguishing media. This is the type of extinguisher or suppression system that is needed to put out a fire involving the substance.

Special fire-fighting procedures. This lists any special methods that are needed to fight fires involving the substance. Peroxides such as those used to cure polyester resins, for example, supply oxygen when burned and cannot be extinguished by ordinary methods that smother or cut off air.

Unusual fire and explosion hazards. This applies to chemicals that can ignite spontaneously or exhibit some unusual fire or explosion characteristics.

Section V: Reactivity Data

This section covers very technical data, including chemical stability, chemicals with which the product would react dangerously if mixed, and hazardous chemicals that are emitted when the product is burned. If you are not trained to read and understand these data, *never* experiment with the product or use it in any way other than how the manufacturer directs.

Section VI: Health Hazard Data

Routes of entry. These are the ways this product could enter your body. They are inhalation, skin contact, and ingestion. (See chapter 8 for details.)

Acute data. This section should include LD50 and LC50 data.

Chronic. This section should report known chronic hazards, such as cancer, reproductive or developmental damage, neurological or other organ damage to animals or humans related to repeated or long-term exposure. *Failure to see data in this section should never be interpreted to mean that the material has no chronic hazards.*

Carcinogenicity. There are three agencies whose opinions regarding carcinogenicity must be reported on MSDSs. These are the NTP (the National Toxicology Program), the IARC (the International Agency for Research on Cancer), and OSHA. The categories for these agencies are as follows:

NTP

K: Known to be a human carcinogen.

R: Reasonably anticipated to be a carcinogen from limited evidence in humans, sufficient evidence in experimental animals, or some combination of these.

IARC

1: Carcinogenic to humans: sufficient evidence of carcinogenicity.

2A: Probably carcinogenic to humans; limited human evidence; sufficient evidence in experimental animals.

2B: Possibly carcinogenic to humans; limited human evidence in the absence of sufficient evidence in experimental animals.

3: Unclassifiable as to carcinogenicity to humans.

4: Probably not carcinogenic to humans.

OSHA

X: Carcinogen defined with no further categorization.

If the MSDS says this chemical is not listed as a carcinogen by these agencies, assume that it has not been sufficiently tested for cancer.

Reproductive hazards. Data on effects on the fetus or the male and female reproductive systems would be listed here. Very few chemicals have been studied for these effects.

California Proposition 65 warnings. Although this is optional, many MSDSs will include whether the chemical is considered a carcinogen or a reproductive or development hazard under Proposition 65.

Signs and symptoms of exposure. These are usually acute large-dose symptoms, because chronic exposure often produces no clear symptoms for years.

Medical conditions aggravated by exposure. Here the MSDS should list medical conditions that are known or suspected to be exacerbated by the chemical. For example, chemicals that are respiratory irritants may aggravate asthma or emphysema.

Emergency and first-aid procedures. These should be clearly listed here.

Section VII: Precautions for Safe Handling/Use

Steps to be taken if the material is released or spilled. The MSDS should list methods for spill control.

Waste-disposal method. Unless the material can be rendered completely innocuous, MSDSs usually only advise users to dispose of the material in accordance with local, state, and federal regulations, because these regulations vary so greatly from location to location.

Precautions to be taken in handling and storing. Here the MSDS should list safe storage conditions (e.g., a cool, dry area).

Other precautions. If needed, other precautions should include any special equipment that would be necessary or that is required to be held in a storage area with the material.

Section VIII: Control Measures

This section should provide information about protective equipment that is needed for normal use of the product. The manufacturer decides what constitutes "normal use."

Respiratory protection (specific type). If respiratory protection is needed during normal use, a good MSDS tells the user whether there is a filter or a cartridge capable of collecting the substance or whether an air-supplied system will be necessary. The MSDS cannot be completely specific about respiratory protection, however, because the type of respirator is determined by the concentration of the substance in the air.

Ventilation. If ventilation is needed during normal use, a good MSDS specifies the type of ventilation system that provides proper protection. Merely advising the consumer to "Use with good ventilation" is not very helpful.

Protective gloves. Good MSDSs list the specific type of glove material needed (rubber, nitrile, etc.) and other glove attributes. It is the user's responsibility to contact the technical department of the glove supplier and obtain precise information about glove permeability.

Eye protection. Good MSDSs indicate the type of eyewear that is needed.

Other protective clothing or equipment. If additional protection, such as aprons, boots, face shields, or eye-wash stations, is required, it should be listed here.

Work/hygienic practices. Practices such as proper daily cleanup methods and equipment after normal use should be detailed here.

Other Sections

There may be additional information on environmental hazards, but it is not directly relevant to your health and safety.

Appendix C
NEW YORK DISCLOSURE
AMENDMENT

A memorandum filed with Assembly Bill Number 6963-A titled "An Act to . . . amend the environmental conservation law, in relation to the regulation of household cleansing products" was signed by then governor Nelson Rockefeller in June 1971. That memorandum clearly defines the law's intent as follows:

Labeling:

In the use of household cleansing products, the consumer has been given little or no information about the ingredients of the product or the impact of these ingredients upon the environment. No consumer wishing to purchase a detergent for washing clothes or dishes or for cleansing the human body, can realistically gauge the detrimental effects of such products unless informed as to the ingredients of the product.

Legislation enacted last year requiring that detergents and soap sold after January 1, 1971 be plainly labelled as to trisodium phosphate content is helpful. The technical wording of the law is open to varying interpretations, however, which could result in different labelling descriptions and consequent confusion to the consumer.

This bill will obviate misunderstandings under present law by requiring labelling of ingredients of household products that the Environmental Conservation Commissioner determines may affect adversely human health or the environment including phosphates and, in addition, provide the consumer with meaningful ingredient information on a recommended use level basis.

Then further on in the memorandum, under "Phosphates," it says,

By delaying outright elimination of phosphorus from household cleansing products, the bill recognizes the serious problems of developing phosphate substitutes that will not be more harmful to our health and environment than phosphates themselves. The legislation will be effective in 1972, in order to enable the industry to develop the necessary substitutes and to assure the safety and acceptability of such substitutes.

The governor's memorandum went on to explain that the law's phosphate restrictions "should be recognized as a preliminary step to avoid possible further undesirable ecological changes in our State's waters" and represent "the minimum requirement which can be realistically justified at this time." In time, it may be found that "other ingredients of washing compounds may be found to adversely affect human health and the environment." So the memorandum declares that

Accordingly, the bill will permit the Commissioner of Environmental Conservation to set further restrictions on ingredients of household detergent products based on the effect those products may have on human health and the environment.

This gave the commissioner the right to restrict any ingredients without having to legislate chemical by chemical.

In 1976, the New York State Department of Environmental Conservation promulgated regulations implementing the cleaning products law. These regulations were published in Part 659 in chapter 6 of the New York Code of Rules and Regulations (6 NYCRR

Part 659). Of particular importance is the part of the regulations codified as §659.6 Disclosure of Information.

(a) Manufacturers of household cleansing products distributed, sold or offered for sale in this State shall furnish to the commissioner for public record such information regarding such products as the commissioner may require, in such form as may be prescribed by the commissioner.

NOTES

Preface

1   It is important to be able to prove a statement like this—and I can. In 1964, I was married to Jack Holzhueter, who was and still is a Wisconsin state historian with a mind like a file cabinet. When I told Jack what Littleton had said, he couldn't believe it. At the time, we were living in a Frank Lloyd Wright house that Littleton had expressed an interest in seeing, so Jack invited him over. Jack asked Littleton the same question and got the same answer. So, if you doubt my account, I'll put you in touch with Jack Holzhueter, who, bless his heart, became an instant women's rights advocate after this incident.

2   I also told this story in a magazine article and, in 2004, the then chair of the University of Wisconsin Art Department, Jim Escalante, sent a formal letter of apology. It's forty years late but deeply appreciated.

1. Your Body Is a Chemistry Experiment

1   G. Werth, "Disturbances of the Heredity Pattern, and Formation of Tumors by Experimental Tissue Anoxia," *Arzneimittel-Forschung*, vol. 8, pp. 735–744, 1958.

2   Neil A. Littlefield, et al., "Chronic Toxicity and Carcinogenicity Studies of Gentian Violet in Mice," *Fundamentals of Applied Toxicology*, vol. 5, pp. 902–912, 1985.

3   Neil A. Littlefield, et al., "Chronic Toxicity/Carcinogenicity Studies of Gentian Violet in Fischer 344 Rats: Two-Generation Exposure," *Food and Chemical Toxicology*, vol. 27, no. 4, pp. 239–247, 1989.

4   *Bureau of National Affairs-Occupational Safety and Health Reporter*, vol. 24, no. 5, June 29, 1994.

5   *Federal Register*, vol. 64, pp. 4535–4540, esp. 4538, January 29, 1999. This document reclassifies phenolphthalein and danthron from Category I to Category II.

6   *Federal Register*, vol. 64, pp. 4535–4540, esp. 4537.

7   T. Leon Lassiter, et al., "Exposure of Neonatal Rats to Parathion Elicits Sex-Selective Programming of Metabolism and Alters the Response to a High Fat Diet," *Environmental Health Perspectives*, vol. 116, no. 11, pp. 1456–1462, 2008.

226

2. Dying for Your (Child's) Art

1   The ACMI was once called the Crayon, Water Color and Craft Institute. At the Center for Occupational Hazards (later called the Center for Safety in the Arts), we had a plastic package of this papier-mâché product to use as an example of the labeling problem.

2   See the entire article: Jeffry R. Young, "Student's Death at SUNY Plattsburgh Was Caused by Fraternity Hazing, Police Say," *Chronicle of Higher Education*, reprinted in *The Stony Brook Statesman*, vol. XLVII, no. 55, May 5, 2003, p. 5.

3   For Canadian readers, almost identical rules are in the Canadian Federal Hazardous Products Act.

4   Emilio Sartorelli, et al., "Lead Silicate Toxicity: A Comparison among Different Compounds" (University of Siena), *Environmental Research*, vol. 36, pp. 420–425, 1985.

5   *Morbidity and Mortality Weekly Report*, Centers for Disease Control, vol. 41, no. 42, pp. 781–783, October 23, 1992.

6   Ibid.

7   Ashley Rose Witt, a minor, by and through her mother and natural guardian, Patty Moore and Ronald Witt vs. Duncan Enterprises; American Art Clay, Co.; Mayco Colors, Inc.; C and R Products, Inc.; and Robert R. Umhoefer, Inc., in the Circuit Court, Sixth Judicial Circuit of Florida, Pinellas Co., Civil Division, No. 92-5392-CI-20. The case settled for approximately $500,000. See also, Sherrell McClendon, wife of/and Richard A. Duggan Jr., individually and as natural tutors of the minors, Richard A. Duggan, III, Jordan E. Duggan, and Michelle L. Duggan. vs. Duncan Ceramics D/B/A/ Duncan, Mayco, D/B/A Mayco Colors, and Allstate Insurance Company USDC, in the U.S. District Court, Eastern District of Louisiana, No. 94-2183. The case settled for approximately $865,000.

8   Taken from page 69 of the deposition given on April 1, 1991, in the Ashley Rose Witt case.

9   Press release, ACMI, Inc., Boston, *Institute Items*, vol. 39, no. 4, December 1997.

10   *Daily Hues*, Golden Artist's Colors, Inc., pp. 1–2, April 2000.

11   "EPA Announces Public Health Emergency in Libby, Montana; EPA to Move Aggressively in Cleanup and HHS to Assist Area Residents with Medical Care," Environmental Protection Agency Press Release, June 17, 2009. See also, Patricia A. Sullivan, "Vermiculite, Respiratory Disease, and Asbestos Exposure in Libby, Montana: Update of a Cohort Mortality Study," *Environmental Health Perspectives*, vol. 115, no. 4, April 2007. Available online at http://ehp03.niehs.nih.gov/article/fetchArticle.action?articleURI=info:doi/10.1289/ehp.9481.

12   M. Kleinfeld, J. Messite, O. Kooyman, et al., "Mortality among Talc Miners and Millers in New York State," *Archives of Environmental Health*, vol. 14, pp. 663–667, 1967.

13   M. Kleinfeld, J. Messite, and M. H. Zaki, "Mortality Experiences among Talc Workers: A Follow-up Study," *Journal of Occupational Medicine*, vol. 16, pp. 345–349, 1974. Arthur N. Rohl and Arthur M. Langer, "Identification and Quantitation of Asbestos in Talc," *Environmental Health Perspectives*, vol. 9, pp. 95–109, 1974.

14   John M. Dement, et al., NIOSH Technical Report: *Occupational Exposure to Talc Containing Asbestos (Morbidity, Mortality, and Environmental Studies of Miners and Millers)*, NIOSH, 1980.

15 M. Rossol, "In Memoriam," *Art Hazards News*, Center for Occupational Hazards, p. 1, November 1981.

16 Andrew Schneider and Carol Smith, various articles in the *Seattle Post-Intelligencer*, May 23, 24, 26, 27, 30, and June 1, 2000; e-mails between ASTM D01.57 committee members; and reports from other news media.

17 The full statement was posted online at www.acminet.org/ACMI_Response.htm, but is no longer there. The site seems to have been sanitized of any mention of talc except for a link that led to a nineteen-page study submitted to the Consumer Product Safety Commission by Dr. Stopford. It quantifies the amounts of asbestos fibers by Stopford's definition that are in the talcs and calculates the exposures to artists based on studies he made of artists, which in my opinion does not reflect the way most artists use their materials. He concludes that if the talc was used in art materials, his calculations indicate the risk "is considerably less than that risk considered acceptable to either USEPA or OEHHA." I have to wonder why working with art materials should ever involve any level of exposure to asbestos fibers. Perhaps determining if the risk is acceptable or not should be left to the artists themselves or the parents of the children using art materials.

18 Personal communication, June 29, 2007.

3. Calling a Product Green Doesn't Make It Stop Being Poison

1 Phthalates banned by the CPSC in children's toys or child-care articles at levels greater than 0.1% are DEHP (di-2-ethylhexyl phthalate), and DBP (dibutyl phthalate). The phthalates banned at the same level in toys or articles that could be put in a child's mouth are BBP (benzyl butyl phthalate), DINP (diisononyl phthalate), DIDP (diisodecyl phthalate), and DNOP (di-n-octyl phthalate). California also regulates DnHP (di-n-hexyl phthalate) under Proposition 65.

2 Hazardous Substances Fact Sheet, New Jersey Department of Health, 2-butoxyethanol, latest revision: August 2008. This is one of over 1,600 data sheets that can be accessed at http://web.doh.state.nj.us/rtkhsfs/indexfs.aspx. You can search for chemicals by name or CAS number. These data sheets are updated regularly.

3 *Federal Register*, vol. 64, pp. 69358–69364, December 10, 1999; quote is from p. 69359.

4 You can learn more about this study, called "Hidden Hazards: Health Impacts of Toxins in Polymer Clays," by visiting the Web site www.vpirg.org or writing to VPIRG, 141 Main Street, Suite 6, Montpelier, VT 05602. Or you can get it directly from www.uspirg.org/uploads/Zu/sM/SusMU1w2maKOQllc4uVn4A/HiddenHazards.pdf.

5 Woodhall Stopford, "Questions Concerning the Risk Assessment for Polymer Clays," October 23, 2000. This document is only available from VPIRG and other researchers who obtained a copy in the past. It is no longer available from Dr. Woodhall Stopford's Web site. In this document, Dr. Stopford stated that "no more than 25% of polymer clay weight would be made up of phthalate ester plasticizers."

6 H. M. Stapleton, J. G. Allen, S. M. Kelly, et al., "Alternate and New Brominated Flame Retardants Detected in U.S. House Dust," *Environmental Science and Technology*, vol. 42, no. 18, 6910–6916, 2008.

4. "All-Natural" Doesn't Mean Safe, Either

1   *Federal Register*, vol. 62, pp. 33089, June 18, 1997.

2   Martin Stote, "Fashion Girl Killed by Her Special Hair Fixing Glue," *Express* (UK), June 9, 2000.

3   21 CFR 801.437(h).

4   "Lemon appeal," *Chemical & Engineering News*, June 26, 2006, p. 56. This short article quotes Lia Leendertz, a gardening expert, from a British article in the *Guardian*'s weekend supplement (May 20, 2006, p. 104). She notes that tiger worms inhabit compost heaps and help recycle stale bread, fruit and vegetable waste, used teabags, and other organic waste. Yet the worms are put off by the antiseptic properties of d-limonene. She suggests keeping citrus peels in a separate bin until they turn furry and green, indicating that the d-limonene is degraded and the peels will be accepted by the worms.

5   The *Federal Register* proposed rule was published January 18, 1995 (*Federal Register*, vol. 60, p. 3607), and comments/petitions were published January 31, 1995 (*Federal Register*, vol. 60, p. 64164).

6   *Federal Register*, vol. 61, pp. 11359–11362, March 20, 1996; *Federal Register*, vol. 62, pp. 25518–25524, May 9, 1997.

7   *Federal Register*, vol. 61, pp. 50685, September 26, 1996.

8   Richard J. Lewis, *Sax's Dangerous Properties of Industrial Materials*, 8th ed. (New York: Van Nostrand Reinhold, 1992), p. 2117.

9   "Grumtine Odor a Hazard?" *Art Hazards News*, Center for Occupational Hazards, vol. 6, no. 6, July 1982.

10 *Federal Register*, vol. 62, pp. 8659–8663, February 26, 1997.

11 "Toxicology and Carcinogenesis Studies of d-Limonene in F344/N Rats and B6C3F1 Mice (Gavage Studies)" (TR 347), NTP Public Information Office, Research Triangle Park, NC, January 1990.

12 Jill D. Haag, et al., "Limonene-Induced Regression of Mammary Carcinomas," *Cancer Research*, vol. 52, pp. 4021–4026, July 15, 1992.

13 Randy L. Jirtle, et al., "Increased Mannose 6-Phosphate/Insulin-like Growth Factor II Receptor and Transforming Growth Factor B1 Levels during Monoterpene-Induced Regression of Mammary Tumors," *Cancer Research*, vol. 53, pp. 3849–3852, September 1, 1993.

14 "d-Limonene," *Workplace Environmental Exposure Level Guide*, American Industrial Hygiene Association, Fairfax, VA, 1993.

15 *Federal Register*, vol. 68, pp. 65585–65619, November 20, 2003. Part III. EPA 40 CFR Parts 260 and 261, "Hazardous Waste Management System: Identification and Listing of Hazardous Waste: Conditional Exclusions from Hazardous Waste and Solid Waste for Solvent-Contaminated Industrial Wipes"; Proposed Rule, p. 65600.

16 Michael McCann, *Artist Beware*, 2nd ed. (New York: Lyons & Burford, 1993), p. 181.

17 There were other standards for d-limonene in the United States in the past. The American Industrial Hygiene Association (AIHA) set a Workplace Environmental Exposure Limit of 30 ppm for d-limonene in the 1990s, but it was withdrawn around 2005 without explanation. See the yearly *Workplace Environmental Exposure Level Guides*, AIHA, 2700 Prosperity Avenue, Suite 250, Fairfax, VA 22031.

18   The International Agency for Research on Cancer lists styrene in category 2B.

19   J. Raloff, "Lemon-Scented Products Spawn Pollutants," *Science News*, vol. 158, p. 375, December 9, 2000.

20   Xiaoyu Liu, et al., "Full-Scale Chamber Investigation and Simulation of Air Freshener Emissions in the Presence of Ozone," *Environmental Science and Technology*, vol. 38, no. 10, pp. 2802–2812, 2004.

21   The 2009 MSDS is a "globally harmonized" version, meaning that the phrasing is consistent with the European Unions and other countries' standards. In this case, the new wording leaves you to determine what the full implications of "no data" mean, rather than being more explicit as the earlier versions were.

22   Derek V. Henley, Natasha Lipson, Kenneth S. Korach, and Clifford A. Bloch, "Prepubertal Gynecomastia Linked to Lavender and Tea Tree Oils," *New England Journal of Medicine*, vol. 356, no. 5, pp. 479–485, February 1, 2007.

23   You can see these data at www.nih.gov/news/pr/jan2007/niehs-31.htm. By doing a Google search for "lavender oil," you can also find several entries that say that it is not responsible for the breast development in boys, but these Web sites appear to be maintained by sellers of the oil.

24   *Federal Register*, vol. 63, pp. 68775–68777, December 14, 1998.

25   Ibid.

26   *Physicians' Bulletin*, San Diego Department of Health Services, May 1996, reprinting Press Release no. 31-96 from the California Department of Health Services, Sacramento.

27   *Mortality and Morbidity Weekly Report*, Centers for Disease Control, vol. 45, no. 19, pp. 400–403, May 17, 1996.

28   Ibid., vol. 45, no. 29, pp. 633–635, July 26, 1996.

29   "Wood Dust," *Documentation of TLVs and BEIs*, American Conference of Governmental Industrial Hygienists, pp. 1728–1731, 1997.

5. Why Not Just Use Soap?

1   This mechanism is not the same in the special case of the nonionic and some cationic detergents. Yet these detergents are not very common in household products.

2   J. Dachs, D. A. Van Ry, and S. J. Eisenreich, "Occurrence of Estrogenic Nonylphenols in the Urban and Coastal Atmosphere of the Lower Hudson River Estuary," *Environmental Science and Technology*, vol. 33, pp. 2676–2679, 1999.

3   *Federal Register*, vol. 72, pp. 50954–50955, September 5, 2007.

6. Of Wall Paint and Face Paint

1   R. E. Train, "Decision of the Administrator on the Cancellation of Pesticides Containing Mercury," EPA, February 17, 1976, FIFRA dockets no. 246, et al., *Federal Register*, vol. 41, p. 76; R. E. Train, "Decision of the Administrator on Reconsideration," EPA, May 27, 1976, FIFRA dockets no. 246, et al.

2   *Morbidity and Mortality Weekly Report*, Centers for Disease Control, vol. 39, no. 8, pp. 125–126, March 2, 1990.

3   *Federal Register*, vol. 56, pp. 31403–31405, July 10, 1991. Troy Chemical Corporation's Troysan PMA-100 and Cosan Chemical Corporation's Cosan PMA-100, two phenylmercuric acetate biocides, were canceled effective July 1, 1991, at the request of their makers. The EPA permitted the sale and distribution of existing stocks until September 30, 1991.

4   Common "in-the-can" biocides include substances in one of two classes: the iso-thiazolinone class or the amine adduct class.

5   Common dry film biocides include chlorothalonil, n-octyl isothiazolin, iodoproy-nylbutyl carbamate (IPBC), or zinc pyrithione. Products that specifically advertise their antifungal properties such as KILZ are likely to actually identify their biocide. Other paints usually do not.

6   Per www.cfsan.fda.gov/~dms/cos-tan4.html as of 2004. The Web site still said basically the same thing in 2009, but the text no longer included the numbers of the regulations nor did it quote the rule.

7   Ibid.

8   Susan Green, "Oil Secret Has Nasty Side Effect," *Denver Post*, July 24, 2008.

7. You Have the Right to Know

1   *Federal Register*, vol. 74, pp. 50279–50549, September 30, 2009.

2   Globally Harmonized System of Classification and Labelling of Chemicals, 3rd rev. ed., United Nations Web site.

8. Your Air Filter May Be Polluting Your Air

1   S. G. Lilley, T. M. Florence, and J. L. Stauber, "The Use of Sweat to Monitor Lead Absorption through the Skin," *Science of the Total Environment*, vol. 76, pp. 267–278, 1988. This study was financed by a grant from the Australian National Occupational Health and Safety Commission and was also presented in the letters department of the journal *Lancet*. "Skin Absorption of Lead," pp. 157–158, July 16, 1988; J. L. Stauber, T. M. Florence, B. L. Gulson, and L. S. Dale, "Percutaneous Absorption of Inorganic Lead Compounds," *Science of the Total Environment*, vol. 145, pp. 55–70, 1994; Sun Chee-Ching, et al., "Percutaneous Absorption of Inorganic Lead Compounds," *AIHA Journal*, vol. 63, pp. 641–646, September–October 2002.

2   A team headed by Elizabeth Triche of the Yale University School of Medicine studied 691 women with three- to five-month-old infants from nonsmoking households in and around Roanoke, Virginia. Sixty-one of the mothers had asthma, signaling that their babies were at risk of developing the disease. The researchers collected daily respiratory data, as reported by the mothers, on all of the children for eighty-three days in the summer—the peak ozone season. These data were correlated with outdoor air pollutant levels.

As ozone rose, so did the risk of wheezing and troubled breathing in the babies. Other pollutants, such as fine particulates, didn't show that correlation. Each 11.8 parts per billion (ppb) increase in average daily concentrations in ozone increased the likelihood of wheezing by 41 percent in all infants and 91 percent in those with asthmatic moms. Each 11.8 ppb increase in ozone also increased the risk of labored breathing by almost 30 percent in all of the infants. Ozone was not associated with cough.

The mean concentration for maximum eight-hour average ozone levels during the 166 days of the study was 54.5 ppb. Peak measurements averaged 60.8 ppb. These levels did not exceed the EPA's moderate air quality eight-hour standard for ozone. Elizabeth Triche, J. F. Gent, T. R. Holford, K. Belanger, M. B. Bracken, et al., "Low-Level Ozone Exposure and Respiratory Symptoms in Infants," *Environmental Health Perspectives*, vol. 14, no. 6, pp. 911–916, June 2006.

3 "Ozone Generators: Two Judged Not Acceptable," *Consumer Reports*, p. 661, October 1992, and "Ozone Generators Generate Prison Terms for Couple," Paula Kurtzweil, *FDA Consumer*, November–December, pp. 36–37, 1999.

4 Fred Brown, "Ozone Purifier Maker Found Guilty of Misleading Advertising, Minnesota Fines Alpine Air Products," *Indoor Air Review*, p. 11, October 1992.

5 "'Air Purifier' Manufacturer Ordered to Pay $1.49 Million," Press Release 154, U.S. Department of Justice, April 09, 2001, www.justice.gov/opa/pr/2001/April/154civ.htm.

6 "Proposed Settlement in Sharper Image Air Purifiers Case," *Consumer Reports*, www.ConsumerReports.org, February 2007.

7 Pallavi Gogoi, "Dim Prospects for Sharper Image," *Bloomberg Businessweek*, October 19, 2007. "Sharper Image Dims," Eva Woo, *Bloomberg Businessweek*, February 21, 2008, www.businessweek.com.

9. Silver Socks Rocked by Toxic Shocker!

1 Try M. Benn and Paul Westerhoff, "Nanoparticle Silver Released into Water from Commercially Available Sock Fabrics," *Environmental Science and Technology*, vol. 42, no. 11, April 9, 2008, pp., 4133–4139, also reported in "Toxic Socks," Rachel Petkewich, *Chemical and Engineering News, April* 14, 2008, p. 10.

2 L. Geranio, M. Heuberger, and B. Nowack, "The Behavior of Silver Nanotextiles during Washing," *Environmental Science and Technology*, vol. 43, no. 21, pp. 8113–8118, 2009.

3 *Federal Register*, vol. 74, pp. 30070–30073, June 24, 2009.

4 Alison Elder, et al., "Translocation of Inhaled Ultrafine Manganese Oxide Particles to the Central Nervous System," *Environmental Health Perspectives*, vol. 114, no. 8, pp. 1172–1178, August 2006.

5 Grace E. Ziem and Barry I. Castleman, "Threshold Limit Values: Historical Perspectives and Current Practice," *Journal of Occupational Medicine*, vol. 31, no. 11, pp. 910–918, November 1989.

6 You may see numbers other than 428 when reading about this notice. The differences depend on whether they count TLVs with different exposure times for the same substance as one TLV or count each time-dependent standard separately.

7 *Federal Register*, vol. 54, pp. 2332–2983 , January 19, 1989.

8 Comment in quote in *Federal Register*, vol. 58, pp. 40191, July 27, 1993.

9 *Federal Register*, vol. 58, p. 28517, May 14, 1993.

10 *Today! Online*, www.acigh.org, vol. 12, no. 4, Fall 2004.

11 Matthew Toussant, the senior vice president of editorial operations for CAS, writing on the Editor's Page, "A Scientific Milestone," *Chemical and Engineering News*, vol. 87, no. 37, p. 3, September 14, 2009.

12 "Regulation (EC) No. 1907/2006 of the European Parliament and of the Council of 18 December 2006," *Official Journal of the European Union*, Annex X, "Standard Information Requirements for Substances Manufactured or Imported in Quantities of 1000 Tonnes or More," pp. 360–370, December 30, 2006.

13 *Chemical Regulation: Options Exist to Improve EPA's Ability to Assess Health Risks and Manage Its Chemical Review Program* (GAO-05-458), Report to Congressional Requesters, pp. 1–69, esp. pp. 50–52.

14 *Corrosion Proof Fittings v. EPA*, 947 F.2d 1201, 33 ERC 1961 (U.S. Court of Appeals for the Fifth Circuit), 1991.
15 Denise Grady, "When Body Piercing Causes Body Rash," *New York Times*, October 20, 1998, p. F8.
16 Regulation (EC) No. 1907/2006 of the European Parliament and of the Council of December 18, 2006, pp. 422–424.
17 David Michaels, speech at the NIOSH Going Green Workshop, Washington, D.C., December 16, 2009 (visit www.OSHA.gov for more information).

INDEX